Keep. 8/18/16 MR

1001 Colorado Place l

D0447565

1001 Colorado Place Names

Maxine Benson

Illustrations by Robin Richards

University Press of Kansas

Quotations in entries for Fondis, Jansen, Manitou Springs, Ninaview, Rockvale, Sawpit, Silver Plume, Sunbeam, Victor, and Villa Grove courtesy Colorado Historical Society

Lyrics from C. W. McCall, "Wolf Creek Pass" (New York: PolyGram Records, 1978), used with permission of C. W. McCall

Post Office information from William H. Bauer, James L. Ozment, and John H. Willard, *Colorado Post Offices, 1859–1989* (1990), courtesy Colorado Railroad Museum

Published by the University Press of Kansas (Lawrence, Kansas 66049), which was organized by the Kansas Board of Regents and is operated and funded by Emporia State University, Fort Hays State University, Kansas State University, Pittsburg State University, the University of Kansas, and Wichita State University

Library of Congress Cataloging-in-Publication Data

Benson, Maxine.
    1001 Colorado place names / Maxine Benson ; illustrations by Robin Richards.
       p. cm.
    ISBN 0-7006-0632-7 (cloth : alk. paper). — ISBN 0-7006-0633-5 (paper : alk. paper))
    1. Names, Geographical—Colorado. 23. Colorado—History, Local.
I. Title. II. Title: One thousand one Colorado place names.
III. Title: One thousand and one Colorado place names.
F774.B46   1994
917.88'0014—dc20   94-13556

British Library Cataloguing in Publication Data is available.
Printed in the United States of America
10 9 8 7 6 5 4 3 2 1

To
my husband, Benjamin L. Cook
my mother, Frances L. Benson
and the memory of my father, Mac W. Benson

Contents

Introduction

Within its rectangular boundaries, Colorado encompasses 104,247 square miles on which Indians and explorers, prospectors and politicians, surveyors and settlers, have placed thousands of names. Some describe natural features—rivers, forests, peaks, passes; others denote places people have called home, from mining camps to cities to tiny rural crossroads. Some names that once existed are no longer on any map; others have endured for centuries. All reflect the influence of those who have lived in or passed through the area called Colorado.

The earliest namers were the Ute, who once ranged over the mountains and western plateau country and left many names still used today: Cochetopa, Uncompahgre, Saguache. Some of their leaders are remembered by such place names as Ouray, Ignacio, Chipita Park, and Mount Antero. On the plains lived the Arapaho, Cheyenne, Kiowa, Comanche, and other tribes, known today more for the names they inspired than for those they gave.

Beginning in the seventeenth century came Spanish explorers, military men, and priests, including the Franciscan friars Francisco Atanasio Domínguez and Silvestre Vélez de Escalante, who led a 1776 expedition through the present-day Four Corners states. Searching for a route from Santa Fe to the California missions, they also produced a journal that provides the first written glimpse of much of western Colorado. Later came Hispanic settlers whose influence is strongly felt in the southern part of the state. Numerous place names reflect this Spanish heritage: Sangre de Cristo, San Juan, and San Luis; La Plata, Conejos, and Huerfano. To the north, the French contributed such names as Platte and Cache la Poudre.

In 1806, the first United States explorer raised the American flag in present-day Colorado. He was Zebulon Montgomery Pike, now remembered by the famous peak that he neither climbed nor named. Stephen H. Long and his party of naturalists and artists explored the area in 1820, followed by John C. Frémont and his five expeditions (1842-1854) and John W. Gunnison (1853), who was searching for a central railroad route through the Rockies. Ferdinand V. Hayden and George W. Wheeler led government surveying parties in the 1860s and 1870s. All these men recorded names already in use and bestowed new ones; in turn, they were honored with the names of peaks, passes, forests, rivers, towns, and counties.

From 1858 onward, gold and silver discoveries brought English-speaking prospectors, town builders, farmers, and shopkeepers, who named countless mines, camps, and towns. From the mountain wealth they coined Oro City, Gold Hill, and Goldfield; Silverton, Silver Cliff, and Silver Plume; Placerville, Platoro, and Rico. Settlers also brought names from their former homes; honored wives, husbands, children, postmasters, ministers, politicians, and soldiers; and drew inspiration from such common objects as a rifle, a frying pan, a tin cup, a coffee pot, and a wagon wheel. Railroad officials and land agents made their contributions as they named the stations around which many communities developed, while postal officials in far-off Washington, D.C., sometimes had the last word.

As the namers named, historians and guidebook authors followed with pen in hand. Frank Fossett included some Spanish names in *Colorado: Its Gold and Silver Mines* (1880), while George A. Crofutt listed "Spanish-Mexican and Indian Names" in his *Grip-Sack Guide of Colorado* (1881, 1885). Michael Beshoar, an early Trinidad doctor remembered today by Beshoar Junction, featured a section on "Geographical Names in Las Animas County" in his 1882 county history. Larger works, such as the four-volume *History of the State of Colorado* (1889-1895) by former territorial secretary Frank Hall, also paid attention to place name origins, and shortly after the turn of the century appeared the landmark *Gazetteer of Colorado* (1906) by Henry Gannett, then chairman of the United States Board on Geographic Names and earlier a member of the Hayden Survey.

Although these pioneering works recorded valuable information, the real basis of Colorado place name studies was formed as a part of the Depression-era projects supported successively between 1933 and 1941 by the Civil Works Administration (CWA), the Federal Emergency Relief Administration (FERA), and the Works Progress (later Work Projects) Administration (WPA). Directed by the State Historical Society of Colorado (now termed the Colorado Historical Society), researchers and librarians interviewed old-timers, classified thousands of books, and indexed journals, newspapers, and documents. In addition, the society sent numerous letters to postmasters and long-time community residents as part of a place-name survey, conducted principally during 1935. "The State Historical Society of Colorado is making a special study of Place Names in Colorado; compiling data on the towns, cities, rivers, and mountains in the State," wrote employee Julia Stokes. "We are endeavoring to determine the origin of each name, when and by whom applied." Back came the answers, which the thrifty respondents often wrote on the original queries.

Concurrently, the Colorado Writers' Project, a separate WPA program, also was employing writers and researchers. *Colorado: A Guide to the Highest State,* published in 1941 and reissued in 1987 as *The WPA Guide to 1930s Colorado,* is the best-known result of their work. In addition, Writers' Project researchers continued and expanded the society's work on place names. More letters were sent out—551 to postmasters, 287 to school principals, 62 to county superintendents of education, and 14 to forest supervisors, according to one summary. The results were published in a nineteen-part series, "The Names of Colorado Towns," in the *Colorado Magazine* between January 1940 and May 1943. Project writers also prepared brief community histories now filed as the "1000 Towns" notebooks in the society's library.

As this work was proceeding, Ruth Estelle Matthews was writing "A Study of Colorado Place Names" for her M.A. degree in English from Stanford University (1940). Matthews too canvassed postmasters, school officials, and "a great number of persons not in official positions but known to be interested in the stories of their communities." The information she received, combined with the material gathered by the federally sponsored projects, forms a good picture of what people knew or believed about the origins of many Colorado place names on the eve of World War II.

Two books on Colorado place names were published subsequently. The first, *Place Names in Colorado,* by J. Frank Dawson, appeared in 1954, followed some twenty years later by *Colorado Place Names* by George R. Eichler (1977). A long-time newspaper reporter and public relations professional, Eichler was working on a more comprehensive gazetteer at the time of his death in 1980. In 1993, William Bright, a retired linguistics professor from UCLA, issued a revised edition of Eichler's study that gives greater attention to Spanish and Native American names.

The present work discusses 1001 Colorado place names chosen for their historical, geographical, or geological significance, or, in a few cases, because the stories associated with their naming seemed worth telling. All sixty-three present-day counties are included, as well as one (Greenwood) no longer on the map. Settlements ranging from cities to villages to crossroads account for another 716 names, including 595 listed in the index to the official 1993 state highway map. Represented also are the fifty-six peaks over 14,000 feet—the Fourteeners—as designated in "Elevations of Named Summits over 14,000 Feet above Sea Level" in *Elevations and Distances in the United States,* issued by the United States Geological Survey in 1990. Controversy abounds here about the number, since many mountain climbers accept only fifty-three or fifty-four as true Fourteeners because of such factors as the "saddle drop" between two nearby summits. A few lower peaks also are featured, including some former Fourteeners since demoted by surveyors. The remaining names range from national parks, sites, forests, and grasslands to major rivers and mountain passes to past and present military installations, all forming a diverse overview of Colorado nomenclature.

The components included in an entry are the following:

a. The place name

b. The county: In all instances the present county location for both current and extinct places is given. For example, Auraria, which existed for only a short time in Kansas Territory, was situated on a site in what is now the City and County of Denver and is so identified. Many another community began life in one county, only to find itself in a different one after legislators redrew the lines. Here, too, only the current county is listed. Forests, rivers, and other such features are usually described more generally, i.e., Northwest Colorado.

c. Pronunciation: Pronunciations are taken from Floyd Baskette, *Pronunciation Guide, Colorado* (n.d.). Baskette, a longtime faculty member of the University of Colorado College of Journalism, compiled the guide "with the cooperation and assistance of Colorado broadcasters."

d. Body of entry: Here the emphasis is historical and reflects the source and meaning of the name today, although usually previous names and predecessor towns are mentioned. Often more than one version of the name origin is given, for as Fred Tarpley aptly remarks in *1001 Texas Place Names* (1980), "often no hope remains for authenticating the motives of the namegivers, and the folklore might as well be enjoyed."

e. Post office history: Information on post office names is derived from *Colorado Post Offices, 1859-1989,* by William H. Bauer, James L. Ozment, and John H. Willard, published by the Colorado Railroad Museum in 1990. This work was used as the authority in cases where local sources provided conflicting data. The *Rand-McNally Commercial Atlas and Marketing Guide* (1992) also was helpful.

f. Population: Population figures are taken from the 1990 census and the *Rand-McNally Commercial Atlas.* When information is for an area denoted as a Census Designated Place (CDP), that fact is indicated in parentheses following the number: (CDP). The Census Bureau defines CDPs as "densely settled concentrations of population that are identifiable by name, but are not legally incorporated places."

g. Elevation

h. County seat: Communities that are county seats are designated CS following the population figure.

Place-name scholars or onomasticians have often devised systems to classify names. The Place Name Survey of Texas, for example, used eleven categories for its computerized analysis, while George R. Stewart, author of the 1945 classic *Names on the Land*, proposed ten: descriptive, associative, possessive, incidental, commemorative, commendatory, coined, transfer, folk etymology, and mistake. Most Colorado place names fit into the descriptive, transfer, and commemorative categories; all tell something about the people who gave them. Here, then, are the stories behind Happyville, Heartstrong, Wideawake, Firstview, Last Chance, and 996 more of Colorado's "names on the land."

Acknowledgments

In addition to the sources mentioned in the Introduction, a number of other basic works were indispensable to the research for *1001 Colorado Place Names*. Erl Ellis, *Colorado Mapology* (1983) is invaluable for tracing county development. A convenient compilation of current maps is the *Colorado Atlas and Gazetteer: Topo Maps of the Entire State* (1991). Thomas J. Noel, Paul F. Mahoney, and Richard E. Stevens include maps on boundaries, transportation, mining, and settlement in the *Historical Atlas of Colorado* (1994). Railroad history is capsulized in Tivis E. Wilkins, *Colorado Railroads: Chronological Development* (1974), and Donald B. Robertson, *Encyclopedia of Western Railroad History, Vol. 2: The Mountain States: Colorado, Idaho, Montana, Wyoming* (1991). On the names of the Fourteeners, the classic history is John L. J. Hart, *Fourteen Thousand Feet: A History of the Naming and Early Ascents of the High Colorado Peaks* (1925; rev. ed. 1931). Also helpful is William M. Bueler, *Roof of the Rockies: A History of Colorado Mountaineering* (1986). On passes, see Marshall Sprague, *The Great Gates* (1964), and Don Koch, *The Colorado Pass Book* (2d ed., 1987).

Several works on specific areas or topics were useful. These include Louisa Ward Arps and Elinor Eppich Kingery, *High Country Names: Rocky Mountain National Park* (1966; rev. ed. 1972); Virginia McConnell Simmons, "Hispanic Place Names of the San Luis Valley," *San Luis Valley Historian* (1991); Ray L. Newburn, Jr., "Postal History of the Colorado San Juan," *Western Express* (1975-1984); Ruben Cobos, *A Dictionary of New Mexico and Southern Colorado Spanish* (1983); Richard M. Pearl, *Nature's Names for Colorado Communities* (1975); Charles A. Page, *What's in a Name? In the Gunnison Country* (1974); and Ray Shaffer, *A Guide to Places on the Colorado Prairie, 1540-1975* (1978). On individual counties, see Shaffer's separate works on Adams, Arapahoe, Boulder, Elbert, Jefferson, and Weld counties (1989-1991); Etholine Aycock and Mary Hagen, *Larimer County Place Names* (1984); and, in a class by itself, Carol Rein Shwayder, *Weld County Old and New: Gazetteer and Dictionary of Place Names* (1992), a 659-page computerized compilation. Noteworthy regional or county histories include Janet Lecompte, *Pueblo, Hardscrabble, Greenhorn* (1978); Robert C. Black III, *Island in the Rockies: The Pioneer Era of Grand County, Colorado* (1969; 2d ed., 1977); Allan Nossaman, *Many More*

Mountains: Vol. 1: Silverton's Roots (1989); Mary Ellen Gilliland, *Summit: A Gold Rush History of Summit County, Colorado* (1980); and three books by Virginia McConnell Simmons: *Bayou Salado: The Story of South Park* (1966); *The San Luis Valley: Land of the Six-Armed Cross* (1979); and *The Upper Arkansas: A Mountain River Valley* (1990). Much important information can also be found in the histories that many counties have issued to celebrate the Colorado Centennial in 1976 or their own anniversaries.

The library of the Colorado Historical Society, directed by Rebecca Lintz, holds invaluable card files with material collected by the federally supported projects during the 1930s and early 1940s. The files also contain references to newspapers, manuscripts, and interviews. Of equal importance are the clipping files and indexes of the Western History Department, Denver Public Library, directed by Eleanor M. Gehres. Staff members of both Denver institutions were invariably cheerful, helpful, and courteous as they retrieved the countless bits of information needed for this work.

Special mention should be made of the extensive place name card files compiled by James Grafton Rogers (1883-1971), a lawyer, scholar, and diplomat and a founder of the Colorado Mountain Club in 1912. Rogers had a lifelong interest in place names, and he indexed references to Colorado communities and natural features in maps and published works. Held by the Colorado Historical Society, the files are available on microfilm in both the society's library and in the Western History Department.

Today, place name research has joined the computer age with the Geographic Names Information System (GNIS), an automated data system developed by the United States Geological Survey (USGS). One component of GNIS is the National Geographic Names Data Base, which ultimately will include published volumes for all states in the *National Gazetteer of the United States of America*. The first phase of data compilation, representing names derived from USGS maps, is now available for Colorado.

These sources, along with many specialized works, were used to prepare the entries in *1001 Colorado Place Names*. Lois Anderton, Boulder; Robert C. Black III, Denver; Jo Cole, Greenwood Village; Robert McQuarie, Littleton; Rheba Massey, Fort Collins; Duane A. Smith, Durango, and many other individuals throughout the state helped solve particularly difficult problems, as did the "map makers" of the Geographic Information Systems Unit of the Colorado Department of Transportation. All sources are cited in an annotated copy of the manuscript on file in the library of the Colorado Historical Society and in the Western History Department of the Denver Public Library. Thomas J. Noel and Donald L. Baars read the manuscript and made a number of helpful suggestions. I am grateful as well to Fred Woodward, director of the University

Press of Kansas, for suggesting this companion volume to *1001 Kansas Place Names* (1989) and for his patience in awaiting its completion. Much research remains still to be done on Colorado place names, and I hope that this work not only will serve as a useful reference but will also stimulate additional scholarship. Any corrections or new information that readers supply will be welcomed for future revisions of this book.

1001 Colorado Place Names

Agate

Abarr *(Yuma)* [AB-ahr]

Abarr took the maiden name of postmistress Ethel Abarr Hoffman.
PO: February 26, 1923–November 30, 1947

Adams County *(Established November 15, 1902)*

Democrat Alva Adams served two gubernatorial terms (1887–1889, 1897–1899) and was elected again in 1904, a victory that was contested in the legislature. Several months later, Colorado had three governors in twenty-four hours when Adams was unseated and Republican James H. Peabody took the oath of office, but only on condition that he resign immediately in favor of Lieutenant-governor Jesse F. McDonald.
Pop. 265,038

Agate *(Elbert)* [AG-it]

Was there "a gate" in the area through which travelers (or cattle) had to pass? Was there a store known as Agate? Or were agates found nearby? "Moss agates are said to abound in the neighborhood of this station," wrote George A. Crofutt in his 1885 *Grip-Sack Guide of Colorado*. In any event, after a brief stint as *Gebhard*, for rancher Henry Gebhard, the post office name was changed to *Agate*.
PO: April 8, 1881–April 24, 1882, as Gebhard; April 24, 1882–;
Pop. 90

Aguilar *(Las Animas)* [AG-ih-lar]

José Ramón Aguilar, who served two terms in the 1880s as a Las Animas County representative to the Colorado legislature, was remembered when this community was named.
PO: December 16, 1890–; Pop. 520

Air Force Academy *(El Paso)*

"This is the greatest thing that has happened to Colorado since Pikes Peak was discovered by Zebulon Pike," exulted

Senator Edwin C. Johnson upon learning in June 1954 that
the new United States *Air Force Academy* would be built near
Colorado Springs. Five years later, the first cadets received
their diplomas on the modernistic campus after having spent
most of their college days at Lowry Air Force Base, the interim
headquarters.
*PO: June 28, 1958–, as United States Air Force Academy; Pop.
9,062 (CDP)*

Akron *(Washington)* [AK-run]

The wife of a Burlington Railroad official named *Akron* for her
Ohio home. *Akron*, which means "summit" in Greek, was an
apt description for this townsite situated at a high point along
the line.
PO: January 30, 1883–; Pop. 1,599; CS

Alamosa *(Alamosa)* [al-uh-MOH-suh]

When the Denver and Rio Grande Railway reached this spot
in 1878, officials briefly called the place *Rio Bravo* before
choosing the name *Alamosa* for the new townsite. The Spanish
word means "place of cottonwoods."
PO: March 12, 1878–; Pop. 7,579; CS

Alamosa County *(Established March 8, 1913)*

The sixty-third and last Colorado county to be created, *Alamosa County* took the name of its county seat town.
Pop. 13,617

Allenspark *(Boulder)*

Allenspark took its name from pioneer Alonzo N. Allen, who
built a cabin near the present resort community. (*See also* Gunbarrel.)
PO: August 18, 1896–November 30, 1905; May 5, 1906–; Pop. 300

Allison *(La Plata)* [AL-uh-son]

Allison Stocker, secretary of the Colorado Development and
Ditch Company, which helped build the community, was
honored with the post office name after officials rejected the
earlier choice of *Vallejo* because mail might be missent to Vallejo, California.
PO: August 22, 1904–November 30, 1954; Pop. 60

Alma *(Park)*

Who was Alma? She might have been Alma James, a merchant's wife; Alma Graves, whose husband ran the Alma

Mine; or Alma Trevor, reportedly the first child born at the place. Or maybe she was Alma Jaynes, daughter of an apparently unpopular early settler. According to one old-timer, residents balked at calling the community *Jaynesville,* for her father, but enthusiastically accepted the daughter's name.
PO: March 7, 1873–; Pop. 148

Almont *(Gunnison)* [AL-mahnt]

A horse called Almont inspired the naming of the Denver and Rio Grande station on rancher Samuel Fisher's land. Almont was the sire of Fisher's horse Firmont and a direct descendant of the famed trotting horse Hambletonian (1846–1879).
PO: March 6, 1882–May 3, 1893; April 21, 1904–October 31, 1908; April 28, 1910–January 31, 1913; July 21, 1913–; Pop. 5

Altman *(Teller)*

Sam Altman, who counted mining claims and a sawmill among his business interests, laid out *Altman* in the Cripple Creek mining district.
PO: January 18, 1894–February 20, 1895; March 21, 1895–May 20, 1911

Amache *(Prowers)*

During World War II, the United States government moved thousands of people of Japanese descent from the West Coast to inland internment camps. The Colorado facility, which operated between 1942 and 1945, was officially called the *Granada Relocation Center,* for the nearby town; the post office, however, took the name *Amache,* the daughter of a Cheyenne chief killed at the 1864 Sand Creek Massacre and wife of John Prowers, namesake of the county.
PO: September 15, 1942–February 9, 1945 (branch of Lamar)

Amherst *(Phillips)* [AM-erst]

Amherst is thought to be a "transfer name" brought from Amherst, Massachusetts. Like nearby Holyoke, named for another Massachusetts town, *Amherst* was platted by the Lincoln Land Company subsidiary of the Burlington Railroad.
PO: February 18, 1888–August 18, 1899; April 18, 1907–; Pop. 60

Amity *(Prowers)* [AM-i-ti]

Little remains of *Amity,* which traced its origins to the short-lived Fort Amity farm colony, one of three such turn-of-the-century Salvation Army ventures in the United States. The source of the name, which means "good will," is uncertain,

although United States Salvation Army Commander Frederick Booth-Tucker has been credited with suggesting it.
PO: July 18, 1898–February 27, 1937

Anaconda *(Teller)*

In Montana, the developer of the famed Anaconda Mine named it for Union General Winfield Scott's strategy, described as encircling the Confederate forces "like an anaconda," or South American snake. A Colorado Anaconda Mine between Cripple Creek and Victor gave its name to this mining town, first called *Barry* for Horace Barry.
PO: March 1, 1892–December 7, 1893, as Barry; December 7, 1893–March 31, 1909; February 15, 1911–November 15, 1917.

Animas Forks *(San Juan)* [AN-i-muhs]

"At what is called the Three Forks or the junction of the three creeks which form the head of the Animas [River], we found several cabins with a number of miners about, who kindly showed us specimens of ore from their various mines," reported Hayden Survey topographer Franklin Rhoda in August 1874. The camp, known early as *Three Forks* and *Forks of the Animas,* became simply *Animas Forks* when the post office was established in 1875. A century earlier, the Franciscan missionaries Domínguez and Escalante had recorded the Spanish name for the Animas River, *El Río de las Ánimas,* "River of Souls," when they traveled through the area in 1776.
PO: February 8, 1875–February 26, 1889; October 21, 1889–November 14, 1891; July 25, 1904–November 30, 1915

Antero Junction *(Park)* [an-TEH-roh]

Like nearby Antero Reservoir and Mount Antero, to the southwest, this crossroads commemorates the Uintah Ute chief Antero.

Anton *(Washington)*

Maurice S. Walters, a teacher and Washington County homesteader, took credit for naming the *Anton* post office, although he said that he had really suggested *Canton,* for Canton, Nebraska. Somehow the *c* was omitted, and the settlement thus became *Anton.*
PO: July 18, 1916–October 15, 1928; June 30, 1934–; Pop. 50

Antonito *(Conejos)* [an-tuh-NEE-toh]

With the arrival of the Denver and Rio Grande in 1880, the railroad station and settlement were first known as *San Antonio Junction* or *San Antonio,* "Saint Anthony" in Spanish, for

anton

San Antonio Mountain in New Mexico and the San Antonio River. Within a short time, the railroad changed the names of a number of stations along the line, and *San Antonio* became *Antonito*, "Little Anthony."

PO: November 26, 1880–January 24, 1881, as San Antonio; January 24, 1881–; Pop. 875

Apishapa River *(Southern Colorado)* [uh-PISH-uh-puh]

"Apishapa, (a-pish-a-pa) is so-called because the stream usually ceases to flow during the summertime, and the holes of water remaining in the river bed become stagnant and offensive to the smell," wrote pioneer Trinidad doctor Michael Beshoar in *All About Trinidad and Las Animas County.* "The Indians for that reason gave it the name it bears, meaning the 'Stinking River,' or 'Stinking Water.' " Beshoar also said that "early settlers chose St. Anthony as their patron saint, and for that reason sometimes speak of it as Rio San Antonio."

Arapahoe *(Cheyenne)* [uh-RAP-uh-hoh]

Although a townsite and post office called *Arapahoe* existed briefly in the early 1860s, development of the present *Arapahoe* did not begin until 1906. Like the county, the town took its name from the Arapaho Indians.

PO: January 17, 1860–October 12, 1861; May 5, 1906–; Pop. 100

Arapahoe County *(Established November 1, 1861)*

Arapahoe County was created by the first territorial legislature and named for the Arapaho Indians. The original *Arapahoe*

County boundaries extended from Denver to the Kansas state line before the present, smaller county borders were established in 1902. An earlier *Arapahoe County* also existed in what was then Kansas Territory between 1855 and 1861.
Pop. 391,511

Arapaho National Forest *(North Central Colorado)*

Combining parts of the Medicine Bow, Leadville, and Pike national forests, the *Arapaho National Forest* was created in 1908. The name, which commemorates the Indian tribe, can be spelled either with or without the *e*, although the United States Board on Geographic Names and other government agencies today officially use *Arapaho*.

Arboles *(Archuleta)* [AHR-boh-lees]

In 1899, the Arboles Land and Water Company began laying out a townsite at the Denver and Rio Grande station of *Arboles*, which means "trees" in Spanish.
PO: December 13, 1882–April 4, 1899; April 13, 1899–; Pop. 70

Archuleta County *(Established April 14, 1885)*

Taos-born Antonio Archuleta was reportedly the youngest member of the first state House of Representatives when he was elected in his early twenties from Conejos and Costilla counties in 1876. Archuleta later won a seat in the Colorado Senate and was serving in that body when *Archuleta County* was created from Conejos County in 1885.
Pop. 5,345

Argentine *(Summit)*

Argentine took its third and final name from nearby Argentine Pass. The camp was first called *Decatur*, for founder and promoter "Commodore" Stephen Decatur; it would have been *Bross*, if Decatur had used his real name. Although he steadfastly denied the connection, Decatur actually was Stephen

Decatur Bross and the brother of Illinois lieutenant-governor William Bross, remembered in Colorado by Mount Bross. Decatur had left behind several previous lives and wives on his way to Colorado; newspaper editor Samuel Bowles, who toured the territory with William Bross in 1868, aptly described him as "the prince of prospectors, the character of all Colorado characters." Despite Decatur's renown, his town did not perpetuate even his chosen name. It later became *Rathbone* and then *Argentine*, eventually falling victim to mining's boom-bust cycles as well as a devastating avalanche. (*See also* Mount Bross.)
PO: October 3, 1879–January 28, 1885, as Decatur; September 19, 1891–July 11, 1895, as Rathbone; November 18, 1901–February 28, 1907

Argentine Pass *(Clear Creek, Summit)*

Today only hikers can ascend the steep, rocky western approach to *Argentine Pass*. First called *Sanderson* and then *Snake River Pass*, this highest Continental Divide crossing in the Rocky Mountains later took the name *Argentine* for the East Argentine mining camp and district. The word *argentine*, meaning "silvery" or "silver-like," comes from the Latin *argentum*, or "silver."
Elevation: 13,207 feet

Argo *(City and County of Denver)*

Argo was founded in 1878 when the Boston and Colorado Smelting Company moved its operations from Black Hawk to the Denver area. As Frank Fossett remarked in *Colorado: Its Gold and Silver Mines* (1880), "the very appropriate name of Argo was applied, after the good ship in which a hero of Grecian mythology is reputed to have set sail in search of the golden fleece." Once separately incorporated, *Argo* became part of the City and County of Denver in 1902.
PO: April 11, 1881–March 21, 1890; June 11, 1890–January 15, 1904; May 18, 1904–September 15, 1911

Arikaree River *(Yuma)* [uh-RIK-uh-ree]

This tributary of the Republican River took the name of the Arikaree (or Arikara) Indians. In 1868, the "Battle of the Arikaree," one of the last Indian engagements on the Colorado plains, was fought on an island later named for Lieutenant Frederick H. Beecher. (*See* Beecher Island.)

Arkansas River *(Southern Colorado)* [AR-k'n-sah]

Rising near Leadville, the *Arkansas River* acquired Spanish, Indian, and French names on its way across the southern plains to join the Mississippi River in Arkansas. Spaniards with Coronado, crossing the river in present-day Kansas on the saint's day of Peter and Paul in 1541, called the river *El Río de San Pedro y San Pablo,* while eighteenth-century Spanish explorers reported that Indians they encountered used the name *Napestle* or *Napeste.* Other Indian names for the river included the Pawnee *Kits-ka* and the Osage *Ne Shutsa.* Ultimately, because the French used the name Akansa (probably an Algonquin word) for an Indian village situated near the mouth of the river, the name became *Arkansas,* although not before frontier settlers and travelers spelled it *Acansas, Akansas, Arcansas,* or, like Thomas Jefferson, *Arkanzas.* Such spellings reflected the differing pronunciations of the word. Even today, the river is the "Arkansaw" in Colorado, Oklahoma, and Arkansas, but the "Arkansas," with the accent on the second syllable, in Kansas.

Arlington *(Kiowa)*

Once an important cattle-shipping point, the station was first called *Joliet* when the Pueblo and State Line Railway, a subsidiary of the Missouri Pacific, came through in 1887. The later name of *Arlington* is said to honor a railroad official.
PO: August 16, 1887–; Pop. 5

Aroya *(Cheyenne)* [uh-ROY-yuh]

Aroya (sometimes *Arroya*) is still shown on Colorado maps, although only a few structures survive to mark the community that grew up around a Kansas Pacific railroad station. In the western United States the word *arroyo,* Spanish for "rivulet" or "small river," refers to a gully carved out by a usually dry stream; such an *arroyo* goes through *Aroya.*
PO: September 17, 1889–March 26, 1965

Arriba *(Lincoln)* [AIR-uh-buh]

Don't say Ar-RI-ba out here on the plains—residents pronounce the Spanish word AR-ri-ba, which means "high" or "above." Settled as the Rock Island Railroad moved westward to ever-higher altitudes, *Arriba* has an elevation of 5,228 feet, more than 1,000 feet higher than Burlington, which is near the Kansas border.
PO: February 4, 1889–; Pop. 220

Arriola *(Montezuma)* [ahr-ee-OH-luh]

A "Spanish general," otherwise unidentified, is said to be the source of this community's name. H. F. Morgan, an old-timer interviewed in 1934, credited an early schoolteacher with making the suggestion.

PO: December 18, 1894–June 15, 1904; June 20, 1908–August 15, 1933; Pop. 75

Arvada *(Adams, Jefferson)* [ahr-VAD-uh]

After the Colorado Central Railroad came through the area in 1870, early settler and first postmaster Benjamin F. Wadsworth gave his wife Mary the privilege of naming the community. She chose *Arvada* to honor her brother-in-law Hiram Arvada Haskin. The name may refer to Arva, one of the sons of Canaan and a founder of the Arvadites in the Bible.
PO: February 16, 1871–; Pop. 89,235

Ashcroft *(Pitkin)*

Prospector and town promoter T. E. Ashcraft gave his name (with a slight change in spelling) to this once-booming mining camp near Aspen. Now being restored, *Ashcroft* was also briefly called *Castle Forks* or *Castle Forks City* and *Chloride*.
PO: August 12, 1880–August 5, 1881; August 5, 1881–January 3, 1882, as Chloride; January 3, 1882–November 30, 1912

Aspen *(Pitkin)* [AS-p'n]

Promoter, town surveyor, and later mayor B. Clark Wheeler named the townsite in 1880 for the many aspen trees in the area. Replacing an earlier camp known as *Ute City, Aspen* became one of Colorado's richest nineteenth-century silver towns; after World War II, skiing, music festivals, and cultural seminars brought renewed prominence to the community.
PO: June 7, 1880–; Pop. 5,049; CS

Atwood *(Logan)* [AT-wood]

Early settler Victor Wilson, a Unitarian, is credited with naming the town for a minister of that faith, the Reverend John S. Atwood of Boston, Massachusetts.
PO: August 10, 1885–; Pop. 200

Ault *(Weld)* [AWL't]

Ault grew up around the Denver Pacific siding first called *McAllister,* for a railroad official, and then *Burgdorf,* for a road master. Before storage facilities were built, Fort Collins grain dealer Alexander Ault bought quantities of wheat during hard times of drought and depression, thus saving many farmers from bankruptcy. Grateful residents renamed the community in his honor when they obtained a post office.
PO: March 29, 1898–; Pop. 1,107

Auraria *(City and County of Denver)*

In the fall of 1858, gold seekers established the Auraria Town Company near the confluence of Cherry Creek and the South Platte River. Dr. Levi J. Russell, one of a party of argonauts from the gold-mining district of Georgia, suggested naming the settlement for his hometown of Auraria in Lumpkin County—"auraria" is from the Latin word *aurum* for gold. Although *Auraria* merged with rival Denver City across Cherry Creek in 1860, today the Auraria Higher Education Center on the site recalls the pioneer town.
PO: January 18, 1859–February 11, 1860

Aurora *(Adams, Arapahoe)* [aw-ROH-ruh]

Incorporated in 1891, the city was first called *Fletcher,* for real estate promoter Donald Fletcher. After the Panic of 1893, however, Fletcher left both the community and his debts; in 1907, residents decided to adopt the name *Aurora* from a *Fletcher* subdivision. Colfax Avenue, the original main street, both bisects *Aurora* and divides it into two county jurisdictions—Adams and Arapahoe.
PO: January 15, 1908–; Pop. 222,103

Austin *(Delta)* [AWS-tin]

Austin Miller gave land for the townsite and the Denver and Rio Grande Railroad right of way.
PO: May 19, 1905–

Avon *(Eagle)* [AY-v'n]

The name *Avon* reflects the English background of a pioneer Anglo resident.
PO: November 26, 1900–; Pop. 1,798

Avondale *(Pueblo)* [AV-uhn-dale]

According to most accounts, early settler Sam Taylor remembered his hometown of Stratford-on-Avon, England, when he named this community. An alternate version traces the name to the Avondale addition in Pueblo, which J. Eire Green developed before platting *Avondale.*
PO: March 22, 1892–; Pop. 950

Baca County *(Established April 16, 1889)*

When Las Animas County was divided in 1889, Casimiro Barela, who was then representing the county in the state senate, suggested naming the new entity for the prominent Felipe Baca family in Trinidad; a Baca reportedly had been the first settler along Two Buttes Creek, which flows through the northwestern part of the county. In 1861, New Mexican sheep-

herder and rancher Felipe Baca came to Trinidad, where he served as president of the school district and representative to the territorial legislature before his death in 1874. Today the adobe Baca home on Main Street is maintained as a museum restoration by the Colorado Historical Society.
Pop. 4,556

Bailey *(Park)* [BAY-lee]

In 1864, Ann Bailey and Elizabeth Entriken, sisters of the famed Methodist circuit-riding minister John L. Dyer, and Ann's husband, William Bailey, arrived in Colorado Territory from Wisconsin. They settled on the North Fork of the South Platte River, where they operated a popular hotel and stage stop at Bailey's Ranch. Although the railroad supplanted the stage coach in 1878, the town that grew up around the Denver, South Park, and Pacific station kept the Bailey name.
PO: November 20, 1878–; Pop. 150

Barela *(Las Animas)* [bahr-EL-uh]

Elected to the state senate in 1876, prominent southern Colorado rancher and merchant Casimiro Barela served as a legislator the next forty years, thus earning the nickname "The Perpetual Senator."
PO: May 19, 1873–July 28, 1874, as Glenham; July 28, 1874–May 21, 1886; March 19, 1887–October 19, 1896; April 9, 1902–September 30, 1931

Barnesville *(Weld)*

Charles and George Barnes hoped that their town on the Union Pacific Greeley-Briggsdale branch would prosper, but today little remains of their dream. Even one *e* is gone from the designation on the official Colorado state highway map, which lists the site as *Barnsville*.
PO: June 9, 1910–September 14, 1935

Barnum *(City and County of Denver)*

Contrary to local legend, the Barnum circus animals never wintered in this Denver neighborhood. Once separately incorporated but now part of the city, *Barnum* took its name from showman Phineas T. Barnum, who invested in the subdivision in 1878. Disappointed by lack of water and other deficiencies, Barnum soon transferred the property to his daughter Helen; she and her husband, Dr. William Buchtel, developed the area with some success.
PO: February 5, 1892–June 30, 1901

Barnum

Barr Lake *(Adams)*

A Burlington Railroad civil engineer named Barr is remembered by *Barr Lake,* which grew up around a station briefly called *Platte Summit* when the Chicago, Burlington, and Quincy line came through in 1882. Developers soon enlarged a nearby buffalo wallow, now part of Barr Lake State Park, and formed a company in 1887 to promote the townsite of *Barr City.*
PO: March 15, 1883–October 17, 1914, as Barr; October 17, 1914–August 31, 1952; Pop. 180

Bartlett *(Baca)*

Bartlett was born in 1926 with the arrival of the Dodge City and Cimarron Valley Railway, an Atchison, Topeka, and Santa Fe subsidiary. Twelve years later, the *Bartlett* postmaster told the Colorado Writers' Project that the place had been named for an AT&SF official.
PO: September 5, 1928–March 31, 1938

Basalt *(Eagle, Pitkin)* [buh-SAHLT]

First known as *Frying Pan* or *Frying Pan Junction,* for the river that here joins the Roaring Fork River, the community later became *Aspen Junction* and finally *Basalt* for nearby Basalt Mountain, which had been named for the abundant dark volcanic rock in the area.
PO: February 13, 1890–June 19, 1895, as Aspen Junction; June 19, 1895–; Pop. 1,128

Battlement Mesa *(Garfield)*

Although the first schoolhouse in the area was built in 1889, the present settlement was developed initially by the Exxon Corporation to provide employee housing. Situated on Battlement Mesa, which was probably named for rock formations that look like medieval battlements, the town became a recreational and retirement community after the company shut down its Western Slope oil shale project in 1982.
PO: January 31, 1988– (branch of Parachute); Pop: 1,477 (CDP)

Baxter *(Pueblo)*

O. H. P. Baxter, who ranched and farmed in the area after coming to the gold fields in 1858, gave his name to this settlement east of Pueblo. Active in southern Colorado business and politics, Baxter served in the territorial legislature during the mid-1860s.

Bayfield *(La Plata)*

First called *Los Pinos,* for the nearby river, the settlement was renamed after farmer William A. Bay surveyed and laid out the townsite on his land.
PO: January 18, 1889–February 25, 1899, as Los Pinos; February 25, 1899–; Pop. 1,090

Bedrock *(Montrose)*

Bedrock seemed appropriate to those who named this post office and hamlet built amidst sandstone outcrops in the Paradox Valley. In recent years *Bedrock* has received mail addressed to "the Flintstones" as well as an actual rock mailed from England.
PO: November 8, 1883–September 15, 1903; October 12, 1911–; Pop. 60

Bedrock

Bellvue

Beecher Island *(Yuma)*

Beecher Island in the Arikaree River took its name from Lieutenant Frederick H. Beecher, who was killed during the "Battle of the Arikaree" as troops on the island commanded by Major George A. Forsyth withstood an attack by Cheyenne and Sioux Indians in September 1868. The small nearby settlement also honored the memory of Beecher, a nephew of the Reverend Henry Ward Beecher.
PO: November 13, 1924–February 1, 1925, as Glory; February 1, 1925–May 31, 1958

Bellvue *(Larimer)*

In the 1870s, B. F. Flowers came to the area with his father Jacob, who with others bought land and started a community. The younger Flowers told an interviewer in 1934 that as the settlement developed, he and his father decided on the name *Bellevue*, meaning "beautiful view" in French, but accidentally misspelled it as *Bellvue*.
PO: June 24, 1884–; Pop. 250

Bennett *(Adams)*

Bennett grew up near the Kiowa Stage Station at the junction of the Smoky Hill North Trail and the Fort Morgan Cut-Off. The post office was established in 1877 as *Bennet* for Hiram Pitt Bennet of Denver, a prominent lawyer and politician who had served as Denver postmaster from 1869 to 1874. In 1878, flooding on nearby Kiowa Creek washed out the railroad bridge, with the result that a Kansas Pacific engine and several cars plunged into the river. Some local sources assert that the name came from the maiden name of the two sisters who were the widows of the engineer and fireman, although this incident took place a year after the post office opened as *Bennet* (the second *t* was added in 1907).
PO: March 16, 1877–June 1, 1907, as Bennet; June 1, 1907–; Pop. 1,757

Bent County *(Established February 11, 1870)*

Bent County was named for Bent's Old Fort and for founders Charles and William Bent. Ironically, when *Bent County* was

divided in 1889, Bent's Old Fort ended up just beyond the western boundary in the new Otero County.
Pop. 5,048

Bent's Old Fort *(Otero)*

Charles and William Bent and Ceran St. Vrain completed their adobe castle on the north bank of the Arkansas River in 1833–1834. Here Indians exchanged bison robes for trade goods—here, too, marched Stephen Watts Kearny's troops en route to their conquest of New Mexico during the Mexican War. Now a National Historic Site, *Bent's Old Fort* was reconstructed as a Bicentennial project by the National Park Service.

Bergen Park *(Jefferson)*

Bergen Park took the name of early settler Thomas C. Bergen.
Pop. 30

Berkeley *(City and County of Denver)*

Incorporated in 1892 as *North Denver,* this community encompassed land that had once been the Berkeley Farm, which owner John Brisben Walker perhaps named for his former home of Berkeley Springs, Virginia. Initially, only the post office was called *Berkeley;* the town did not take that name until 1898. Four years later *Berkeley* joined the newly created City and County of Denver; today Berkeley Lake and Berkeley Park perpetuate the name of this early suburb.
PO: October 24, 1890–May 18, 1896; May 18, 1896–June 30, 1904, as Alcott

Berthoud *(Larimer)* [BER-thud]

An earlier settlement about a mile to the south of *Berthoud* was called *Little Thompson,* for the nearby river, but after the Colorado Central Railroad arrived in 1877 the name was changed to honor Edward L. Berthoud, surveyor and engineer with the line, and the buildings were soon moved to the present, higher location.
PO: April 5, 1875–April 4, 1878, as Little Thompson; April 4, 1878–; Pop. 2,990

Berthoud Pass *(Clear Creek, Grand)*

In mid-May 1861, shortly after the Civil War broke out in the East, engineer Edward L. Berthoud led a small party searching for this rumored mountain passageway. Today, U.S. Highway 40 carries travelers bound for Middle Park ski resorts over Berthoud's discovery.
Elevation: 11,315 feet

Berwind *(Las Animas)*

Edward J. Berwind, president of the Colorado Coal and Iron Company between 1889 and 1892, gave his name to this once-active coal mining camp.
PO: March 10, 1892–May 30, 1931

Beshoar Junction *(Las Animas)*

Beshoar Junction commemorates Dr. Michael Beshoar, who came to Trinidad after the Civil War. Born in Pennsylvania, Beshoar earned his medical degree from the University of Michigan before establishing a practice in Randolph County, Arkansas. During the war he ministered to both Southern and Northern casualties, first as a Confederate surgeon and later as a Union captive. In Colorado, Beshoar held many local political offices, served in the state legislature, and wrote *All about Trinidad and Las Animas County, Colorado,* published in 1882.
PO: January 25, 1901–June 30, 1903, as Beshoar

Bethune *(Kit Carson)* [beth-YOON]

Early in 1889, a post office called *Bethune* was established along the newly completed Rock Island line in eastern Colorado. A schoolhouse also soon served area families, but not until 1918 did J. J. Delaney plat a townsite. Because the community developed at the end of World War I, later residents thought that the name might refer to the battle-scarred French town of Béthune. Clearly, however, the post office name predated that conflict by some thirty years.
PO: January 19, 1889–May 15, 1905; September 17, 1906–; Pop. 173

Beulah *(Pueblo)* [BYOO-lah]

Once known as *Fisher's Hole,* for Mountain Man Robert Fisher, the valley around *Beulah* was later called *Mace's Hole* for legendary outlaw Juan Mace. In 1873, a *Mace's Hole* post office was established, but settlers soon decided that the cattle-rustling, horse-stealing Mace deserved no honor in their town. Discarding *Silver Glen, Glen Eden,* and *Spruce Valley,* they chose in 1876 to christen the community with the biblical name of *Beulah.*
PO: April 23, 1873–October 25, 1876, as Mace's Hole; October 25, 1876–; Pop. 600

Big Sandy Creek *(Eastern Colorado)*

Although on maps this often dry stream is labeled *Big Sandy Creek,* history will always know it as *Sand Creek,* site of the Sand Creek Massacre. Here, on November 29, 1864, troops led by Colonel John M. Chivington killed hundreds of Cheyenne and Arapaho Indians encamped some nine miles northeast of present-day Chivington, the town named later for the controversial commander.

Big Thompson River *(Larimer, Weld)*

"After diligent search through all the authorities at command and consulting many of the pioneers, we have been unable to trace the origin of the names given the Big and Little Thompson streams," wrote Ansel Watrous in his 1911 *History of Larimer County*. Watrous speculated, however, that the name honored North West Company fur trader and explorer David Thompson, although this Thompson probably stayed far to the north. A more likely candidate is Mountain Man Philip F. Thompson, who is known to have been at Fort Vasquez in 1837 and 1839. In any case, by 1842, when John C. Frémont traveled through the area, the name *Thompson's Creek* was in use. More than a century later, on July 31, 1976, the eve of Colorado's centennial observance, the Big Thompson Canyon was the scene of a disastrous flood.

Big Timbers *(Bent)*

Big Timbers, a grove of large cottonwoods, offered welcome shelter to Indians, trappers, and travelers along the Arkansas River. Later settlers cut down the trees, but the name of this well-known plains landmark is preserved by the Big Timbers Museum in Lamar.

Bijou Creek *(Northeast Colorado)*

Joseph Bijou, interpreter and guide with the 1820 Stephen H. Long exploring party, left his name on this eastern Colorado stream, which was shown as *Bijeaus Cr.* on the expedition map. A noted trapper, Bijou had been born Joseph Bissonet in St. Louis in 1778, but he often used his stepfather's name after his mother remarried.

Black Canyon of the Gunnison National Monument *(Montrose)*

Deep walls shadowed from the sunlight inspired the name of this dark, narrow Gunnison River canyon. Twelve miles of the spectacular gorge are protected in the *Black Canyon of the Gunnison National Monument*, established in 1933.

Black Forest *(El Paso)*

Situated northeast of Colorado Springs, the community grew up in the midst of the Black Forest. Local sources suggest that

the area of dark, thick ponderosa pines may have reminded an early settler of his homeland, the Black Forest in Germany.
PO: April 16, 1960–; Pop. 8,143 (CDP)

Black Hawk *(Gilpin)*

In 1860, so the story goes, a mining company hauled a stamp mill emblazoned with the name of the famed Sauk war chief Black Hawk to the Gregory diggings. Made by the Black Hawk Company in Rock Island, Illinois, the quartz mill, which was used to crush ore and thus free the gold for further processing, soon gave its name to the new camp.
PO: December 6, 1862–February 8, 1871, as Black Hawk Point; February 8, 1871–January 30, 1895, as Black Hawk; January 30, 1895–July 1, 1950, as Blackhawk; July 1, 1950–; Pop. 227

Blakeland *(Arapahoe)*

Landowner Ethel Blake is credited with coining the name *Blakeland,* once the site of a poultry farm.

Blanca *(Costilla)* [BLANG-kuh]

Blanca began in 1908 when a land lottery drew thousands of prospective settlers to a site on the Denver and Rio Grande Railroad west of Fort Garland. The town that emerged from this promotion was named for the snowclad peak. (Earlier, a *Blanca* post office had existed nearer Blanca Peak between 1894 and 1902.)
PO: October 28, 1908–; Pop. 272

Blanca Peak *(Alamosa, Costilla)*

Blanca means "white" in Spanish, an apt name for this snow-covered Fourteener. Wheeler Survey members who made the first documented ascent in 1874 found signs that Indians, probably Ute, had earlier reached the top; native traditions also tell of Arapaho ascents of Longs Peak.
Elevation: 14,345 feet

Blue Mountain *(Moffat)*

From the air, wrote David Bradley in *This Is Dinosaur* (1955), Blue Mountain appears "washed and splotched with blue—the blue of ponderosa pine and Douglas fir, of sage and juniper and distance and the shadows of cliff and cloud." The community of *Blue Mountain* took its name from this "gathering of hills and sharp ridges and benches and chasms" at the southern edge of Dinosaur National Monument.
PO: September 1, 1949–January 31, 1957; Pop. 15

Blue River *(Grand, Summit)*

Rising near Hoosier Pass, the *Blue River* enters the Colorado River near Kremmling in Middle Park. In the mid-nineteenth century, the name, which the 1853-1854 John W. Gunnison expedition reported as the "Nah-un-kah-rea, or Blue river of the Indians and mountain men," was often applied to the Grand (Colorado) River between its headwaters and the junction with the Gunnison River, not to the present *Blue River* tributary.

Blue River *(Summit)*

This southside suburb of Breckenridge is situated along the Blue River in Summit County.
Pop. 440

Boggsville *(Bent)*

Descended from Daniel Boone and related by marriage to Kit Carson, scout and trader Thomas O. Boggs gave his name to *Boggsville,* the spot where he, Carson, and others long active on the frontier settled in the mid-1860s. Here on the Purgatoire River, southeast of present Las Animas, Carson was buried in 1868 after his death at nearby Fort Lyon; his remains later were reinterred in Taos, New Mexico.

Bonanza City *(Saguache)* [boh-NAN-zuh]

"Boys, she's a bonanza," exclaimed the prospector who discovered a rich claim in the mountains north of Saguache. Meaning "prosperity" or "success" in Spanish, the name was appropriate for the booming camp. Anne Ellis, who lived there as a child, recalled in *The Life of an Ordinary Woman* (1929) that *Bonanza* once had thirty-six saloons and seven dance halls.
PO: August 12, 1880–May 14, 1938; Pop. 16

Boncarbo *(Las Animas)* [bahn-KAR-boh]

Boncarbo represents an attempt to say "good coal" in French. Whereas *bon,* of course, means "good," the French word for coal is *charbon,* for carbon, *carbone.*
PO: November 15, 1917–; Pop. 40

Bond *(Eagle)*

Salt Lake City was 173 miles closer to Denver when the Dotsero Cutoff connected Dotsero on the Denver and Rio Grande Western Railroad and Orestod on the Denver and Salt Lake Railway (the Moffat Road). West of Orestod, the *Bond* station and the community that grew up around it were named for this "bonding" of the rails.
PO: December 4, 1935–; Pop. 55

The Dance Hall Girls

Bonanza City

Boone *(Pueblo)*

First called *Booneville* or *Boonetown,* the community took its name from founder and postmaster Albert Gallatin Boone, grandson of Daniel and a noted trapper, trader, and Indian agent in his own right.

PO: January 2, 1863–December 5, 1891, as Booneville; December 5, 1891–; Pop. 341

Boreas Pass *(Park, Summit)*

Known to early prospectors as *Breckenridge, Hamilton,* or *Tarryall,* this pass became *Boreas,* for the Greek god of the north wind, when Denver, South Park, and Pacific tracks spanned the summit in 1882. Samuel Bowles, a newspaper editor who had crossed the pass in August 1868, probably would have found the new name appropriate. Bowles wrote that as he and his party approached the top, "a cold storm gathered upon the snow-fields above us, wheeled from peak to peak in densely black clouds, and soon broke in gusts of wind, in vivid lightning, in startlingly close and loud claps of thunder, in driving snow, in pelting hail, in drizzling rain. . . . one moment we felt like 'fleeing before the Lord,' the next charmed and awed into rest in His presence."

Elevation: 11,481 feet

Boulder *(Boulder)*

Gold discoveries in the nearby mountains prompted the formation of *Boulder* (first *Boulder City*) early in 1859. With numerous large boulders in the vicinity, the name was a natural.
PO: April 22, 1859–; Pop. 83,312; CS

Boulder County *(Established November 1, 1861)*

Taking its name from *Boulder*, the county seat, *Boulder County* was one of seventeen counties created by the first territorial legislature in 1861.
Pop. 225,339

Bovina *(Lincoln)* [boh-VEE-nuh]

Bovina, a Spanish adjective meaning "belonging to cattle," was an appropriate name for this townsite, platted on the Rock Island Railroad near a waterhole long used by north-moving trail herds.
PO: January 8, 1899–November 30, 1955

Bowie *(Delta)* [BOH-ee]

Bowie was named for Alexander Bowie, who had come to the North Fork valley in 1906 to manage the Juanita Coal and Coke Company mine.
PO: February 5, 1907–July 14, 1967

Bovina

Bow Mar *(Arapahoe, Jefferson)*

A suburban residential community, *Bow Mar* combined the names of Bowles Lake and Marston Lake, which in turn honored pioneers Joseph Bowles and John Marston.
Pop. 854

Boyero *(Lincoln)* [boy-YER-oh]

Spanish-English dictionaries define *boyero* as "oxdriver" or "cowherd." The settlement grew up around a Kansas Pacific (later Union Pacific) cattle-shipping point.
PO: March 3, 1902–; Pop. 20

Brandon *(Kiowa)* [BRAN-duhn]

In 1889, the newspaper published at nearby Stuart said that *Brandon* was named for "Brandon, Canada," probably referring to the Manitoba community.
PO: May 19, 1888–May 3, 1893; May 28, 1908–; Pop. 35

Branson *(Las Animas)* [BRAN-suhn]

A. L. Branson, president of the Trinidad Chamber of Commerce, is usually credited with inspiring the naming of *Branson*, which was known first to the postal department as *Coloflats*. An alternate version traces the name to townsite owner F. J. Branson.
PO: August 19, 1915–July 30, 1918, as Coloflats; July 30, 1918–; Pop. 58

Breckenridge *(Summit)*

As prospectors flocked to the area following the discovery of gold in 1859, a community soon developed along the Blue River. According to an oft-told story, B. D. Williams, then in Washington lobbying for the interests of the Pikes Peak country, advised settlers to name the town for vice-president John C. Breckinridge if they wanted quick action on a post office application; apparently the ploy succeeded. As for Breckinridge, at the end of his term in 1861 he became a United States Senator from Kentucky but soon left to join the Confederacy. Breckinridge's defection was too much for the town's Unionists, who changed the name to *Breckenridge*.
PO: January 18, 1860–; Pop. 1,285; CS

Breen *(La Plata)*

Breen took its name from Thomas Breen, who served as superintendent of the nearby Fort Lewis Indian School from 1894 to 1903. Housed on the former army post, the institution was the forerunner of present Fort Lewis College in Durango.
PO: July 19, 1901–November 30, 1954

Briggsdale *(Weld)*

"We own and have platted the new town of Briggsdale at the terminus of the Union Pacific Railroad," advertised Frank N. Briggs and Edwin L. Layton about their 1910 venture, assuring prospective residents that the area was "surrounded by 80,000 acres of the finest agriculture land under Colorado's blue skies."
PO: August 1, 1910–; Pop. 95

Brighton *(Adams, Weld)*

Mrs. Daniel F. Carmichael, whose husband platted the town, honored her birthplace of Brighton Beach, New York. *Brighton* developed around the station where the Denver and Boulder Valley Railroad joined the Denver Pacific; it was called Hughes or Hughes Junction for Bela M. Hughes, first president of the Denver Pacific.
PO: April 13, 1871–August 4, 1879, as Hughes; August 4, 1879–; Pop. 14,203; CS

Bristol *(Prowers)* [BRIS-t'l]

C. H. Bristol, a Santa Fe manager, should have been honored with the naming of the townsite near his property. Instead, clerks in the Chicago office of the railroad erroneously called the proposed settlement Hartman, for George Hartman, who was also associated with the line; the intended Hartman townsite (close to land Hartman owned) was named *Bristol*. (*See also* Hartman.)
PO: July 1, 1908–; Pop. 250

Brookside *(Fremont)*

A mine opened in 1888 by the Canon City Coal Company formed the nucleus of *Brookside,* situated near the Arkansas River southeast of Canon City.
PO: May 21, 1888–March 15, 1909; Pop. 183

Broomfield *(Adams, Boulder, Jefferson, Weld)*

Broom corn growing in the vicinity inspired the naming of this community, which grew up around the railroad station known as Zang's Spur for Adolph Zang, a Denver brewing company executive who raised Percheron horses on a nearby farm. *Broomfield* boomed after the Denver-Boulder Turnpike (U.S. Highway 36) opened in 1952, soaring from a population of 176 in 1950 to 24,638 in 1990.
PO: September 26, 1884–; Pop. 24,638

Broomfield

Brown's Park *(Northwest Colorado)*

In June 1844, John C. Frémont and members of his second expedition came to an area called "Brown's hole." The place was "well known to trappers," wrote Frémont of the "narrow but pretty valley" that stretches across present northwest Colorado and northeast Utah. Several early travelers spoke of a man named Brown who had lived in the Green River Valley, while John Wesley Powell wrote in 1869 that Brown was "an old-time trapper who once had his cabin here and caught beaver and killed deer." Some thirty years later, in *The Old Santa Fe Trail* (1897), Colonel Henry Inman offered a portrait of trapper Baptiste Brown, leading some to accept him as the namesake of *Brown's Park*. Historian Janet Lecompte has shown, however, that Inman's account, which borrowed heavily from earlier works about other frontier characters, is "a specious and contrived tale, full of blunders." Thus, whether Inman's Baptiste Brown was a historical figure associated with *Brown's Park* remains open to question, although there seems little doubt that *someone* named Brown was there long enough to be remembered.

Brush *(Morgan)*

Brush took the name of prominent cattleman and farmer Jared L. Brush, who later served two terms as lieutenant governor of Colorado (1895-1899).
PO: September 19, 1882–; Pop. 4,165

Buckingham *(Weld)* [BUHK-ing-h'm]

C. D. Buckingham, a Chicago, Burlington, and Quincy superintendent, gave his name to *Buckingham*.
PO: December 21, 1888–January 8, 1890; April 8, 1910–July 1, 1966

Buckley Air National Guard Base *(Arapahoe)*

Opened early in World War II and first called *Buckley Field,* this Colorado Air National Guard base honors First Lieutenant John Harold Buckley from Longmont, who was killed in France during World War I.
PO: July 6, 1942–October 1, 1946, as Buckley Field branch of Denver

Buckskin Joe *(Park)*

His fellow prospectors called Joe Higganbottom "Buckskin Joe" for the deerskin clothes he wore, and named the camp where they discovered gold in 1859 *Buckskin Joe's Diggings.* A year later, residents renamed the growing settlement *Lauret,* sometimes spelled *Laurette.* "The desire was to have named it by compounding the names of the only two ladies in the gulch, (for there are two here, God bless them,) wives of the two Dodge brothers," a correspondent told the *Rocky Mountain News* in September 1860. But because either Laura or Jeannette Dodge objected, *Lauret* "was adopted as a compromise for Lauranette." Most folks, however, continued to call the place *Buckskin Joe* or *Buckskin,* which became the post office name in 1865. Only a cemetery survives at the original site, although a new Buckskin Joe "Old West town" amusement park near Canon City perpetuates the historic name.
PO: November 14, 1861–December 21, 1865, as Laurette; December 21, 1865–January 24, 1873, as Buckskin

Buena Vista *(Chaffee)* [BYOO-nuh-vihs-tuh]

This descriptive Spanish name means "beautiful view." Nationally, the name grew in popularity after United States soldiers turned back Santa Anna's troops at the 1847 Mexican War Battle of Buena Vista.
PO: September 18, 1879–; Pop. 1,752

Buffalo Creek *(Jefferson)*

Once a station called *Buffalo* on the Denver, South Park, and Pacific (later the Colorado and Southern), *Buffalo Creek* shares the name buffalo with the nearby stream and many other Colorado natural features.
PO: August 16, 1878–; Pop. 225

Buford *(Rio Blanco)* [BYOO-f'rd]

In 1941, the Buford postmaster said that an early rancher had named the town for "a Civil War general." Union officer Napoleon Bonaparte Buford (1807-1883) is one likely candidate for the honor; after the war, Buford spent a short time in Colo-

rado as superintendent of the Federal Union Mining Company before settling in Chicago.
PO: March 19, 1890–June 30, 1919; December 6, 1921–December 15, 1961; Pop. 5

Buick *(Elbert)*

Buick honored, in slightly modified form, local rancher August Bueck.
PO: September 19, 1916–March 23, 1918; May 1, 1918–August 15, 1925

Burlington *(Kit Carson)*

For a short time in 1887 two townsites existed side by side: Lowell, named for the man who platted it, and *Burlington*, named by settlers for their former homes of Burlington, Kansas, and Burlington, Iowa. After Lowell was abandoned, *Burlington* residents moved a mile or so east and replatted the townsite, keeping the name *Burlington*. In 1889, the *New Burlington* addition was platted to the west, where the Rock Island railroad had placed a depot; consequently Lowell/Burlington became known as *Old Burlington*.
PO: April 29, 1887–; Pop. 2,941; CS

Burns *(Eagle)*

Burns took the name of trapper Jack Burns, who had a cabin in the area.
PO: May 14, 1895–; Pop. 25

Byers *(Arapahoe)* [BIGH-ers]

First known as *Bijou*, this station and settlement on the Kansas Pacific Railway soon took the name of William N. Byers, who counted among his many positions that of general manager for Colorado of the National Land Company, agent for the sale of Kansas Pacific and Denver Pacific railroad lands. On April 23, 1859, Byers had founded Colorado's first newspaper, the still-published *Rocky Mountain News*. In his history of the *News*, Robert Perkin says that Oliver P. Wiggins, the first postmaster of *Byers*, helped ink the type for the initial issue of the paper and later named the town "to show his gratitude for being tapped as a printer's devil."
PO: February 27, 1873–; Pop. 1,065 (CDP)

Cache la Poudre River *(Larimer, Weld)* [kash-luh-POO-d'r]

At least two accounts, both dating from the Mountain Man era and reflecting the influence of French trappers, record the naming of this river. According to one version, the William H. Ashley party, which included Antoine St. Charles Janis, camped on the stream in 1825. To hide their supplies from Indians while making nearby excursions, they "cached the powder" under the bank. (Janis's son, also Antoine and an early Larimer County settler, is often given credit for taking this enterprising action while with American Fur Company trappers in 1836—an erroneous but widely accepted story.) A second version has Quebec-born Pierre Lesperance and other Frenchmen making the cache on another expedition. At any rate, by 1835, when Colonel Henry Dodge led his dragoons along the South Platte River, he wrote that they traveled by the mouth of the "Cache de la Poudre."

Caddoa *(Bent)* [kuh-DOH-uh]

Caddoa is situated to the east of John Martin Reservoir, whose waters now cover an earlier townsite. The name recalls a group of Caddo Indians who refused to join the Confederate cause and fled northward from Indian Territory (present-day Oklahoma). Although the government set aside land near Fort Lyon, built housing, and purchased farming supplies for them during 1863–1864, the Caddo ultimately planted their crops farther down the Arkansas River.
PO: November 7, 1881–June 9, 1884; June 12, 1884–March 7, 1958; Pop. 35

Cahone *(Dolores)* [kuh-HOHN]

Cahone took its name from nearby Cahone Canyon. The word "cahone" comes from the Spanish *cajón*, which means "box." A canyon which is "boxed in" by three high, vertical walls is called a "box canyon."
PO: May 21, 1916–November 30, 1917; June 12, 1920–; Pop. 50

Calhan *(El Paso)* [KAL-un]

A Chicago, Rock Island, and Pacific contractor named Callahan or Calhan gave his name to this townsite, founded when the railroad came through in 1888.
PO: November 24, 1888–; Pop. 562

cahone

Cameo *(Mesa)* [KAM-i-oh]

A cameolike face in a nearby cliff suggested the name for this
Colorado River coal-mining town.
PO: December 14, 1907–February 28, 1969

Cameron Pass *(Jackson, Larimer)*

Cameron Pass honors its discoverer, Brooklyn-born and Indi-
ana-educated Robert A. Cameron, who came to Colorado after the Civil War. Involved first with organizing the Union
Colony at Greeley, Cameron later helped develop Colorado
Springs and Fort Collins and served as warden of the state
penitentiary.
Elevation: 10,276 feet

Camp Bird *(Ouray)*

"Whiskey Jack," "Camp Robber," and "Camp Bird" are all
names for the Gray or Canada Jay, which likes to steal food
and objects from mountain campsites. Thomas Walsh gained a
fortune from the nearby Camp Bird gold mine; his daughter,
Evalyn Walsh McLean, gained fame as the owner of the Hope
Diamond.
PO: April 28, 1898–March 15, 1918, as Campbird; Pop. 10

Camp Hale *(Eagle)*

Little remains to mark the site of *Camp Hale* at the base of Tennessee Pass, where Tenth Mountain Division soldiers trained
on skis during World War II. The post honored Brigadier General Irving Hale, a West Point graduate who had led Colorado
troops in the Philippines during the Spanish-American War.

Camp Bird

Campion *(Larimer)*

Campion honors John F. Campion, whose extensive and varied business interests ranged from mining and railroads to the sugar beet industry. *Campion* is noted for the Campion Academy, a Seventh Day Adventist school.
Pop. 1,692 (CDP)

Campo *(Baca)* [KAM-poh]

Early settler and first postmaster Frank Wheeler is credited with choosing the name *Campo*, a Spanish word whose meanings include "field" and "flat country."
PO: April 10, 1913–; Pop. 121

Camp Weld *(City and County of Denver)*

Established in 1861 to house troops of the Colorado Volunteers, *Camp Weld* honored Territorial Secretary Lewis Ledyard Weld, who also gave his name to Weld County. The camp was abandoned in 1865 after fire destroyed most of the buildings; today a monument at West Eighth Avenue and Vallejo Street in Denver marks the site. (*See also* Weld County.)

Canon City *(Fremont)* [KAN-y'n]

Canon City took its name from the nearby Royal Gorge, a narrow, deep canyon carved out by the Arkansas River. Zebulon Pike camped at present-day *Canon City* in December 1806 and January 1807; in 1820, when the Stephen H. Long expedition came through the area, Captain John R. Bell noted in his journal that the party was "surrounded by the grandest & most romantic scenery I ever beheld—what a field is here for the naturalist, the mineralogist, chemist, geologist and landscape painter."
PO: December 13, 1860–July 30, 1904, as Canon City; July 30, 1904–December 15, 1904, as Canyon City; December 15, 1904–; Pop. 12,687; CS

Capitol City *(Hinsdale)*

George S. Lee counted a sawmill and a smelter among his business interests, but he wanted more. He thought that his town, originally called *Galena City*, should become the capital of Colorado, and to that end he built an elegant brick mansion. Lee, of course, would be governor. Although *Galena* was renamed *Capitol City*, Denver remained the capital, Lee's political ambitions were unfulfilled, and the walls of the "governor's mansion" tumbled into dust. In 1974, the state declared that *Capitol City* was officially abandoned; as Hinsdale County

Assessor Lowell B. Swanson had testified, no town election had been held "since the sinking of the Titanic."
PO: May 18, 1877–October 30, 1920

Capitol Peak *(Pitkin)*

Members of the 1870s Hayden Survey thought that *Capitol Peak*, named for the United States Capitol, was an appropriate label for this prominent, ridged summit.
Elevation: 14,130 feet

Capulin *(Conejos)* [kap-yoo-LEEN]

Capulin in Spanish means "chokecherry" or "wild cherry." In neighboring New Mexico a community, a creek, and a mountain are also named Capulin.
PO: August 10, 1881–July 14, 1922; September 21, 1923–; Pop. 400

Carbondale *(Garfield)*

One of *Carbondale*'s founders is credited with naming the community for his Pennsylvania home.
PO: January 6, 1887–February 14, 1887; May 14, 1887–; Pop. 3,004

Caribou *(Boulder)* [KAIR-i-boo]

Only a few relics survive to mark the bleak and windswept site of this once prosperous mining camp. George Lytle, who was among the first 1869 prospectors, had formerly mined in the Cariboo region of British Columbia, and he named the great silver lode the *Cariboo*. Soon rendered *Caribou*, the mine gave its name to the community. However spelled, the word is derived from an Algonquin Indian word and refers to the North American reindeer.
PO: January 31, 1871–March 31, 1917

Carlton *(Prowers)*

C. H. Frybarger was the chief boomer and prime mover of *Carlton* and of the Colorado Land and Town Company, which promoted the site in the late 1880s. By 1900 Frybarger was listed in the *Colorado Business Directory* as a storekeeper, justice of the peace, and notary active in real estate in the "prosperous agricultural town"; his wife, Louise, served as postmistress. The records are silent, however, on the reason why the community was named *Carlton*.
PO: January 14, 1891–March 5, 1960

Carr *(Weld)*

Carr developed around the Denver Pacific railroad siding named for Robert E. Carr, who was serving as president of the Kansas Pacific Railway when he also became president of the allied Denver Pacific, which connected Cheyenne and Denver, in 1872.
PO: March 26, 1872–November 19, 1878; October 17, 1884–; Pop. 45

Cascade *(El Paso)*

Anticipating the arrival of the Colorado Midland Railway in the late 1880s, Kansas town promoters formed the Cascade Town Company, named, like the nearby creek, for the many area waterfalls or "cascades." First called *Cascade Canon* by the railroad, *Cascade* soon became a popular summer resort.
PO: August 16, 1887–; Pop. 1,479 (Cascade–Chipita Park CDP)

Castle Peak *(Gunnison, Pitkin)*

Members of the Hayden Survey climbed and named this castellated peak in 1873.
Elevation: 14,265 feet

Castle Rock *(Douglas)*

Aptly named, the town of *Castle Rock* grew up around the nearby castlelike erosional remnant. In July 1820, much to the

Centennial
Peak

confusion of later historians, members of the Stephen H. Long expedition named and sketched a "castle rock" as they journeyed along the Front Range from the South Platte to the Arkansas rivers. The explorers were not describing this *Castle Rock*, however, but present-day Elephant Rock, southeast of Palmer Lake and some twenty miles distant.

PO: May 18, 1874–; Pop. 8,708; CS

Cedaredge *(Delta)*

Cedaredge developed on land once part of the Henry Kohler ranch named "Cedar Edge" for its border of cedar trees, as easterners called the Utah junipers here.

PO: December 5, 1894–; Pop. 1,380

Cedarwood *(Pueblo)*

Ranch owner J. H. White, a minister from Pittsburgh, Pennsylvania, suggested the post office name *Cedarwood* for the abundant cedar trees nearby.

PO: March 22, 1912–March 15, 1943

Centennial Peak *(Montezuma)*

Banded Mountain was renamed *Centennial Peak* in 1976 to honor the one-hundredth birthday of Colorado, the "Centennial State," which entered the Union one hundred years after the Declaration of Independence.

Elevation: 13,062 feet

Center *(Saguache)*

First called *Centerview, Center* took its name from its location in the middle of the San Luis Valley.
PO: April 22, 1898–July 1, 1899, as Centerview; July 1, 1899–; Pop. 1,963

Central City *(Gilpin)*

Soon after John H. Gregory discovered Colorado's first lode gold in May 1859, thousands of prospectors poured into Gregory Gulch and the surrounding area. *Central City* was so named because of its central location among the various camps, which included Black Hawk, Mountain City, and Nevadaville. Today this Victorian mining community draws visitors to the famed 1878 Opera House, where summer operatic and theatrical productions have been presented since the 1932 reopening.
PO: October 8, 1869–; Pop. 335; CS

Chaffee County *(Established February 10, 1879)*

Prominent in territorial mining, banking, and Republican politics, Jerome B. Chaffee led the fight for statehood and became one of the first two United States senators from Colorado after it joined the Union in 1876.
Pop. 12,684

Challenger Point *(Saguache)*

Challenger Point in the Sangre de Cristo Range was named in 1987 to honor the astronauts who died in the 1986 Challenger explosion.
Elevation: 14,080 feet

Chama *(Costilla)* [CHAH-muh]

Early settlers from Chamita, "Little Chama," New Mexico, are credited with naming this San Luis Valley settlement. The Spanish *chama* comes from the Tewa Indian word *tzama*, which is said to mean either the color red or "here they have wrestled." The Chama River and the community of Chama, New Mexico, also took this Spanish name.
PO: May 3, 1907–; Pop. 250

Cheney Center *(Prowers)* [CHEE-nee]

Cheney Center took its name from Cheney, Kansas, named for Atchison, Topeka, and Santa Fe director Benjamin P. Cheney, Sr.
PO: February 24, 1917–June 30, 1936

Cheraw *(Otero)* [chair-AW]

Probably of Siouan origin, the Cheraw Indians lived in Virginia and the Carolinas, where Cheraw, South Carolina, was named for them. From the southeast the name made its way to Colorado, where it was given to the town and a nearby lake. Some local sources state that "cheraw" is a term for "sparkling waters," although according to South Carolina place name scholars the meaning is unknown.
PO: August 13, 1910–; Pop. 265

Cherry Creek *(Central Colorado)*

Colorado has a number of *Cherry Creeks*, including the storied stream that joins the South Platte River in Denver. Near this confluence gold seekers in 1858 erected the first crude buildings of the future capital. Here, too, Francis Parkman had camped in 1846, as he recalled in *The California and Oregon Trail* (1849). The young Bostonian noted the "great abundance of wild-cherries, plums, gooseberries, and currants" at the site. Both Parkman and pathfinder John C. Frémont, who camped in the area in 1843, referred to the creek by its present name. Earlier, however, in July 1820, the Stephen H. Long expedition had called the stream *Vermilion Creek:* "In some part of its course, its valley is bounded by precipitous cliffs of a red sand-rock, whence the name of the creek." Between 1869 and about 1886, a *Cherry Creek* post office operated south of Denver; today, the name appears on everything from shopping centers to housing developments.

Cherry Hills Village *(Arapahoe)*

In 1922, the *Denver Post* reported that "a large cherry orchard, located on an attractive knoll on the club grounds," had inspired the name of the new Cherry Hills Country Club. The residential community that developed around the club thus became *Cherry Hills Village.*
Pop. 5,245

Cheyenne County *(Established March 25, 1889)* [shigh-AN]

Along with their allies, the Arapaho, the Cheyenne Indians roamed the plains of present-day Colorado from the beginning of the nineteenth century.
Pop. 2,397

Cheyenne Wells *(Cheyenne)*

When writer and lecturer Bayard Taylor stopped at the *Cheyenne Wells* stage station on the Smoky Hill Trail in 1866, he "found a large and handsome frame stable for the mules, but no dwelling. The people lived in a natural cave, extending for

some thirty feet under the bluff." Nonetheless, the travelers soon "sat down to antelope steak, tomatoes, bread, pickles, and potatoes—a royal meal, after two days of detestable fare." Named for nearby wells and for the Cheyenne Indians who frequented the region, the station was about five miles north of the present town, which was founded after the Kansas Pacific Railway came through the area in 1870.
PO: May 8, 1876–August 21, 1895; October 2, 1895–; Pop. 1,128; CS

Chimney Rock *(Archuleta)*

Chimney Rock took its name from the spires that serve as a prominent landmark. The *Chimney Rock* post office was established in 1950 when the Dyke post office, named for rancher William Dyke and his postmistress wife Lena, was moved.
PO: November 1, 1950–; Pop. 50

Chipita Park *(El Paso)* [chuh-PEE-tuh]

Chipita Park commemorates Chipeta (usually spelled with an *e*), the wife of the Ute chief Ouray. Forced with other Ute to leave Colorado in 1881, a year after her husband's death, Chipeta lived at Bitter Creek, Utah, until her own death in 1924. Her body subsequently was interred in Colorado near the home where she and Ouray had once lived; today the site is maintained by the Colorado Historical Society as part of the Ute Indian Museum complex in Montrose.
PO: March 9, 1935–ca. 1981; Pop. 1,479 (Cascade–Chipita Park CDP)

Chivington *(Kiowa)* [CHIV-ing-t'n]

Founded while the Pueblo and State Line Railway built across southeastern Colorado in 1887, the town took the name of John M. Chivington, one of the most controversial figures in Colorado history. A Methodist minister, Chivington had led Colorado troops in an 1864 attack against Indians camped on nearby Big Sandy Creek; many women and children were killed. Despite the association with the Sand Creek Massacre, *Chivington* residents apparently did not consider the name a liability; on November 11, 1887, the first issue of the *Chivington* newspaper boomed the fledgling settlement as "Chivington! A pretty pick of the prairie!" (*See also* Big Sandy Creek.)
PO: October 24, 1887–; Pop. 20

Chromo *(Archuleta)* [KROH-moh]

Initially *Price,* for first postmaster Charles W. Price, this settlement was renamed *Chromo,* from the Greek *khrōma* ("color")

so that mail would not be misdirected to Price, Utah. In 1935, Price's son told the State Historical Society that his father had suggested the name for a Chromo Mountain in New Mexico, which he also had named.
PO: September 27, 1880–August 31, 1882, as Price; October 30, 1885–; Pop. 20

Cimarron *(Montrose)* [sim-uh-ROHN]

Cimarron took its name from the nearby Cimarron River (not to be confused with the more famous Cimarron River that flows across the southeastern corner of Colorado). The Spanish word *cimarrón*, meaning "wild" or "unruly," specifically came to refer to the Rocky Mountain bighorn sheep.
PO: August 28, 1883–; Pop. 20

Clark *(Routt)*

Clark probably honored stagecoach operator Worthington Clark.
PO: September 16, 1889–; Pop. 500

Clarkville *(Yuma)*

Clarkville developed around a service station established in the early 1930s. The community took the name of Ted Clark, who was operating the business when he became the first postmaster.
PO: May 18, 1938–April 30, 1954

Clear Creek County *(Established November 1, 1861)*

Clear Creek County took its name from the stream that flows through the area on its way from the Continental Divide to join the South Platte River. "The reason we gave Clear Creek that name was because of its very clear water," said gold-rush prospector Anselm Barker. Earlier, Mountain Men called the creek Vasquez Fork for the trading post that Louis Vasquez had at the confluence of the creek and the South Platte River before establishing the better-known Fort Vasquez.
Pop. 7,619

Cleora *(Chaffee)*

"Cleora" was Cleora Bale, whose father William operated Bale's Tavern and stage stop. The settlement boomed in the late 1870s on the expectation that the Atchison, Topeka, and Santa Fe would establish a station there. Instead, the railroad that came was the Denver and Rio Grande, which built its station a short distance northwest at South Arkansas. Thus eclipsed, *Cleora* residents and businesses left for the new town, soon to be called Salida.
PO: December 5, 1876–March 7, 1882

Clifton *(Mesa)*

Clifton developed around a Denver and Rio Grande station apparently named for the nearby Book Cliffs, so termed, as Hayden Survey topographer Henry Gannett wrote, "from the characteristic shape of the cliff, which, with its overhanging crest and slight talus, bears considerable resemblance to the edge of a bound book."
PO: August 18, 1900–; Pop. 12,671 (CDP)

Climax *(Lake)*

When the Denver, South Park, and Pacific Railroad completed its line to Leadville in 1884, the station at the top of Fremont Pass was called *Climax*. "The name was suggested as indicating that the effort to overcome all obstacles in railroad building, had been overcome at this point," George A. Crofutt told readers of his 1885 *Grip-Sack Guide of Colorado*. Nearby were vast deposits of molybdenum, and when World War I and the burgeoning automobile industry created a demand for the rare metal, used in hardening steel, the Climax Molybdenum Company's operations and mining town perpetuated the historic name.
PO: April 22, 1887–April 12, 1898; December 5, 1917–; Pop. 20

Coal Creek *(Fremont)* [KOHL-kreek]

Coal Creeks meander through Colorado counties both east and west of the Continental Divide. This mining town took its name from the Fremont County Coal Creek, where outcroppings of coal could be seen along the banks.
PO: November 4, 1873–May 31, 1894, as Coal Creek; May 31, 1894–July 1, 1964, as Coalcreek; July 1, 1964–; Pop. 157

Coaldale *(Fremont)*

This settlement had post office names of *Hayden Creek, Palmer,* and *Hendricks* before nearby coal mining operations suggested *Coaldale*. Later, gypsum production became more important than coal to the regional economy.
PO: May 4, 1878–February 10, 1880, as Hayden Creek; February 10, 1880–January 31, 1887, as Palmer; January 31, 1887–February 16, 1891, as Hendricks; February 16, 1891–; Pop. 100

Coalmont *(Jackson)*

Nearby coal mines inspired the naming of *Coalmont*.
PO: March 11, 1912–December 21, 1983; Pop. 5

Coffeepot Pass

Cochetopa Pass *(Saguache)* [kohch-i-TOH-puh]

Indians, Spaniards, and American trappers and explorers all crossed historic *Cochetopa Pass,* one of several gateways through the Cochetopa Hills. Gwinn Harris Heap, chronicler of the 1853 Edward F. Beale expedition searching for a central railroad route, explained the meaning of the name. *"Coochatope* signifies, in the Utah language, *Buffalo gate,"* he wrote in *Central Route to the Pacific* (1854), "and the Mexicans have the same name for it, *El Puerto de los Cibolos."* Today the highway between Saguache and Gunnison goes over *North Cochetopa Pass,* usually shown on maps as simply *North Pass.*
Elevation: 10,032 feet

Coffeepot Pass *(Gunnison, Pitkin)*

Prospectors in the late 1870s found a coffee pot on this pass, abandoned perhaps by an earlier Hayden Survey party. According to some reports, the pot survived at least until 1906. "It was gone, however, when I looked for it in 1918," wrote longtime forest ranger Len Shoemaker in *Roaring Fork Valley* (1973).
Elevation: 12,500 feet

Cokedale *(Las Animas)*

Cokedale was founded by a subsidiary of the American Smelting and Refining Company to house workers who toiled at the company-operated coke ovens.
PO: December 26, 1906–; Pop. 116

Colfax *(Custer)*

In 1870, Carl Wulsten led members of the German Colonization Society from Chicago to the Wet Mountain Valley. Their
cooperative endeavor soon foundered, as did the town they
named for Schuyler Colfax, who served as vice-president of
the United States between 1869 and 1873. In the Denver area,
another Colfax existed as a separately incorporated suburb on
West Colfax Avenue from 1891 to 1895, when it was annexed
to the capital city.
PO: May 2, 1870–January 16, 1879

Collbran *(Mesa)* [KOHL-bruhn]

During 1890 the Colorado Midland and Denver and Rio
Grande railroads were building a line between Rifle and
Grand Junction through the jointly owned Rio Grande Junction Railway. The route passed through De Beque, and apparently a railroad official, probably Henry Collbran of the Colorado Midland, thought that it would be nice to change the
name of De Beque to *Collbran*. Not surprisingly, De Beque's pioneer settler, Dr. W. A. E. deBeque, objected, and a vigorous
debate ensued; when the smoke cleared, residents of *Hawxhurst*, to the southeast, had changed the name of *their* community to *Collbran*. Henry Collbran later went to Korea, where
he was involved in a number of railroad and mining enterprises.
PO: January 9, 1892–; Pop. 228

Colorado

Tampa, Idaho, Nemara, San Juan, Lula, Weapollao, Arapahoe,
and Tahosa were only a few of the names Congress considered before establishing *Colorado Territory* on February 28,
1861. Lafayette, Franklin, and Columbus also had their supporters along with Jefferson, which residents of the mining regions had chosen when they created their own extralegal Jefferson Territory in 1859. Republicans, however, objected, as
did those who thought that George Washington should be the
only president honored with a state or territorial name. Finally, *Colorado* emerged the winner, even though the river that
inspired the name was in fact outside the territory. Fifteen
years later, on August 1, 1876, *Colorado* became the *Centennial
State,* but not until 1921, when the legislature renamed the
Grand River, did *Colorado* have a Colorado River within its
boundaries. (*See also* Colorado River, Jefferson County.)

Colorado City *(El Paso)*

Settled in 1859 as a supply center and named because early
prospectors believed that the mines were at the headwaters of
the Colorado River, *Colorado City* quickly supplanted the ear-

lier townsites of *El Paso* and *Eldorado.* "This appears to have been the first application of the name 'Colorado' in this region," noted Jerome C. Smiley in his 1901 *History of Denver.* In 1861, the Colorado territorial assembly designated *Colorado City* as the first capital, but legislators met there for only four days in July 1862 before they reconsidered and moved the capital to Golden, which held the honor until 1867. Now part of Colorado Springs, *"Old Colorado City"* has undergone a renaissance in recent years as a restored historic district.
PO: March 24, 1860–June 30, 1917

Colorado City *(Pueblo)*

Some one hundred years after the first Colorado City was founded, a new, planned community, also named *Colorado City,* took shape south of Pueblo. At the October 1963 opening, Colorado Governor John A. Love commented that "the first Colorado City, which was at the foot of Ute Pass, was created to serve the miners and ranchers. This new Colorado City is to provide a new way of life incorporating a great climate and beautiful scenery."
PO: September 1, 1964–; Pop. 1,149 (CDP)

Colorado National Monument *(Mesa)*

Established in 1911, the *Colorado National Monument* might have been called Centennial, Mammoth, Monolithic, Mile High, Columbine, or one of many other proposed names. It might even have been known as Hooper for S. K. Hooper, longtime head of the Denver and Rio Grande passenger department. Ultimately, Colorado Representative Edward T. Taylor, who took the lead in securing monument designation for the area, chose the name his wife suggested—*Colorado.*

Colorado River *(Central and Western Colorado)*

During the sixteenth and seventeenth centuries, almost every Spanish explorer who came upon this great river in the Southwest gave it a different name: *Río de Buena Guía* ("River of Good Guidance"), *Río del Tizon* ("Firebrand River"), *Río Grande de Buena Esperanza* ("Great River of Good Hope"), *Río de los Martires* ("River of the Martyrs"). Indian names, too, abounded—it was *Javill* or *HahWeal* to the Yuma, *Buqui Aquimuri* to the Pima; both phrases describe the reddish color of the water. By the late eighteenth century *Río Colorado,* the Spanish name that also referred to the reddish hue, was becoming more accepted. "Colorado was a word of common speech," as George R. Stewart observed in *Names on the Land,* "comfortable to the tongue and fitted to the stream." Until 1921, however, the branch of the river from the Colorado high country to the junction with the Green River in southeastern Utah was known as the *Grand River,* giving rise to such place names as Grand County, Grand Junction, and Grand Lake. In that year the Colorado legislature changed the name of the *Grand* to the *Colorado.* The United States Congress and the state of Utah concurred, and thus for the first time, part of the river for which Colorado was named actually was within the state borders. (*See also* Colorado.)

Colorado Springs *(El Paso)*

When Union Army veteran and railroad entrepreneur William Jackson Palmer fell in love with Mary Lincoln "Queen" Mellen in 1869, he was planning a north-south narrow-gauge railroad that would stretch from Denver into Texas and Mexico. Palmer determined to build a resort along the Denver and Rio Grande fit for the sheltered daughter of a Long Island lawyer, and soon after the couple married in 1870 a settlement developed at the confluence of Fountain and Monument creeks. Nearby Colorado City was declining, and the community that Palmer first called the *Fountain Colony* prospered to become *Colorado Springs*—the "springs" were the mineral waters at present-day Manitou Springs. Soon the town boasted so many English-born residents that it was nicknamed "Little London," but Queen herself did not like the West, however civilized. Ac-

companied by her three daughters, she fled to the East Coast and then to England, where she died in 1894. *Colorado Springs* thrived without her, becoming Colorado's second largest city.
PO: December 1, 1871–; Pop. 281,140; CS

Columbine *(Routt)* [KAHL-uhm-bighn]

Inspired by the many columbine plants blooming in the area, residents called their settlement *Columbine*. A few years before the post office was established, Colorado schoolchildren had voted on Arbor Day, April 17, 1891, for the blue-and-white *Aquilegia coerulea* as the state flower; the legislature made it official in 1899.
PO: June 5, 1896–May 19, 1967

Columbine Valley *(Arapahoe)*

Incorporated in 1959, this one-square-mile affluent Denver suburb developed around the Columbine Country Club.
Pop. 1,071

Comanche National Grassland *(Southeast Colorado)* [koh-MAN-chee]

During the eighteenth century the Comanche, who had ranged in the northern regions of present-day Colorado, began to move toward the south, eventually occupying the southeastern corner of the state as well as portions of present-day New Mexico, Texas, Oklahoma, and Kansas. Today the *Comanche National Grassland*, consisting of scattered areas retired from cultivation near Springfield and La Junta, commemorates the tribe.

Commerce City *(Adams)*

This descriptively named Denver suburb is home to numerous oil refineries and grain elevators. Incorporated in 1952 as *Commerce Town*, which included Rose Hill and southern Adams City, the community gained city status with the annexation of part of Derby in 1962.
PO: February 1, 1963–; Pop. 16,466

Como *(Park)* [KOH-moh]

Italian coal miners brought the name *Como* from the lake and city in their native land.
PO: July 23, 1879–; Pop. 25

Conejos *(Conejos)* [kuhn-AY-us]

Settled in the mid-1850s, *Conejos*, meaning "rabbits," took its name from the nearby river, christened by the Spanish per-

haps because the current was so rapid or because so many rabbits were seen in the vicinity. *Conejos* is home to Our Lady of Guadalupe, the oldest church in present-day Colorado, which was organized as a Catholic parish about a year after the original adobe chapel was dedicated in 1857.
PO: February 25, 1862–; Pop. 100; CS

Conejos County *(Established November 1, 1861)*

First called *Guadaloupe,* this county originally stretched westward from the Rio Grande to the Utah border. Almost immediately, the name was changed to *Conejos,* for the river and the town; the present borders were set in 1913.
Pop. 7,453

Conifer *(Jefferson)*

Conifer is the most recent name for the place known in early territorial days as *Bradford Junction* for Robert B. Bradford, whose wagon road joined others here before heading toward South Park. In 1865, a post office called *Hutchinson,* with George Hutchinson as postmaster, opened at the junction. Later, the settlement became *Conifer,* either for a George or a Jim Conifer or, more likely, for the abundant coniferous or cone-bearing trees in the vicinity.
PO: April 27, 1865–September 25, 1869, February 19, 1872–January 3, 1881, and June 15, 1881–November 16, 1894, as Hutchinson; November 16, 1894–February 28, 1929; October 1, 1960–; Pop. 550

Conundrum Peak *(Pitkin)*

Nearby Conundrum Creek was so named, according to one story, because prospectors who found placer gold never discovered the "Mother Lode." Puzzled, one said, "It sure is a conundrum," wrote forest ranger Len Shoemaker in *Roaring Fork Valley* (1958), and thus West Castle Creek became Conundrum Creek. Although the United States Geological Survey lists *Conundrum Peak* in its "Elevations of Named Summits over 14,000 Feet above Sea Level," the Colorado Mountain Club's *Guide to the Colorado Mountains* (1992) considers it "not a true fourteener because of inadequate distance and saddle drop" from Castle Peak.
Elevation: 14,022 feet

Cope *(Washington)* [KOHP]

In the late 1880s, the Burlington Railroad asked Jonathan C. Cope to establish a terminal point for a proposed line. Cope agreed, but said that he would stay only if trees could be grown in the area. The forest that Cope nurtured became known as *Cope's Grove*, the site evolved into the town of *Cope*, and "Daddy Cope," as he was fondly known, remained in the area until his death in 1921 at age eighty-six.
PO: July 16, 1889–; Pop. 130

Copper Mountain *(Summit)*

Copper Mountain is the name of both a 12,441-foot peak and a ski resort that opened in 1972. In 1881, the *History of the Arkansas Valley* predicted that "the development of the present season will bring Copper Mountain prominently before the mining public." A century later, however, it was "white gold"—snow—that created *Copper Mountain*'s prosperity.
PO: September 8, 1977–; Pop. 200

Cortez *(Montezuma)*

Situated in the Montezuma Valley, which like the county recalls the Aztec king, the town took its name from Cortez, the sixteenth-century Spanish conqueror of Mexico.
PO: June 21, 1887–; Pop. 7,284; CS

Costilla *(Taos County, New Mexico)*

"This night we camped on Rib Creek, the Costilla of the New Mexican hunters," wrote the young Englishman George F. Ruxton, who traveled through the area in the mid-1840s. Shortly thereafter a settlement named for Costilla Creek was founded on land encompassed in the future Colorado Territory; an 1868 boundary survey, however, placed the community in New Mexico.
PO: November 13, 1862–

Costilla County *(Established November 1, 1861)*

Costilla County took its name from the settlement of Costilla, originally in Colorado but now in New Mexico.
Pop. 3,190

Cotopaxi *(Fremont)* [koh-toh-PAK-see]

Cotopaxi apparently was named for the Cotopaxi volcano in Ecuador. The site also was known as *Saltiels* for Emanuel Saltiel, a mine owner who hoped to promote settlement on land he owned in the area. In 1882, he persuaded a colony of Russian and Polish Jewish immigrants to come to *Cotopaxi,* but they soon left after finding reality quite different from Saltiel's rosy representations.
PO: May 25, 1880–; Pop. 100

Cottonwood Pass *(Chaffee, Gunnison)*

Miners and freighters in the late nineteenth century used a wagon road over *Cottonwood Pass,* but after the boom days ended the route fell into disrepair. Not until the United States Forest Service opened a new summertime road in 1959 could automobiles traverse this Continental Divide crossing. The name Cottonwood appears frequently in the West; the most common cottonwood in the northern Rocky Mountains is the narrowleaf "mountain" or "black" cottonwood, found at elevations between 3,000 and 8,000 feet.
Elevation: 12,126 feet

Cowdrey *(Jackson)* [KOU-dree]

Early resident Charles Cowdrey gave his name to the community.
PO: December 21, 1901–January 15, 1907; April 5, 1915–; Pop. 60

Craig *(Moffat)* [KRAYG]

First called *Yampa, Craig* took its name from the Reverend William B. Craig, who with others had invested in the Craig Land and Mercantile Company that laid out the town. Related by marriage to Mrs. John L. Routt, wife of Colorado's last territorial and first state governor, Craig had come to Denver in 1882, where he served as pastor of the Central and South Broadway Christian churches. He later was chancellor of Drake University in Des Moines, Iowa.
PO: January 12, 1883–August 28, 1889, as Yampa; August 28, 1889–; Pop. 8,091; CS

Crawford *(Delta)* [KRAW-f'rd]

Editor and town promoter George A. Crawford had been nominated several times as governor of Kansas (he was even

elected in 1861, but the election was deemed illegal). In Colorado, after the former Western Slope Ute lands were opened for settlement following the 1880 agreement with the United States government, he helped found Grand Junction, Delta, and his namesake community of *Crawford*.
PO: April 14, 1883–; Pop. 221

Creede *(Mineral)* [KREED]

> Here's a land where all are equal—
>   Of high or lowly birth—
> A land where men make millions,
>   Dug from the dreary earth.
> Here the meek and mild-eyed burros
>   On mineral mountains feed.
> It's day all day in the daytime,
>   And there is no night in Creede.

So wrote newspaper editor and poet Cy Warman about the silver camp that materialized after Nicholas C. Creede and other prospectors discovered a bonanza lode in 1889. Soon the hills along East and West Willow creeks were teeming with miners who threw up shacks and shanties, communities as fluid as their changing names—*Weaver, Willow, North* or *Upper Creede* (once called simply *Creede*), *Bachelor, Amethyst, Sunnyside,* and *Gintown* or *Jimtown*, present-day *Creede*. Yet all of Creede's fortune did not make him a happy man. In 1897, while living in Los Angeles, he committed suicide by taking an overdose of morphine because, as one contemporary account put it, "his wife, from whom he had separated, insisted on living with him."
PO: May 12, 1891–July 1, 1891, as Willow; July 1, 1891–November 28, 1908 (moved to North Creede); February 9, 1909–; Pop. 362; CS

Crested Butte *(Gunnison)* [KREST'd-BYOOT]

A one-time coal town transformed into a skiing center, *Crested Butte* took its name from the 12,162-foot mountain christened by the Hayden Survey in 1874. Although the peak is often described as having the appearance of a rooster's comb, at least one early visitor didn't see it that way. When writer and former survey member Ernest Ingersoll was touring the area in the early 1880s with a feminine companion, he pointed out the distinctive feature as the train pulled into the *Crested Butte* station. Unable to see anything resembling a crest, the woman concluded that she was glad nonetheless that *Crested Butte* had been so named, because it now had "a name worth remembering, something you can't say of too many of these mountain villages."
PO: May 26, 1879–; Pop. 878

Crestone *(Saguache)* [kres-TOHN]

Crestone and Crestone Creek took their names from nearby Crestone Peak. Buddhist, Catholic, and New Age religious communities have settled here in recent decades, transforming a fading mining town into a modern-day Mecca.
PO: November 16, 1880–; Pop. 39

Crestone Needle *(Custer, Saguache)*

Along with its higher neighbor, Crestone Peak, *Crestone Needle* was first climbed in 1916.
Elevation: 14,197 feet

Crestone Peak *(Custer, Saguache)*

The name *Crestone* reflects the influence of the Spanish in southern Colorado. Spanish-English dictionaries define *crestón* as the "crest of a helmet in which the feathers are placed" and "an outcropping of a vein, ore," while *cresta* can mean a cock's comb, the crest of a helmet, or a mountain summit.
Elevation: 14,294 feet

Cripple Creek *(Teller)*

Almost every old-timer had a story to tell about the naming of *Cripple Creek,* which later gave its name to the mining camp. One account described the misfortunes of a cowboy chasing a cow over the creek. The cow stumbled, the horse fell over the cow, and the rider was thrown to the ground. Both animals had broken legs, the cowboy a broken arm. In another version, early rancher Alonzo Welty said that when he and his brother George were building a log cabin in the 1870s, George tumbled from the roof. Not long afterward, a hired hand fell from a horse and broke his leg. "Cripple Creek," another hand suggested, was an apt name for the stream. At any rate, after gold was discovered, ranching soon gave way to prospecting and town promotion. In 1891, a townsite named Fremont was platted next to Hayden Placer, known popularly as *Cripple Creek*—and where, to add to the confusion, the Fremont post office, named for John C. Frémont, was situated. All was resolved in 1893 when Fremont and Hayden Placer–Cripple Creek combined to become *Cripple Creek.*
PO: July 29, 1891–December 9, 1891, as Fremont; December 9, 1891–February 4, 1892, as Morland; February 4, 1892–June 20, 1892, as Fremont; June 20, 1892–; Pop. 584; CS

Crisman *(Boulder)*

Obed Crisman built an ore concentration mill in the mid-1870s and gave his name to *Crisman.*
PO: July 20, 1876–June 15, 1894; January 4, 1898–May 31, 1918

Cripple Creek

Crook *(Logan)* [KRUHK]

Crook took its name from General George Crook, who commanded troops on the Indian frontier after the Civil War.
PO: May 26, 1882–; Pop. 148

Crowley *(Crowley)* [KROW-lee]

Settlers in the community forming around the Missouri Pacific station decided to honor State Senator John H. Crowley for his role in establishing Crowley County.
PO: December 18, 1914–; Pop. 225

Crowley County *(Established May 29, 1911)*

When Otero County was divided in 1911, the northern section was named in honor of John H. Crowley, a prominent fruit grower then serving as state senator from Otero County. *Pop. 3,946*

Cuchara *(Huerfano)* [koo-CHAH-ruh]

Several southern Colorado place names are derived from the Cucharas River—*cuchara* means "spoon" in Spanish. Along with *Cuchara*, which is southwest of La Veta, are Cucharas Pass, the Cucharas Reservoir, and Cuchara Junction northeast of Walsenburg.
PO: January 20, 1916–June 15, 1957, as Cuchara Camps; June 15, 1957–; Pop. 400

Culebra Peak *(Costilla)* [koo-LAY-brah]

Culebra Peak took its name from Culebra Creek, shown on the map of Zebulon Pike's 1806-1807 expedition as the *Río de Culebra*. The word *culebra* means "snake" in Spanish.
Elevation: 14,047 feet

Cumbres Pass *(Conejos)* [KUHM-burs]

During 1880–1881, the Denver and Rio Grande Railway spanned this southern Colorado pass, named for the Spanish word meaning "summits." The railroad discontinued regular passenger service over the pass in 1951; today, however, tourists can ride the Cumbres and Toltec Scenic Railroad, which operates summer passenger trains over sixty-four miles of historic D&RG narrow-gauge track between Antonito, Colorado, and Chama, New Mexico.
Elevation: 10,022 feet

Curecanti National Recreation Area *(West Central Colorado)* [koo-ri-KAN-tee]

Recreational opportunities abound on the lakes within the *Curecanti National Recreation Area,* named for the Uncompahgre Ute Chief Curecante. Created by three Gunnison River dams built to provide irrigation water and hydroelectric power, the reservoirs are part of the Bureau of Reclamation's Upper Colorado River Storage Project.

Custer County *(Established March 9, 1877)*

With memories of the 1876 Battle of the Little Big Horn fresh in their minds, legislators honored George Armstrong Custer when the county was created in 1877.
Pop. 1,926

Dacono *(Weld)* [day-KOH-noh]

Daisy, Cora, and Nora (or Nona) were remembered when
mine owner Charles L. Baum named *Dacono,* using the first
two letters of each name. Daisy was Baum's wife; whether the
other women were her friends, his sisters, or a friend and a
woman minister who married the Baums has not been settled.
PO: December 21, 1907–; Pop. 2,228

Dailey *(Logan)*

According to the Burlington Railroad "Colonization Department," the line named the siding around which the town developed for trainmaster James Dailey.
PO: June 28, 1915–July 7, 1961

Dallas *(Ouray)*

George M. Dallas, diplomat and vice-president in the James
K. Polk administration (1845-1849), is often said to have been
honored with Dallas, Texas. He is similarly credited as the
namesake of this Colorado stage stop, mining camp, and railroad station. Fred Tarpley notes in *1001 Texas Place Names,*
however, that the city might actually have been named for Joseph Dallas, a friend of town founder John Neely Bryan. In
any event, whether named for the politician or the place, *Dallas,* Colorado, declined after the Rio Grande Southern Railroad established nearby Ridgway at its junction with the Denver and Rio Grande tracks.
PO: February 11, 1884–October 31, 1899

Dallas Divide *(Ouray, San Miguel)*

Colorado Highway 62 crosses the Uncompahgre Plateau at
Dallas Divide, which perpetuates the Dallas name in Colorado.
The pass was spanned in earlier days by the tracks of the Rio
Grande Southern Railroad, which had a flag stop at the sum-
mit called *Dallas Divide* or *Peake.*
Elevation: 8,970 feet

Dearfield *(Weld)*

Led by Oliver T. Jackson, who had been inspired by Booker T.
Washington's *Up from Slavery* (1901), blacks hoping for a better
life established an agricultural colony southeast of Greeley in
1910. The fields "will be very dear to us," said black Denver
physician J. H. Westbrook, "so why not incorporate that senti-
ment into the name we select and call our colony Dearfield?"
Although at its height *Dearfield* had a population of some
seven hundred, lack of farming experience, insufficient funds,
and hard times took their toll; just twelve persons were

counted in the 1940 census. Today, only a few dilapidated buildings remain to mark the site.

De Beque *(Mesa)* [di-BEK]

Born in Canada, Dr. W. A. E. deBeque served with a Maine cavalry unit in the Civil War before migrating west to Colorado. By 1884, he had settled on a ranch he called Ravensbeque, where the post office of Ravens (soon Ravensbeque) was established in 1885. In 1888, deBeque relocated some three miles north to the new townsite named in his honor. Soon, however, some factions suggested changing *De Beque* to *Collbran,* probably for Henry Collbran, an official of the Colorado Midland and later the Midland Terminal railroads. After a spirited contest, residents of Hawxhurst to the southeast were induced to change the name of *their* town to Collbran, thereby leaving *De Beque* as a memorial to its "first citizen."
PO: March 23, 1888–April 28, 1894; April 28, 1894–May 27, 1902, as Debeque; May 27, 1902-; Pop. 257

Deckers *(Douglas)*

First called *Daffodil,* this hunting and fishing community was renamed for storekeeper Steve Decker.
PO: April 11, 1896–February 19, 1908, as Daffodil; February 19, 1908–November 15, 1933; Pop. 100

Deer Ridge *(Larimer)*

Deer Ridge and Deer Mountain commemorate the popular Rocky Mountain National Park residents. "Usually anyone on a trip into the park who really looks for deer will see them," write Louisa Ward Arps and Elinor Eppich Kingery in *High Country Names.*

Deer Trail *(Arapahoe)*

Deer are also common on the Colorado plains. Situated east of Denver, *Deer Trail* claims the honor as the site where the first rodeo recorded with rules and prizes took place on July 4, 1869.
PO: June 3, 1875–May 17, 1894; May 17, 1894–October 1, 1950, as Deertrail; October 1, 1950-; Pop. 476

Delhi *(Las Animas)* [DEL-ee]

Michael Beshoar listed *Delhi* in his 1882 history of Las Animas County, although the pioneer doctor gave no information on the origin of the name. It is logical to assume that the community, situated between Bloom and West (Edwest) on the Santa Fe line, took its name from the city in India; George R. Stew-

Deckers

art commented in *American Place Names* (1970) that Delhi has been "generally applied as an exotic name without much reason."

PO: March 16, 1908–April 19, 1913; December 26, 1919–May 30, 1975

Del Norte *(Rio Grande)* [del-NOHRT]

Río del Norte ("River of the North") and *Río Grande del Norte* ("Great River of the North") are two of the Spanish names given through the centuries to the Rio Grande, the "great river" that inspired the naming of *Del Norte*. (*See also* Rio Grande.)
PO: January 28, 1883–; Pop. 1,674; CS

Delta *(Delta)*

Western Slope town builder George A. Crawford, who spear-headed the founding of Grand Junction and gave his name to Crawford, also served as president of the Uncompahgre Town Company that established *Delta*. As Frank Hall wrote in his *History of the State of Colorado,* the community was "situated upon the broad and fertile delta at the junction of the Gunni-son and Uncompahgre Rivers, whence its name."
PO: January 5, 1882–; Pop. 3,789; CS

Delta County *(Established February 11, 1883)*

This county took its name from the county seat town.
Pop. 20,980

Denver *(City and County of Denver)*

In November 1858, gold seekers and town promoters from Leavenworth and Lecompton, Kansas, arrived at the conflu-ence of Cherry Creek and the South Platte River. Finding the choice location on the east bank of Cherry Creek already taken by the St. Charles Town Company, they "jumped" the site, using threats of violence and liberal doses of whiskey. This part of future Colorado was then in Kansas Territory, and the group included county officials appointed by Governor James W. Denver. The Kansans decided to honor the gover-nor—and perhaps obtain additional patronage—by naming the new town for him, not knowing that he had resigned while they were en route to the gold fields. Denver first vis-ited his namesake city in 1874. "And such a city!" he wrote to his wife. "It is, indeed, a city in the desert."
PO: February 11, 1860–February 13, 1866, as Denver City; Febru-ary 13, 1866–; Pop. 467,610; CS

Denver, City and County of *(Established December 1, 1902)*

Denver was situated in and served as the county seat of Ara-pahoe County, which extended eastward to the Kansas bor-der, until 1902. Following voter approval of the twentieth (home rule) constitutional amendment in that year, the *City and County of Denver* was created. Thus there is properly no "City of Denver" or "County of Denver" but rather one entity

that combines both municipal and county functions and powers.
Pop. 467,610

Devine *(Pueblo)*

Devine is thought to honor prominent Pueblo lawyer Thomas H. Devine, who died in 1932. At one time Devine was the general attorney for the Colorado branch of the Missouri Pacific Railroad, whose tracks paralleled those of the Atchison, Topeka, and Santa Fe through *Devine*.

Dillon *(Summit)* [DIL-uhn]

Present-day *Dillon* overlooks Dillon Reservoir, which submerged three previous townsites as part of an early 1960s project to channel Western Slope water to Denver. Forced to relocate on higher ground, *Dillon* residents moved the cemetery, preserved several historic buildings, and kept the name of pioneer prospector Tom Dillon.
PO: October 24, 1879–January 5, 1881; June 28, 1881–; Pop. 553

Dinosaur *(Moffat)*

Triceratops Terrace, Brontosaurus Boulevard, and Stegosaurus Freeway are but a few of the streets in *Dinosaur,* where residents renamed both the town and the roadways in 1965 to capitalize on tourist traffic headed to nearby Dinosaur National Monument. First called *Artesia,* for artesian wells in the vicinity and for Artesia, New Mexico, the community boomed after World War II along with the Rangely oil field.

PO: March 20, 1946–January 1, 1966, as Artesia; January 1, 1966–; Pop. 324

Dinosaur National Monument *(Northwest Colorado, Northeast Utah)*

Established in 1915 and enlarged in 1938, *Dinosaur National Monument* took its name from the rich fossil bone deposits protected within its borders.

Divide *(Teller)*

Long a busy railroad center, *Divide* was situated at the high point of the Colorado Midland Railway as it ascended through Ute Pass on the way to Florissant. From *Divide*, the Midland Terminal Railway built southward, reaching booming Cripple Creek in late 1895.
PO: July 26, 1889–; Pop. 600

Dolores *(Montezuma)* [duh-LOH-res]

Dolores was established on the Dolores River after the Rio Grande Southern Railroad bypassed Big Bend, a few miles downstream, in 1891. West of *Dolores* is the Anasazi Heritage Center, opened in 1988, which displays artifacts from the extensive archaeological investigations undertaken before the McPhee Dam and Reservoir were built.
PO: April 5, 1878–; Pop. 866

Dolores County *(Established February 19, 1881)*

Dolores County also took its name from the Dolores River.
Pop. 1,504

Dolores River *(Southwest Colorado)*

In August 1776, the Domínguez-Escalante expedition traveled along the river the Spanish called *El Río de Nuestra Señora de Dolores*, translated as "The River of Our Lady of Sorrows" and today known as the *Dolores River*.

Dominguez *(Delta)*

A few miles northwest of Escalante on the Denver and Rio Grande line is *Dominguez*. The town commemorates Fray Francisco Atanasio Domínguez, the senior member and leader of a 1776 expedition through present western Colorado. While seeking a route from Santa Fe to Monterey, Domínguez and Fray Silvestre Vélez de Escalante compiled a detailed journal describing the terrain and the native inhabitants. A century later, members of the Hayden Survey named *Dominguez* and Escalante creeks in their honor.
PO: August 17, 1907–October 31, 1913

Dotsero *(Eagle)*

"We used to be told that Dotsero got its name from an Indian girl, but I never could learn more about it," recalled early Red Cliff newspaperman William Thom in 1921. Another dubious story traces the origin of the name to a Ute Indian exclamation meaning "something new." More likely, as a Denver and Rio Grande engineer told the State Historical Society, *Dotsero* was derived from "dot zero," referring to a survey starting point.
PO: June 29, 1883–April 12, 1895; August 14, 1895–September 30, 1905; May 19, 1933–February 29, 1948

Douglas County *(Established November 1, 1861)*

Douglas County was named for Stephen A. Douglas, Abraham Lincoln's opponent in the famed debates during the 1858 Illinois senatorial campaign and in the 1860 presidential election. Douglas had died in 1861, several months before the first territorial legislature created the county, which initially extended east to the Kansas border.
Pop. 60,391

Douglas Pass *(Garfield)*

After Agent Nathan Meeker and other employees were killed in the 1879 Ute uprising at the White River Agency, Chief Douglas was imprisoned for almost a year at Fort Leavenworth, Kansas. *Douglas Pass* commemorates the Ute leader, who died in an 1885 dispute with another tribal member. (*See also* Meeker.)
Elevation: 8,268 feet

Dove Creek *(Dolores)*

Dove Creek postmaster W. E. Larrance told the Colorado Writers' Project that a freighter who saw flocks of wild doves christened the stream from which the community took its name.

Dove Creek

Situated in the heart of the southwestern pinto bean-growing region, *Dove Creek* claims the honor as the "Pinto Bean Capital of the World."
PO: January 16, 1915–; Pop. 643; CS

Dowd *(Eagle)*

Dowd, sometimes shown on maps as *Dowd's Junction,* commemorates James and Jack Dowd, who operated an early sawmill in the vicinity.

Doyleville *(Gunnison)*

Gunnison County pioneer Henry Doyle gave his name to *Doyleville.*
PO: October 24, 1881–April 9, 1882; September 4, 1882–February 5, 1883, as Gilman; March 24, 1883–April 4, 1969

Drake *(Larimer)*

Residents of *The Forks,* a settlement situated where the North Fork of the Big Thompson joins the main river, honored stockgrower and longtime state senator William A. Drake for helping them gain a post office.
PO: December 14, 1905–; Pop. 300

Dumont *(Clear Creek)* [DOO-mahnt]

First known as *Mill City, Dumont* was renamed for mine operator John M. Dumont, who around 1880 "undertook the redemption of the town and its neighboring mines from their long and absolute stagnation," as Frank Hall wrote a decade later in his *History of the State of Colorado.*
PO: July 5, 1861–February 10, 1863, and March 12, 1866–May 26, 1879, as Mill City; May 17, 1880–: Pop. 100

Dunton *(Dolores)*

Horatio Dunton, identified in 1890s Colorado business directories as a mine owner, justice of the peace, and proprietor of a hotel and grocery store, gave his name to this mining camp turned resort.
PO: August 9, 1892–November 8, 1895; March 19, 1896–November 30, 1954

Dupont *(Adams)* [DOO-pahnt]

Dupont originated with a storage plant for the E. I. du Pont de Nemours & Company branch explosives factory at Louviers. *(See also* Louviers.)
PO: June 19, 1926–; Pop. 5,200

Durango *(La Plata)* [doo-RANG-oh]

When Animas City refused to grant concessions to the Denver and Rio Grande Railway, the line established rival *Durango,* two miles south, in 1880. Former territorial governor Alexander Hunt, then associated with the railroad, perhaps named the new community for Durango, Mexico; the nearby Durango Mine also might have contributed the name.
PO: November 19, 1880–; Pop. 12,430; CS

Dyersville *(Summit)*

Methodist minister John L. Dyer, who recorded his experiences in *The Snow-Shoe Itinerant* (1890), often turned to mining to supplement his church income. A few miles from Breckenridge, he struck paydirt with the Warrior's Mark Mine; nearby he built a log cabin in 1881 that formed the nucleus of *Dyersville.*

Eads *(Kiowa)* [EEDS]

Eads commemorates engineer James Buchanan Eads, whose Eads Bridge spans the Mississippi River at St. Louis. Eads died in 1887, the same year the townsite was surveyed as the Missouri Pacific subsidiary Pueblo and State Line Railway built across the southern Colorado plains.
PO: November 18, 1887–; Pop. 780; CS

Eagle *(Eagle)*

Eagle was known as *Castle,* for an Eagle County peak; *Brush,* for Brush Creek; *McDonald,* for a settler; *Río Aguila,* for the Spanish name for the Eagle River; and *Eagle River Crossing* before residents settled on just plain *Eagle,* for the river.
PO: February 18, 1885–September 3, 1891, as Castle; September 3, 1891–; Pop. 1,580; CS

Eagle County *(Established February 11, 1883)*

Eagle County took its name from the Eagle River.
Pop. 21,928

Eagle River *(West Central Colorado)*

One way or another, the *Eagle River* seems to have acquired its name from the regal bird. The principal of the Eagle Public Schools told the State Historical Society in 1939 that the river "has as many tributaries coming into it as there are feathers in an eagle's tail." Early Red Cliff newspaperman William Thom recalled in 1921, however, that "the eagle's nest from which was derived the name of Eagle River was still a prominent landmark in the cliffs, about one-fourth of a mile up the river from Red Cliff, as late as 1879."

Eagle

Eastlake *(Adams)*

Annexed to Thornton in 1990, *Eastlake* was named for nearby East Lake.
PO: June 8, 1912–; Pop. 500

East Portal *(Gilpin)*

East Portal, at the eastern entrance to the Moffat Tunnel, had its inception as a camp for tunnel workers and their families.
PO: October 12, 1923–January 31, 1928; February 14, 1933–July 21, 1934; December 18, 1936–January 24, 1962; Pop. 10

Eaton *(Weld)* [EE-t'n]

Eaton commemorates Benjamin H. Eaton, governor of Colorado between 1885 and 1887, who took the lead in founding the town and constructing irrigation projects. First known as *Eatonton,* to avoid confusion with Easton in El Paso County, the town became *Eaton* when Easton became Eastonville.

PO: September 25, 1882–September 28, 1883, as Eatonton; September 28, 1883–; Pop. 1,959

Echo Lake *(Clear Creek)*

Echo Lake Park features a lodge and other facilities for travelers headed to the summit of Mount Evans. In 1928, the *Rocky Mountain News* "automobile editor" offered one version of the origin of the name. "Puzzling to the Utes was the mysterious echo for which the lake was named," he wrote, adding that they "had faith that their own voices were but the return calls of their dead."

Eckley *(Yuma)* [EK-lee]

Laid out by the Lincoln Land Company, a subsidiary of the Burlington Railroad, *Eckley* was named for Adam (or Adams) Eckles, foreman for cattleman J. W. Bowles.
PO: November 15, 1883–June 16, 1884; August 14, 1885–; Pop. 211

Edgewater *(Jefferson)*

Although farmer Thomas Sloan only wanted water to irrigate his crops when he dug a well in the early 1860s, what he got was a lake fed by an artesian spring. Before long, agriculture took second place to recreation, and by 1891 Denverites were flocking to the dance pavilion, theater, zoo, and carousel rides at the Manhattan Beach amusement park on the north shore. Today Sloan's Lake, which gave *Edgewater* its name, is part of a Denver city park.
PO: March 1, 1892–July 15, 1937 (branch of Denver); Pop. 4,613

Edith *(Archuleta)*

Was *Edith,* named for the daughter of New Mexico Lumber Company founder E. M. Biggs, in Colorado or New Mexico? Because of a survey line dispute not fully resolved by the Supreme Court until 1960, even the federal Post Office wasn't sure at times how to list the settlement, which ended up officially in Colorado.
PO: October 28, 1895–May 4, 1904 (Archuleta County, Colorado); May 5, 1904–February 4, 1909 (Rio Arriba County, New Mexico); February 5, 1909–October 31, 1917 (Archuleta County, Colorado)

Edwards *(Eagle)*

Edwards took the name of Melvin Edwards, who was postmaster of Red Cliff before serving as Colorado secretary of state (1883–1887).
PO: July 10, 1883–; Pop. 200

Egnar

Egnar *(San Miguel)* [EGG-ner]

Egnar is a Colorado example of a backward or reversed name, in this case "range."
PO: May 28, 1917–; Pop. 50

Eisenhower Memorial Tunnel *(Clear Creek, Summit)*

President Dwight D. Eisenhower, who often vacationed in his wife Mamie's home state, was remembered when the *Eisenhower Memorial Tunnel* on Interstate 70 was named. The first bore under the Continental Divide opened in 1973 to two-way traffic; the second bore, opened in 1980 for eastbound travelers, was named the Edwin C. Johnson Bore for the Colorado governor (1933–1937, 1955–1957) and longtime senator (1937–1955).

Elbert *(Elbert)* [EL-bert]

Established by the Elbert Townsite, Road, and Coal Mining Company, *Elbert* took its name from the county.
PO: March 12, 1875–July 27, 1880; June 27, 1882–; Pop. 280

Elbert County *(Established February 2, 1874)*

Although he was soon replaced, Samuel Hitt Elbert was serving as governor of Colorado Territory when the legislature created the county in 1874. A former territorial secretary, Elbert had married Josephine Evans, daughter of second territorial governor John Evans, in 1865; tragically, she died only three years after the ceremony. (*See also* Mount Elbert.)
Pop. 9,646

El Diente Peak

El Diente Peak *(Dolores)*

Mountaineer Dwight Lavender, who climbed this peak in
1930, gave it the descriptive Spanish name *El Diente,* "the
tooth." Lavender (1911-1934), brother of western historian
David Lavender, is today remembered by 13,160-foot Lavender
Peak in Montezuma County.
Elevation: 14,159 feet

Eldora *(Boulder)* [el-DOH-ruh]

Eldora, first called *Happy Valley* and then *Eldorado* or *Camp Eldorado,* boomed in the 1890s after gold was discovered. When
the post office was established the name became *Eldora* to
avoid confusion with other Eldorados.
PO: February 13, 1897–September 8, 1977; Pop. 50

Eldorado Springs *(Boulder)* [el-doh-RAD-oh]

Warm springs and the Spanish word for "an imaginary paradise of riches and abundance" combined to provide the name
for *Eldorado Springs.* A farming settlement first called *Moffat
Lakes* and then *Hawthorne, Eldorado Springs* became a popular
resort where Dwight and Mamie Eisenhower spent their hon-
eymoon in 1916.
*PO: September 12, 1906–May 1, 1930, as Hawthorne; May 1,
1930–; Pop. 650*

Elizabeth *(Elbert)*

In the early 1880s, as former territorial governor John Evans debated the naming of stations along his new Denver and New Orleans Railroad, he and his wife Margaret were entertaining her sister Elizabeth in their Denver home. One evening during dinner, according to Evans's daughter Anne, her father declared, "I'll name a town for you, Elizabeth."
PO: April 24, 1882–; Pop. 818

Elk Springs *(Moffat)*

A. G. Wallihan told the State Historical Society that he named *Elk Springs* in 1884 for the elk herds that congregated there. A noted wildlife photographer, Wallihan served as postmaster at Lay, northeast of *Elk Springs,* for almost half a century.
PO: June 9, 1924–March 18, 1944; July 16, 1948–1983; Pop. 25

Ellicott *(El Paso)*

English-born George Ellicott, the first postmaster, gave his name to the town.
PO: April 29, 1895–July 31, 1916; Pop. 300

Ellingwood Point *(Alamosa, Huerfano)*

Ellingwood Point, named for noted technical climber Albert R. Ellingwood, appears on the 1990 United States Geological Survey list of "Elevations of Named Summits over 14,000 Feet above Sea Level." Often disputed, however, is whether the "saddle drop" between this summit and Blanca Peak is sufficient to qualify *Ellingwood* as a Fourteener in its own right.
Elevation: 14,042 feet

El Moro *(Las Animas)* [el-MOH-roh]

George A. Crofutt said in his 1885 *Grip-Sack Guide of Colorado* that El Moro was "from El Moro in Spain"; in Spanish, *el Moro* means "the Moor." According to another story, Alexander C. Hunt, who was associated with the Denver and Rio Grande Railway after serving as territorial governor, reportedly thought that nearby Raton (Fisher's) Peak looked like Morro Castle in Havana, Cuba. Thus inspired, he named the new town of *El Moro* (with only one *r*), founded when the railroad built to the site in 1876.
PO: April 17, 1876–January 1896 as El Moro; January 1896–December 15, 1910, and January 20, 1911–September 15, 1933, as Elmoro

El Paso County *(Established November 1, 1861)*

"The pass" (*el paso* in Spanish) from which the county took its name is Ute Pass west of Colorado Springs. For centuries, the

Ute Indians traveled through this mountain gateway to their hunting grounds in South Park.
Pop. 397,014

El Rancho *(Jefferson)*

Visitors sometimes wonder why the rustic *El Rancho* restaurant, with its spectacular view of the Rockies, has both a postal station and its own Interstate 70 exit sign. In 1988, *Rocky Mountain News* columnist Gene Amole offered one answer. President Dwight D. Eisenhower, he recalled, often dined on prime rib at *El Rancho* ("the ranch" in Spanish). Longtime owner Ray Zipprich, Amole continued, "buddied up to the Eisenhower staff people" and in 1956 obtained a post office (a Golden branch) and a highway sign that said *El Rancho* instead of Evergreen. "This way, Ray was able to get El Rancho on every highway map printed," Amole concluded.
PO: July 1, 1956– (branch of Golden); Pop. 40

Elyria *(City and County of Denver)*

A. C. Fisk, president of the Denver Land and Improvement Company that platted the townsite in 1881, once lived in Elyria, Ohio. Incorporated in 1890, *Elyria* became part of the City and County of Denver in 1902.
PO: March 2, 1885–February 15, 1895, as Lyman; February 15, 1895–January 15, 1904

Empire *(Clear Creek)*

Henry DeWitt Clinton Cowles and several other New York prospectors renamed the mining camp of Valley City for the "Empire State" during the winter of 1860-1861. First *Empire City,* the settlement later became *Empire.*
PO: June 28, 1861–May 7, 1886, as Empire City; May 7, 1886–; Pop. 401

Englewood *(Arapahoe)*

Orchard Place and the eastern part of *Petersburg* combined to form *Englewood,* incorporated in 1903. Residents may have remembered either Englewood, Illinois, or Englewood, New Jersey.
PO: October 24, 1903–; Pop. 29,387

Ent Air Force Base *(El Paso)*

Situated in downtown Colorado Springs and housed partially in a former hospital, this facility served as headquarters for the United States Army Second Air Force during World War II. After the war it took the name of Major General Uzal Ent, who died of injuries suffered while commanding the unit in 1944. Now closed, the base is today the site of the United States Regional Olympic Training Center.

Ephraim *(Conejos)*

This short-lived Mormon settlement in the San Luis Valley was named for a son of Joseph in the Old Testament; the more successful settlement of Manassa took the name of his brother.
PO: July 5, 1881–June 2, 1888

Erie *(Boulder, Weld)*

Erie, which straddles the dividing line between Boulder and Weld counties, was named by a minister for his hometown of Erie, Pennsylvania.
PO: January 24, 1871–; Pop. 1,258

Escalante *(Delta)* [es-kah-LAHN-tay]

This Denver and Rio Grande stop near the confluence of Escalante Creek and the Gunnison River commemorates Fray Silvestre Vélez de Escalante. In 1776, Escalante and Fray Francisco Atanasio Domínguez traveled through much of present western Colorado seeking a route from Santa Fe to the California missions; their journal offers a detailed account of the terrain they traversed and the natives they encountered. A century later, members of the Hayden Survey named *Escalante* and Dominguez creeks in their honor.

Estes Park *(Larimer)* [ES-tiz]

Rocky Mountain News editor William N. Byers first used the name *Estes Park* in 1864 to describe the lush mountain valley discovered and settled a few years earlier by Joel Estes. The resort community that developed later and the lake created by the Colorado–Big Thompson Water Diversion Project also commemorate the Missouri gold seeker turned rancher.
PO: June 2, 1876–; Pop. 3,184

Evans *(Weld)*

Platted by agents of the Denver Pacific Railway in 1869, the townsite was named for John Evans, second territorial governor of Colorado (1862-1865), who was then spearheading construction of the line from Cheyenne to Denver. Before coming to Colorado, Evans had also given his name to Evanston, Illinois, where he helped found Northwestern University.
PO: May 16, 1870–; Pop. 5,877

Evergreen

Evergreen *(Jefferson)*

Trees have often been used as place names; early settlers in this mountain area were so inspired by the abundant evergreens that they named the post office *Evergreen*.
PO: July 17, 1876–; Pop. 7,582 (CDP)

Fairplay *(Park)*

Prospectors who disapproved of the greedy residents in Tarryall nicknamed it "Grab-all." Moving to a new camp nearby, they dubbed it *Fair Play* in rebuke. The name is not unique to Colorado; as George R. Stewart noted in *Names on the Land,* "Justice has made only a rare showing, but Fair Play has served as a popular equivalent. and in the Civil War period reached a total of eleven post-offices." Also known as *Platte City,* the community was renamed *South Park City* in 1869 but five years later again became *Fair Play* (now *Fairplay*).
PO: August 2, 1861–October 1, 1924, as Fair Play; October 1, 1924–; Pop. 387; CS

Falcon *(El Paso)*

Named for the falcons that circle the area, *Falcon* was platted in 1888 around the junction of the Chicago, Rock Island, and Pacific and the Denver, Texas, and Gulf (later the Colorado and Southern) railroads.
PO: October 10, 1888–September 14, 1942; Pop. 150

Farisita *(Huerfano)* [fair-uh-SEE-tuh]

Postmaster A. S. Faris named the post office for his daughter Jeannette, called Farisita, "the little Faris girl," by Spanish-

speaking residents. Later, a grown-up Jeannette Faris also served as postmistress.
PO: April 24, 1923–September 2, 1988; Pop. 5

Federal Heights *(Adams)*

Federal Heights overlooks Denver from a height of land along Federal Boulevard.
Pop. 9,342

Firestone *(Weld)*

Landowner Jacob Firestone gave his name to the townsite, one of the "tri-cities" of *Firestone,* Frederick, and Dacono.
PO: August 30, 1907–; Pop. 1,358

Firstview *(Cheyenne)*

On a clear day you can see forever—or at least to Pikes Peak from this aptly named spot on the Colorado plains. Also spelled *First View,* the townsite was platted in 1904 around a station established when the Kansas Pacific Railway came through in 1870.
PO: June 25, 1907–November 24, 1961

Fitzsimons Army Medical Center *(Adams)*

Built in 1918 as General Hospital Number 21, this facility was renamed *Fitzsimons General Hospital* in 1920 to honor Lieutenant William Thomas Fitzsimons, a physician who was the first United States officer killed in World War I. President Dwight D. Eisenhower, who recuperated from a 1955 heart attack at Fitzsimons, remains the most famous patient at the hospital, which became *Fitzsimons Army Medical Center* in 1973.
PO: November 2, 1921–April 30, 1923

Flagler *(Kit Carson)* [FLAG-ler]

For a brief period in 1888 a storekeeper's favorite dog, Bowser, was honored with a post office name before the station was moved to the new townsite of *Flagler* on the Chicago, Rock Island, and Pacific line. First called *Malowe,* for railroad attorney M. A. Lowe, Flagler was renamed for Henry M. Flagler, a longtime associate of John D. Rockefeller in the Standard Oil Company who later gained fame for extending the Florida East Coast Railway across the Florida Keys.
PO: October 12, 1888–; Pop. 564

Fleming *(Logan)*

H. B. Fleming, who represented the Lincoln Land Company of the Burlington Railroad, was remembered when the town-

site was laid out on the Chicago, Burlington, and Quincy line. Previously, the railroad had established 29 Mile Siding, which had a post-office name of Calvert for superintendent Elwood Calvert, about one-half mile east of present-day *Fleming.*
PO: December 22, 1887–August 8, 1888, as Calvert; August 8, 1888–May 31, 1904; September 16, 1904–; Pop. 344

Florence *(Fremont)*

Early settler James McCandless laid out the townsite in 1872, after the Denver and Rio Grande Railway established Labran a few miles distant. *Florence,* named after McCandless's daughter, eventually prevailed over Labran and became an important oil refining and ore reduction center.
PO: May 8, 1873–; Pop. 2,990

Florissant *(Teller)* [FLOH-ri-s'nt]

Pioneer resident James Castello remembered his former home of Florissant, Missouri, when naming the post office at his ranch and trading post.
PO: November 20, 1872–; Pop. 250

Florissant Fossil Beds National Monument *(Teller)*

Fossil insects, fish, birds, small mammals, and plants as well as petrified tree stumps are protected within the boundaries of the *Florissant Fossil Beds National Monument,* established in 1969 south of Florissant.

Fondis *(Elbert)* [FAHN-dis]

In the mid-1930s, W. S. Burns told the State Historical Society that he and his wife, who was the first postmistress, suggested four possible post office names. One, he said, came from "a newspaper article regarding something happening in an Italian hotel (Fondi de Italia)." The federal Post Office took *Fondi* and added an *s* to make *Fondis.*
PO: November 25, 1895–July 15, 1954

Fort Carson *(El Paso)*

Along with a Colorado town, county, and mountain peak, this army post near Colorado Springs honors frontiersman Kit Carson, whose military service included a stint as commander of Fort Garland (1866-1867). Founded as *Camp Carson* during the early days of World War II, the post became *Fort Carson* in 1954. (*See also* Kit Carson.)
PO: June 25, 1942–November 1, 1954, as Camp Carson; November 1, 1954– (branch of Colorado Springs); Pop. 11,309 (CDP)

Fort Collins *(Larimer)*

In order to protect emigrant trains and stage coaches carrying the United States mail, the *Camp at Laporte* was established along the Cache la Poudre River in the fall of 1863. When troops under Colonel William O. Collins arrived the next spring from Fort Laramie, the name was changed to *Camp Collins*. Severe floods washed out the site in June 1864, and the post was relocated a few miles southeast and called *Fort Collins;* settlers kept the name after the soldiers departed in 1867. Because Colonel Collins, commanding officer at Fort Laramie, had been thus honored in Colorado, the Wyoming post known as Platte Bridge Station was rechristened Fort Caspar (instead of Fort Collins) after his son, Lieutenant Caspar Collins, was killed on July 26, 1865, in an Indian skirmish. (Although spelled with an *e*, the name of the present-day city came from the fort; today the reconstructed buildings are open to the public as historic Fort Caspar—with an *a*.) *PO: June 27, 1865–October 19, 1865; May 12, 1866–; Pop. 87,758; CS*

Fort Crawford *(Montrose)*

In the wake of the Ute uprising against agent Nathan Meeker at the White River Agency in 1879, a post called the *"Cantonment on the Uncompahgre"* was established in 1880 near the future site of Montrose. Renamed *Fort Crawford* in 1886 to honor Captain Emmet Crawford of the Third Cavalry, killed early that year while pursuing Indians in Mexico, the fort closed in 1890.

Fort Davy Crockett *(Moffat)*

Built during the late 1830s, this short-lived fur trading post in the northwest corner of present Colorado was named for the famed frontiersman who died at the Alamo in 1836. When German-born physician F. A. Wislizenus visited the fort during his 1839 travels, he noted that "the whole establishment appeared somewhat poverty-stricken, for which reason it is also known to the trappers by the name of Fort Misery (*Fort de Misère*)."

Fort Garland *(Costilla)*

Fort Garland was established in 1858 in what was then New Mexico Territory when troops were moved from Fort Massachusetts, built six years earlier on a swampy and vulnerable site to the north. Named for Brigadier General John Garland, who commanded the Department of New Mexico, the post furnished protection to settlers in the San Luis Valley and to travelers going south to Taos. Kit Carson, the noted frontier scout, then serving with the New Mexico Volunteers, com-

manded the post during 1866 and 1867. Although *Fort Garland* was abandoned in 1883, the surrounding community kept the name. Today the fort, with some of the original buildings still remaining, is operated as a museum by the Colorado Historical Society.
PO: February 25, 1862–; Pop. 300

Fort Jackson *(Weld)*

Partners Peter Sarpy and Henry Fraeb built this South Platte fur-trading post in the late 1830s near present-day Ione. The name perhaps honored either President Andrew Jackson, who had completed his second term in early 1837, or company employee Gilbert Jackson.

Fort Lewis *(La Plata)*

Established initially at Pagosa Springs in October 1878, *Fort Lewis* took the name of Lieutenant Colonel William H. Lewis, a Union army veteran killed a month earlier in a skirmish with Cheyenne Indians in Kansas. Two years later the post was relocated on the La Plata River southwest of Durango, where troops helped keep the peace between settlers and the nearby Ute and Navajo until 1891. In that year the fort was abandoned, only to begin a new life as an educational institution. In 1892, the facility opened its doors as the Fort Lewis Indian School, evolving into a high school in 1911 after the federal government sold the institution to the state of Colorado; junior college classes began in 1927. In 1956, the school moved to the present campus in Durango, becoming a four-year college in 1962.
PO: October 5, 1880–October 10, 1891

Fort Logan *(Arapahoe)*

Established in 1887, this post near Denver was first unofficially called *Fort Sheridan,* for General Philip H. Sheridan. About the same time, a camp known as Fort Logan was authorized in the Chicago area. General Sheridan wanted to have his name on the Chicago installation, and he got his wish; General John Alexander Logan, for whom Logan County also was named, was honored with the Colorado fort. After World War II, *Fort Logan* was discontinued as a military post and a Veterans Administration hospital was opened at the site; since 1961, the state of Colorado has operated a mental health center at *Fort Logan.* (*See also* Logan County.)
PO: May 3, 1889–August 3, 1971

Fort Lupton *(Weld)*

After he resigned from the army in 1836, West Point graduate Lancaster P. Lupton sought his fortune in the fur trade. Lup-

ton had seen the South Platte River country with Colonel Henry Dodge's 1835 dragoon expedition; the adobe post he built along the river was known as *Fort Lancaster,* while the town that developed later around the site took the name *Fort Lupton.*
PO: January 18, 1869–April 17, 1873; May 9, 1873–; Pop. 5,159

Fort Lyon *(Bent)*

After a name change and a move, *Fort Lyon* became the nucleus of this community on the Arkansas River. Built originally in 1860 some twenty miles downstream near William Bent's new stone fort, the military post was called *Fort Wise* for Virginia Governor Henry A. Wise. With the outbreak of the Civil War, the name was changed to commemorate Union General Nathaniel Lyon, killed at the Battle of Wilson's Creek, Missouri, August 10, 1861. The fort was relocated in 1867 following a flood; here famed frontiersman Kit Carson died in 1868. Later, with the construction of more buildings, the fort served as a tuberculosis sanitarium and more recently as a veterans' hospital.
PO: September 5, 1860–August 2, 1862, as Fort Wise; August 2, 1862–December 26, 1889, and October 25, 1919–June 14, 1920; June 15, 1920–October 31, 1921, as U.S. Fort Lyon; November 1, 1921–

Fort Massachusetts *(Costilla)*

Fort Massachusetts existed for a brief six-year period (1852-1858) before the army abandoned it in favor of the newly established Fort Garland. The name probably reflected the fact that Lieutenant Colonel Edwin V. Sumner, the military department commander who authorized the post, had been born in Boston, Massachusetts. (*See also* Fort Garland.)

Fort Morgan *(Morgan)*

Between 1865 and 1868, a military post at the site of the present town protected travelers along the South Platte River stage route. Known first as *Camp Tyler,* then as *Junction Station* or *Post Junction* and *Camp* or *Fort Wardwell,* the fort was renamed in mid-1866 to honor Colonel Christopher A. Morgan. A Cincinnati native, Morgan had served as an aide to Union General John Pope since the early days of the Civil War. By early 1866, he was stationed at St. Louis, where Pope was commanding the Department of the Missouri. On January 20 he was found dead in his bed, asphyxiated when the fire went out in the gas stove warming his room.
PO: July 16, 1866–June 26, 1868; May 28, 1884–; Pop. 9,068; CS

Fort Reynolds *(Pueblo)*

Fort Reynolds, an army post on the south side of the Arkansas River east of Pueblo, was garrisoned between 1867 and 1872. The name honored West Point graduate and Mexican War veteran John F. Reynolds, who died in action at Gettysburg on July 1, 1863.
PO: June 15, 1869–February 25, 1870

Fort Robidoux *(Delta)* [ROO-bi-doh]

Missouri-born Mountain Man Antoine Robidoux established this fur-trading fort near the confluence of the Gunnison and Uncompahgre rivers about the mid-1820s. Also called *Fort Uncompahgre,* the post flourished until the mid-1840s.

Fort Sedgwick *(Sedgwick)*

Fort Sedgwick protected travelers and settlers along the South Platte River from 1864 to 1871. Established as *Camp Rankin,* the post was renamed in 1865 to honor Union Major General John Sedgwick, killed at Spotsylvania, Virginia, May 9, 1864; Sedgwick earlier had established Fort Wise (Fort Lyon) on the Arkansas River.
PO: May 3, 1866–April 8, 1869

Fort Stevens *(Huerfano)*

Shortly after construction had begun, the army deemed *Fort Stevens* unnecessary and ordered it discontinued in September 1866. The post was to have honored Union Major General Isaac Ingalls Stevens, the first governor of Washington Territory (1853–1857), who was killed at Chantilly, Virginia, September 1, 1862.

Fort St. Vrain *(Weld)*

Established in 1837 by the Bent and St. Vrain Company as an adjunct to Bent's Fort, this short-lived South Platte fur-trading post was first called *Fort Lookout,* then *Fort George* for George Bent, who had directed the construction. The later and more common name honored Ceran St. Vrain's younger brother Marcellan, who managed the enterprise.

Fort Vasquez *(Weld)* [VAS-kes]

Fort Vasquez, a South Platte fur-trading post built by Mountain Men Louis Vasquez and Andrew Sublette in 1835, was reconstructed a century later by the Works Progress Administration. Maintained today by the Colorado Historical Society, the site features exhibits on the fur trade, Indians, and archaeology in an adjacent museum.

Fort Wicked *(Logan)*

In January 1865, shortly after the Sand Creek Massacre, Holon Godfrey and his family held off an Indian attack at their ranch on the South Platte River. The Indians thereupon called Godfrey "Old Wicked," so the story goes, and thus Godfrey's Ranch became known as *Fort Wicked*.

Fountain *(El Paso)*

Fountain took its name from Fountain Creek. An earlier *Fountain City* existed briefly near the confluence of Fountain Creek and the Arkansas River in present-day Pueblo.
PO: August 8, 1864–; Pop. 9,984

Fountain Creek *(Central Colorado)*

French trappers and traders were probably the first to call the mineral waters at present Manitou Springs *Fontaine qui bouille,* or "the spring (or fountain) that boils." Thus the nearby stream became the *Rivière de la Fontaine qui Bouille;* John C. Frémont wrote in July 1843: "Our direction was up the Boiling Spring river, it being my intention to visit the celebrated springs from which the river takes it name, and which are on its upper waters, at the foot of Pike's peak." Later the river was known simply as *Fontaine qui bouille,* which became *Fountain Creek* in English. The Spanish, for their part, called it the *Río Almagre,* using a word meaning "red ochre" or "red earth."

Four Corners

Four states—Colorado, Utah, Arizona, and New Mexico—
meet here at the only such point in the United States. A monument with the four state seals marks the spot, which is surrounded by Ute and Navajo reservation lands.

Fowler *(Otero)*

Shortly before his death in 1887, the noted phrenologist Or-
son Squire Fowler embarked on a new project, the Fowler Colony Irrigation and Industrial Company. His aim, he told prospective investors, was "to organize in Southern Colorado a
wealth and health producing enterprise," where "people
could come from the East and acquire a practical knowledge
of farming, stock raising and other healthful and profitable industries of the West, and thus fit themselves or their children
for independent lives of usefulness and happiness in sur-
roundings of health, comfort and progressive attainments."
The site chosen on the Atchison, Topeka, and Santa Fe Railroad, he noted, was "at the station now known as *Oxford*, but
which will probably be changed to *Fowler*." And so it was, although Fowler did not live to see the town that evolved from
his idealistic vision.
*PO: April 27, 1882–September 6, 1890, as Oxford; September 6,
1890–; Pop. 1,154*

Foxton *(Jefferson)*

Early settler Alvin Morey is credited with bestowing the name
Park Siding on this South Platte River site. The later name of
Foxton, given by a merchant, is said to have come from Fox-
hall, England.
PO: January 21, 1909–; Pop. 50

Franktown *(Douglas)*

Franktown had its origins in a claim called *Frankstown*, settled
by Fifty-Niner James Frank Gardner. A former New Yorker,
Gardner was named the first clerk and recorder after Douglas
County was formed in 1861. He conducted county business at
his *Frankstown* cabin until 1863, when he transferred operations some four miles south to *California Ranch*, which became
present-day *Franktown* (without the *s*) and continued as the
county seat until Castle Rock won the designation in an 1874
election. Gardner also represented Douglas County in both
the territorial and state Colorado legislatures.
PO: September 8, 1862–; Pop. 300

Fraser *(Grand)* [FRAY-z'r]

Fraser was named for the Fraser River, which surveyor and explorer Edward L. Berthoud had called *Moses Creek*, after an assistant, Thomas Moses, in 1861. By the late 1860s, however, *Moses Creek* was shown on maps as the *Fraser River*; the source of the name *Fraser* remains a mystery, although Reuben Fraser or Frazier and a "Dr. Fraser" have been suggested as candidates. In 1876 a *Fraser* post office was established at Cozens's Ranch; it was moved to the Gaskill Ranch, near the present-day town, in 1904. With the arrival of the Denver, Northwestern, and Pacific Railway (the Moffat Road) in 1905, lumber company entrepreneur George Eastom laid out a townsite called Eastom, which soon took the post office name of *Fraser*.
PO: July 26, 1876–; Pop. 575

Frederick *(Weld)* [FRED-rick]

Frederick A. Clark was honored when his heirs laid out the townsite on his estate.
PO: December 21, 1907–; Pop. 988

Fremont County *(Established November 1, 1861)* [free-MAHNT]

John C. Frémont, who traveled through portions of present-day *Fremont County* during his western expeditions, was honored with the county name. Frémont later ran for president on the 1856 Republican ticket, commanded the Department of the West during the Civil War, and served as territorial governor of Arizona (1878–1881).
Pop. 32,273

Fremont Pass *(Lake, Summit)*

Both the Denver and Rio Grande and the Denver, South Park, and Pacific railroads crossed Fremont Pass; explorer John C. Frémont, for whom it was named, did not, although he had traveled over nearby Hoosier and Tennessee passes in the 1840s. Some forty years later, naturalist and writer Ernest Ingersoll took a trip over Fremont Pass on the D&RG line, recounting the experience in *The Crest of the Continent* (1885). Near the top, he wrote, "we curl round a perfect shepherd's crook of a curve, and then climb its straight staff to the summit of Fremont's—the highest railway pass in the world. The pathway is so hidden in great woods, and the grim giants of the Mosquito range are still so inaccessibly far above you, even when you have reached the sterile *ober land*, above the trees, that you hardly realize the fact that you are 11,540 feet—considerably over two vertical miles—above the sea."
Elevation: 11,318 feet

Frisco *(Summit)*

"Frisco City" proclaimed the sign that Henry Learned, who
later became *Frisco*'s mayor, nailed above the door of miner
H. A. Recen's cabin. Settled in the 1870s, the community was
probably named for another Frisco—San Francisco, California.
PO: August 29, 1879–; Pop. 1,601

Front Range *(North Central Colorado)*

In 1874, after Hayden Survey topographer James T. Gardner
visited Denver, he described the mountain range to the west.
"The abruptness with which it rises from the plains," together
with "the great length and height of its serrated crest," made
it "one of the most imposing mountain-facades in the world,
a magnificent front to the Rocky Mountains," he wrote. "Being unnamed, we have called it the Front or Colorado range."

Fruita *(Mesa)* [FROO-tuh]

First called *Mesa* in postal records, *Fruita* is in the fruit-growing district of the Western Slope.
*PO: April 12, 1883–March 4, 1884, as Mesa; April 4, 1884–; Pop.
4,045*

Fryingpan River *(Eagle, Pitkin)*

"We are just going from the frying pan into the fire," said
prospectors who attempted to flee Indians by climbing over
the mountains, only to find a band camped on the other side.
Fryingpan, they thought, was an apt name for the river they
had just left. Or perhaps the name came from other prospectors who lost their supplies and were forced to wash gold-
bearing sands in a frying pan. Yet another tale tells of Indians

who killed all but two of a group of Missouri trappers. Before going for help, one hid his wounded companion in a cave and marked the spot with a frying pan tied to a tree limb. When he returned the trapper was dead, but the frying pan remained.

Fulford *(Eagle)*

On April 27, 1893, the *Denver Republican* reported that "three separate towns known as Fulford, Polar City and Gee's addition" had been consolidated "under the name of Fulford, according to the expressed wish of the people by ballot." Platted in December 1895, *Fulford* honored prospector Arthur H. Fulford, who died in an 1892 avalanche.
PO: February 5, 1892–May 15, 1910

Galatea *(Kiowa)* [guh-luh-TEE-uh]

Galatea was one of the stations named in alphabetical order along the Missouri Pacific subsidiary Pueblo and State Line Railway. The name might have been inspired by Cervantes's late-sixteenth-century work *La Galatea* or W. S. Gilbert's *Pygmalion and Galatea* (1871).
PO: December 22, 1887–July 31, 1948

Galeton *(Weld)*

Briefly called *Zita*, for the daughter of an early settler, the post office and Union Pacific station were renamed for Jesse Gale, a rancher and Greeley banker.
PO: February 21, 1910–September 16, 1910, as Zita; September 16, 1910–; Pop. 170

Garcia *(Costilla)* [gahr-SEE-uh]

Beginning in 1849, settlers in the San Luis Valley established *La Plaza de los Manzanares,* named for the Manzanares brothers. Later the community and post office honored the Garcia family, whose members were among the first plaza residents.
PO: February 6, 1915–; Pop. 75

Garden City *(Weld)*

Adjoining Greeley, often called the "Garden City of the West," this town was organized in 1935 to provide bars and liquor stores for its then-dry neighbor. Rosedale, another "wet" Greeley suburb also founded in the 1930s, merged with *Garden City* in 1987.
Pop. 199

Garden of the Gods *(El Paso)*

Tradition traces the name *Garden of the Gods* to photographer Rufus E. Cable, who visited the spectacular sandstone formations in 1859. When a friend remarked that the area would be "a fine place for a beer garden!" Cable reportedly exclaimed, "Beer garden? Why, this is a fit place for the gods to assemble—a garden of the gods!" A registered National Natural Landmark, the area is now maintained as a Colorado Springs municipal park.

Gardner *(Huerfano)*

In 1941, a *Gardner* resident told the Colorado Writers' Project survey that the community was named for an early settler killed by Ute Indians. It is more likely, however, that the town took the name of rancher Herbert Gardner, whose father, Henry J. Gardner, served as governor of Massachusetts during the mid-1850s.
PO: April 13, 1871–October 3, 1871, and December 1, 1871–December 15, 1871, as Huerfano Canyon; December 15, 1871–; Pop. 75

Garfield *(Chaffee)*

Junction City or *Garfield?* This settlement at the confluence of the Middle Fork and the South Arkansas River as well as at

the junction of the Monarch Pass and Alpine Pass roads was initially referred to by both names. The 1881 *History of the Arkansas Valley* called it "Garfield, or, as more generally known, Junction City," while George A. Crofutt's 1881 *Grip-Sack Guide of Colorado* listed it as "Garfield—Chaffee county, formerly called 'Junction City.'" In 1880, the post office opened as *Garfield*, making clear that at least the place was not renamed in 1883 to honor the assassinated president James A. Garfield, as many accounts have it. In any case, in 1990 the post office took the name *Monarch*, for the nearby pass and ski area, and *Garfield* soon disappeared from the official state highway map. (*See also* Monarch.)
PO: July, 8, 1880–November 9, 1889; January 11, 1905–February 28, 1911; September 9, 1911–January 1990; January 1990, as Monarch

Garfield County *(Established February 10, 1883)*

Created in 1883, *Garfield County* took the name of President James A. Garfield, who was assassinated in 1881.
Pop. 29,974

Garland City *(Costilla)*

Garland City, six miles northeast of its namesake, Fort Garland, was briefly the end-of-track town as the Denver and Rio Grande Railway built across the San Luis Valley. When noted author Helen Hunt Jackson visited the place in mid-1877 she was told that "twelve days ago there was not a house here. Today there are a hundred and five, and in a week more there will be two hundred." Scarcely a year later the railroad moved on, and *Garland City* disappeared as quickly as it had been born.
PO: July 24, 1877–June 27, 1878, as Garland

Garo *(Park)* [GAY-roh]

Garo (also *Garos*) took its name from French-born Adolph Guirard, an early South Park rancher. Little remains today of *Garo*; even the schoolhouse, for example, was moved to South Park City in Fairplay.
PO: June 29, 1880–February 28, 1955

Gateway *(Mesa)*

A nearby "gateway" through the mountains used by Ute Indians inspired the name of this community.
PO: April 25, 1903–July 29, 1903; July 16, 1904–; Pop. 300

Gem Village *(La Plata)*

In 1945, the Durango newspaper reported that the first gem show had been held at *Gem Village,* founded by Frank Morse near Bayfield and described as "a colony where collectors, dealers, and hobbyists in semi-precious stones might settle together."

Genesee *(Jefferson)*

Developed west of Denver in the mid-1970s, the *Genesee* community took its name from nearby Genesee Mountain. The word *genesee,* which means "beautiful valley" in the Iroquoian language, has been applied to a river in New York and Pennsylvania and to towns in Pennsylvania and Wisconsin. New York, Illinois, and Kansas have towns named Geneseo, a variant; the Colorado Geographic Board speculated in 1916 that Genesee Mountain was probably named by former Illinois residents.
Pop. 2,737 (CDP)

Genoa *(Lincoln)* [JEN-oh-uh]

Carrie Echternacht, who served for a time as postmistress, is credited with choosing the name *Genoa.* In addition to Italy, several states have places called Genoa, including Ohio, where Mrs. Echternacht was born, and Nebraska, where she once lived. Earlier the settlement was known as *Creech* (or *Creach*) and then *Cable* for R. R. Cable, president of the Rock Island Railroad. *Genoa* is famed for its combined museum/observation tower, a landmark for plains travelers since the 1930s.
PO: July 19, 1893–January 30, 1895, as Cable; January 30, 1895–June 29, 1895; March 31, 1903–; Pop. 167

Georgetown *(Clear Creek)*

Two nearby communities grew up after brothers David and George Griffith discovered gold along Clear Creek in 1859. One was named *Georgetown,* for George Griffith, while the other honored Elizabeth Griffith, who is usually identified as a sister but who was perhaps the wife of another brother, John. By the time *Georgetown* and *Elizabethtown* merged in 1867, silver had replaced gold as the key to success. Today the fine Victorian buildings in the Georgetown–Silver Plume National Historic District reflect the boom days of this "Silver Queen."
PO: June 19, 1866–; Pop. 891; CS

Gilcrest *(Weld)* [GIL-krest]

Gilcrest grew up around a Union Pacific station first called *Nantes* by the railroad. Later, W. K. Gilcrest bought up land, started a townsite company and a bank, and renamed the community.
PO: May 17, 1907–; Pop. 1,084

Gill *(Weld)* [GIL]

Gill was named for William H. Gill of Greeley, whose firm, the Gill and Decker Improvement Company, sold land for the townsite to the Union Pacific Railroad.
PO: December 27, 1910–; Pop. 200

Gillett *(Teller)*

Platted in 1894, *Gillett* took the name of W. K. Gillett, who was a Santa Fe official when he helped launch the Midland Terminal Railway. Gillett later served as president of the road, which connected the Cripple Creek area to the Colorado Midland line. The *Gillett* community gained notoriety in 1895 when promoters staged a bullfight at the local racetrack with imported Mexican bullfighters. A bloody and controversial spectacle, the event drew the wrath of the sheriff and the humane society, drove away the audience, and ended in financial failure.
PO: August 29, 1894–June 15, 1908; February 2, 1909–March 15, 1913

Gilman *(Eagle)*

Gilman took the name of Henry M. Gilman of Baltimore, Maryland, "a mining man who represented eastern capital on Battle Mountain," in the words of early Red Cliff newspaperman William Thom. "He fell dead in the road near the town not long after the town had received his name."
PO: November 3, 1886–April 22, 1986; Pop. 100

Gilpin County *(Established November 1, 1861)*

Western expansionist William Gilpin had accompanied John C. Frémont to Oregon in 1843 and led troops to victory during the Mexican War before President Abraham Lincoln appointed him the first governor of Colorado Territory in 1861. Vigorously attempting to keep Colorado in the Union, Gilpin issued drafts on the federal treasury without explicit authorization; volunteers provisioned with the resulting funds helped to defeat Confederate forces at Glorieta Pass, New Mexico, in a March 1862 battle often termed the "Gettysburg of the West." Nonetheless, controversy over payment of the "Gilpin drafts"

(later honored by the government) led to his dismissal a short
time later.
Pop. 3,070

Glade Park *(Mesa)*

Glade Park was an appropriate name for this large, parklike region in the midst of forests.
PO: November 11, 1910–; Pop. 250

Gladstone *(San Juan)*

Once a thriving mining community centered around the Gold
King Mine, *Gladstone* honored William E. Gladstone, who
served four times as the British prime minister between 1868
and 1894.
*PO: January 24, 1878–November 6, 1879; June 25, 1883–December
17, 1887; June 17, 1898–January 15, 1912*

Glendale *(Arapahoe)*

An early resident who visited California may have brought
back the name *Glendale* to Colorado. Apparently used first in
the mid-1890s for the Glendale Grange, the name was later
applied to the community, which is bounded on all sides by
Denver.
*PO: March 1, 1959–April 15, 1960; February 16, 1964–August 30,
1968; September 3, 1968– (branch of Denver); Pop. 2,453*

Glendevey *(Larimer)* [glen-DAY-vee]

Situated on Captain Thomas H. Davy's ranch in the Laramie
River Valley, this post office combined a version of Davy's
name with the word "glen," which means valley.
PO: May 19, 1902–January 31, 1975

Glen Haven *(Larimer)*

Glen Haven (first *Glenhaven*) had its origins in a resort incorporated as the Presbyterian Assembly Association. Members
bought stock entitling them to one-acre cabin sites; rental accommodations also were available. Hoping that persons of
"good moral character" would be drawn to this mountain
"haven," the association assured them that there were no
snakes or spiders in the area, "not even a *big bug*. The latter all
go to Estes Park."
*PO: May 28, 1917–July 31, 1919; May 26, 1922–July 31, 1924;
May 18, 1926–; Pop. 150*

Glen Haven

Glenwood Springs *(Garfield)*

Hot mineral springs and an Iowa community combined to give *Glenwood Springs* its name. Known earlier as *Defiance,* and briefly in postal records as *Barlow,* the town was incorporated in 1885 as *Glenwood Springs.* Hiram Pitt Bennet, one of the townsite promoters and a prominent Colorado lawyer and politician, later recalled that the name *Glenwood* was chosen because he had practiced law in Glenwood, Iowa. Other sources credit Sarah Cooper, wife of another town company member, Isaac Cooper, with honoring her hometown—which was also Glenwood, Iowa.
PO: June 25, 1883–March 28, 1884, as Barlow; March 28, 1884–; Pop. 6,561; CS

Globeville *(City and County of Denver)*

Workers at the Globe Smelting and Refining Company lived with their families in *Globeville.* Once separately incorporated but now part of Denver, *Globeville* continues to be a distinct and ethnically diverse city neighborhood.
PO: March 4, 1890–June 16, 1900

Golden *(Jefferson)*

Golden took its name from Thomas L. Golden, who with other prospectors camped at the site during the winter of 1858-1859. Between 1862 and 1867 *Golden* was officially the Colorado territorial capital, although legislators adjourned to Denver so often that Territorial Secretary Samuel Hitt Elbert allegedly remarked that the "first railroad needed in Colorado was the most direct line between its two capitals."

PO: April 6, 1860–June 27, 1876, as Golden City; June 27, 1876–;
Pop. 13,116; CS

Goldfield *(Teller)*

Situated near Cripple Creek and Victor, *Goldfield* was surrounded by rich mines such as the Vindicator, the Portland,
and the Independence.
PO: May 5, 1895–June 3, 1932; Pop. 100

Gold Hill *(Boulder)*

Prospectors who swarmed into the area following gold discov-
eries in January 1859 soon founded the community of *Gold
Hill.* They also organized "Mountain District No. 1, Nebraska
Territory" to register and protect claims, probably the first
such district in the Pikes Peak country.
PO: January 13, 1863–April 17, 1866, and December 26,
1879–June 4, 1894, as Gold Hill; June 4, 1894–May 31, 1920, and
May 25, 1923–May 31, 1952, as Goldhill; Pop. 150

Goodrich *(Morgan)*

Goodrich took the name of G. T. Goodrich, one of the first
commissioners of Morgan County.
PO: December 14, 1908–August 30, 1974; Pop. 30

Gore Pass *(Grand)*

Gore Pass is one of many Colorado natural features bearing the
name of Irish baronet Sir St. George Gore, whom Americans
unfamiliar with rank and title often called simply "Lord
Gore." Guided by Jim Bridger, Gore and his entourage
crossed the summit during an 1854–1857 western hunting expedition that slaughtered thousands of game animals from
the comforts of a luxurious caravan. A century later, the modern *Gore Pass* paved highway opened in 1956.
Elevation: 9,527 feet

Gothic *(Gunnison)*

Gothic (also *Gothic City*) was founded in 1879 near Gothic
Mountain, named, as Hayden Survey topographer Henry
Gannett wrote in 1874, "from the spires and pinnacles in bas-
relief upon its eastern face." Since 1928, the one-time mining
camp has been home to the Rocky Mountain Biological Labo-
ratory, a high-altitude summer field station.
PO: August 5, 1879–June 22, 1896; June 20, 1907–January 31,
1914

Gould *(Jackson)* [GOOL'd]

North Park pioneer Edward Gould, a native of Boston, gave his name to *Gould.*
PO: February 2, 1937–June 1, 1937, as Peneold; June 1, 1937–March 14, 1973; Pop. 10

Granada *(Prowers)* [gruh-NAH-duh]

Granada was initially the end-of-track town for the Atchison, Topeka, and Santa Fe, which arrived on July 4, 1873. Although *"Old Granada"* declined after the railroad moved on in 1875, a new townsite platted a few miles west in the mid-1880s survived as homesteaders came into the area. *Granada,* which means "pomegranate" in Spanish, is also the name of the Spanish city famous for the Alhambra, the Moorish citadel.
PO: July 10, 1873–; Pop. 513

Granby *(Grand)* [GRAN-bee]

Attorney Granby Hillyer, whose career included service as district judge in Trinidad and United States district attorney for Colorado, was recognized for his legal work when the Frontier Land and Improvement Company laid out the townsite in 1905.
PO: October 26, 1905–; Pop. 966

Grand County *(Established February 2, 1874)*

Before 1921, the present Colorado River from its source in *Grand County* to its junction with the Green River in Utah was known as the Grand River. The county, which originally extended from the Continental Divide to the Utah border, took its name from the river. (*See also* Colorado River.)
Pop. 7,966

Grand Junction *(Mesa)*

Even before the former Ute lands were officially opened to settlers, eager promoters selected a townsite in September 1881 at the confluence of the Grand (Colorado) and Gunnison rivers, the "grand junction" that gave the place its name.
PO: February 3, 1882–May 26, 1882, as Ute; May 26, 1882–;Pop. 29,034; CS

Grand Lake *(Grand)*

> "White Man, pause and gaze around,
> For we tread now on haunted ground!"
> So said a chief to me one day,
> As along the shore we wound our way.

Thus begins "The Legend of Grand Lake," composed by first settler Joseph L. Wescott and published in the early 1880s. According to Indian lore, the Ute who often camped around *Grand Lake* were surprised by their enemies, the Arapaho and Cheyenne. For protection the Ute women and children rowed out on rafts to the middle of the lake, where they drowned in a sudden storm. Even today, it is said, one can hear the cries of those who were lost in "Spirit Lake," as the Indians afterward termed it. Both *Grand Lake* (the largest natural lake in Colorado) and the community were named for the Grand River, as the Colorado River in Colorado was called until 1921.
PO: January 10, 1879–January 30, 1895; January 30, 1895–April 1, 1938, as Grandlake; April 1, 1938–; Pop. 259

Grand Mesa National Forest *(Western Colorado)*

Grand Mesa, one of the large, flat-topped mountains that inspired the naming of Mesa County, gave its name to this western Colorado national forest. (*See also* Mesa County.)

Granite *(Chaffee)*

Granite owes its name to the Precambrian granite visible nearby and its existence to gold discoveries dating from 1859. Between 1868 and 1879, booming *Granite* served as the county seat of Lake County, continuing briefly as the seat of the newly formed Chaffee County before bowing to Buena Vista in 1880.
PO: November 30, 1868–; Pop. 25

Grant *(Park)*

A settlement on the Denver, South Park, and Pacific Railroad, *Grant* honored President Ulysses S. Grant. "Grant," observed George A. Crofutt in his 1881 *Grip-Sack Guide of Colorado*, "is not as 'Big Injin' as the Grant for whom it was named, but, it is possible it may make *less noise*."
PO: May 16, 1871–October 13, 1918; August 27, 1936–January 1, 1948, as Olava; January 1, 1948–

Grays Peak *(Clear Creek, Summit)*

Grays Peak honors Asa Gray, author of the *Manual of the Botany of the Northern United States* (1848) and collaborator with John Torrey on the *Flora of North America* (1838–1843). *Grays Peak* and its neighbor, Torreys Peak, were named by botanist Charles C. Parry, who commemorated the two scientists while making an 1861 excursion to the area. Gray later climbed his namesake peak in 1872.
Elevation: 14,270 feet

Great Divide *(Moffat)*

In 1916, editor Volney Hoggatt of the *Great Divide,* then a weekly farm journal published by the *Denver Post,* launched the *"Great Divide colony."* Responding to readers seeking farming opportunities, Hoggatt, a former register of the state land board, had determined that government land in northwestern Colorado was suitable for development. Promising that the magazine would take no commissions or " 'rake off' of any nature," the *Great Divide* encouraged prospective homesteaders to settle in Moffat and Routt counties if they had "$1,000 in cash, three graded milch cows and three heavy work horses." By January 1917, the *Post* reported that one thousand "bona fide farmers" had taken up Hoggatt's offer and that the town of *Great Divide* was under construction.
PO: January 30, 1917–July 31, 1954

Great Sand Dunes National Monument *(Alamosa, Saguache)*

"Their appearance was exactly that of the sea in a storm, (except as to color) not the least sign of vegetation existing thereon," wrote explorer Zebulon Pike after he visited the area on January 28, 1807. Since 1932, these "naked, barren, and mysterious" hills, as the WPA Colorado guide called them, have been protected as the *Great Sand Dunes National Monument.*

Greeley *(Weld)*

In December 1869, prospective members met at the Cooper Institute in New York City to organize the Union Colony. The colony plan, promoted by *New York Tribune* editor Horace Greeley, owed much to the efforts of the paper's agricultural editor, Nathan Meeker, who had lived in an Ohio cooperative settlement in the 1840s and 1850s. Early in 1870 the colonists purchased land from the Denver Pacific Railroad, and the first families arrived in April and May. They named the town in honor of Greeley's contributions.
PO: April 21, 1870–; Pop. 60,536; CS

Green City *(Weld)*

Memphis speculator D. S. Green established *Green City* (or *Greensboro*) as part of his Southwestern Colony promotion. Hoping to capitalize on "colony fever," Green and his associates organized the venture in late 1870 primarily to sell townsite lots. Unfortunately, even though disgruntled residents ousted Green as president in 1872 and changed the name of the settlement to *Corona,* the colony soon fell victim to hard times and a lack of irrigation water.
PO: June 15, 1871–April 14, 1874; April 14, 1874–December 20, 1878, as Corona

Greenhorn Mountain *(Huerfano, Pueblo)*

Near this peak, in 1779, New Mexico governor Juan Bautista de Anza killed the Comanche chief called Cuerno Verde, or "green horn," for his striking headdress. In his report, Anza graphically described the encounter. As some forty Comanche approached, Anza "recognized from his insignia and devices the famous chief Cuerno Verde, who, his spirit proud and superior to all his followers, left them and came ahead his horse curvetting spiritedly." With this, "I determined to have his life and his pride and arrogance precipitated him to this end." Yet although Anza was the victor, it is Cuerno Verde who has been remembered with *Greenhorn Mountain*, Greenhorn, and other place names on the Colorado map.
Elevation: 12,347 feet

Greenland *(Douglas)* [GREEN-l'nd]

Local historians credit Helen Hunt Jackson, remembered for her books *A Century of Dishonor* (1881) and *Ramona* (1884), with coining the descriptive name for this settlement while traveling through the area by train. Born in 1830, Helen Hunt was a well-known writer seeking to improve her health when she came to Colorado Springs in 1873. Two years later she married businessman William S. Jackson and thereafter lived in Colorado Springs intermittently until her death in 1885.

Green Mountain Falls *(El Paso, Teller)*

Like nearby Cascade, this descriptively named community was developed in the late 1880s as a summer resort.
PO: August 28, 1888–September 28, 1894; September 28, 1894–June 25, 1901, as Green; June 25, 1901–; Pop. 663

Green River *(Moffat)*

Rising in Wyoming, the *Green River* cuts across the northwestern corner of Colorado before curving back into Utah. The Crow Indians called it the *Seeds-ka-day* or "prairie chicken river," a name that English-speaking travelers rendered in several other creative and varied spellings. In 1776, the Franciscan priests Domínguez and Escalante christened it the *San Buenaventura* for a theologian and teacher canonized in the fourteenth century, while to later Spanish explorers it was the *Río Verde* or *Green River.* "The refreshing appearance of the broad river, with its timbered shores and green wooded islands in contrast to its dry sandy plains, probably obtained for it the name of Green River," wrote John C. Frémont after his expedition crossed the stream in present Wyoming in 1843.

Greenwood County *(Established February 11, 1870; abolished February 6, 1874)*

Greenwood County was formed in 1870 with Kit Carson as the county seat. The name honored William H. Greenwood, then chief engineer of the Kansas Pacific Railway, who shortly joined his friend William Jackson Palmer in building the Denver and Rio Grande. Four years later, the legislature again redrew county lines, and *Greenwood County* disappeared into Elbert and Bent counties.

Greenwood Village *(Arapahoe)*

In 1950, residents of this suburban Denver area voted to incorporate their community as *Greenwood Village*. Although the town was new, the name was historic, commemorating the Greenwood Ranch which New Englander Cyrus Richardson had established in the late nineteenth century.
Pop. 7,589

Greystone *(Moffat)*

Geological features have often inspired place names. Because the nearby rock formations appeared greyish in color, the first postmaster chose the name *Greystone*.
PO: June 20, 1921–December 5, 1975

Grizzly Peak *(Chaffee, Pitkin)*

Colorado has five summits named Grizzly in addition to lakes, streams, valleys, and other features. This *Grizzly Peak*, so called because the Hayden Survey party that climbed it in 1873 supposedly saw a grizzly bear reclining on ice in a

Grizzly Peak

nearby lake, was listed as a Fourteener at 14,000 feet until it was demoted in a 1965 resurvey.
Elevation: 13,988 feet

Grover *(Weld)* [GROH-v'r]

The family of first postmaster Neal Donovan chose Dolly Grover Donovan's maiden name for the place.
PO: March 3, 1885–; Pop. 135

Guanella Pass *(Clear Creek)*

Guanella Pass honors Byron Guanella, a longtime Clear Creek County road supervisor and county commissioner. Guanella, who died in 1984, had been active in constructing the pass highway, now designated as an official Colorado Scenic Byway between Georgetown and Grant.
Elevation: 11,669 feet

Guffey *(Park)*

Pennsylvania oil baron James M. Guffey, who according to an 1896 Denver newspaper article was "largely interested in mining properties in different sections of the camp," was honored when *Idaville* in the Freshwater mining district was renamed.
PO: April 12, 1895–May 23, 1896, as Idaville; May 23, 1896–; Pop. 50

Gulnare *(Las Animas)* [GUHL-ner]

A horse gave its name to Almont; a cow claims the honor for *Gulnare*. In 1935, the *Gulnare* postmaster told the State Historical Society that settlers had sent several names to the federal Post Office for consideration. The envelope featured a picture of a Holstein named "Princess of Gulnare"; looking no further, officials decreed that the post office would be called *Gulnare*.
PO: December 16, 1890–; Pop. 120

Gunbarrel *(Boulder)*

In 1860, Alonzo N. Allen and a friend were hauling logs to build a cabin northeast of Boulder. As Allen's son told the story in 1937, the men decided on a spot near a cottonwood tree. "Father, acting as bull-whacker, drove as straight toward the tree as possible. The heavily loaded wagon cut a deep rut, which was followed by other teamsters, so that a well defined road was the result. It was called 'Gunbarrel' road on account of its straightness." Although this original road has since disappeared, *Gunbarrel Hill* and the *Gunbarrel* community perpetuate the historic name. Allen himself is remembered by Al-

Princess of

Gulnare

lenspark, the site of the cabin he used while prospecting in the mountains.
Pop. 9,388 (CDP)

Gunnison *(Gunnison)* [GUHN-i-s'n]

Gunnison took its name from Captain John W. Gunnison, who camped in the vicinity in September 1853 while leading a government expedition to survey a central railroad route through the Rockies. Some six weeks later, Gunnison and seven of his men were killed by Indians near Sevier Lake in Utah.
PO: October 2, 1876–; Pop. 4,636; CS

Gunnison County *(Established March 9, 1877)*

Although a larger *Gunnison County* was created in 1877, the borders of the present-day county, named for Captain John W. Gunnison, date from 1883.
Pop. 10,273

Gunnison National Forest *(West Central Colorado)*

In addition to a town, a county, and a river, a national forest also carries the name of Captain John W. Gunnison.

Gunnison River *(Western Colorado)*

In 1776, the Domínguez-Escalante expedition termed this river both the *Río de San Javier* and the *Río de San Francisco Xavier*. Although the official report of the Gunnison survey

called it the *Grand*, today the river honors the leader of that
ill-fated 1853–1854 expedition.

Gypsum *(Eagle)* [JIP-s'm]

Nearby gypsum deposits gave this town its name.
PO: June 14, 1883–; Pop. 1,750

Gypsum Gap *(San Miguel)*

In August 1776, the Domínguez-Escalante expedition traveled
through the area near this gateway, noting that "we saw, on
some small mounts, outcroppings of very good transparent
gypsum."
Elevation: 6,100 feet

Hagerman Pass *(Lake, Pitkin)*

President J. J. Hagerman's Colorado Midland Railway tun-
neled underneath this pass in the mid-1880s.
Elevation: 11,925 feet

Hahns Peak *(Routt)*

Prospector Joseph Henn, or Henne, who perished from snow
and starvation in the spring of 1867, left his name (spelled as
it was pronounced) on both a mountain and on the nearby
community that once served as the county seat.
PO: May 3, 1877–November 26, 1941; Pop. 50

Hale *(Yuma)*

Hale is said to honor Revolutionary War hero Nathan Hale,
hanged by the British as a spy in 1776. The *Hale* post office,
now discontinued, was first established in 1890 with Alonzo
Rockwell as postmaster.
*PO: May 17, 1890–February 16, 1894; October 30, 1900–June 1,
1984*

Hamilton *(Moffat)*

While other Colorado Hamiltons, including a once-prosper-
ous South Park mining camp, have disappeared, this community named for settlers Tom and Riley Hamilton is still on the
map.
PO: July 7, 1896–; Pop. 20

Handies Peak *(Hinsdale)*

In mid-August 1874, a Hayden Survey party made the first recorded ascent of this Fourteener, which topographer Franklin

Rhoda described as "a very high, massive mountain, with a great horizontal band of white running across the face of a high bluff on the northeast side of the peak." Rhoda also said that the mountain "bears on the map the name of Handie's Peak" and reported that his group had found prospect holes "with accompanying notices written on a stake" in the area. Perhaps Handie or Handies was one of the miners who had attempted to find paydirt; so far, however, he has not been identified.
Elevation: 14,048 feet

Happyville *(Yuma)*

Founded by obviously optimistic settlers, *Happyville* declined after a disagreement between store owner Cleve Mason and other *Happyville* businessmen. Mason moved some buildings about two miles west to a site he wanted to call Headstrong but which instead became Heartstrong. (*See also* Heartstrong.)
PO: July 26, 1910–February 28, 1922

Hardin *(Weld)*

Rancher George Hardin, who had served with the First Regiment of Colorado Volunteers during the Civil War, gave his name to *Hardin*.

PO: *November 2, 1881–April 7, 1894; December 6, 1894–February 15, 1955*

Hardscrabble *(Fremont)*

This small agricultural and trading community existed briefly in the mid-1840s in the valley of Hardscrabble Creek, south of the Arkansas River. The place was first known as *San Buenaventura de los Tres Arrollos,* which combined the Spanish word for "good luck" with a reference to the three arroyos of Hardscrabble, Adobe, and Newlin creeks. Here Mexicans, Indians, French, and Americans eked out a bare, "hardscrabble" existence in what was then Mexican territory. As trader George Simpson recalled, "it was rather hard scrabbling to get in a crop—hence the name of the settlement." More fanciful stories later ascribed the name either to the difficult escape made up the creek by survivors of an Indian battle or to the steep, rocky trail from Pueblo to the Hardscrabble Creek mesa.

Harman *(City and County of Denver)*

Edwin P. Harman, a lawyer who came to Denver from Mississippi after the Civil War, founded "Harman's Subdivision" in 1882 on land north of the present Cherry Creek Shopping Center. Incorporated in 1886, *Harman* was annexed to Denver in 1895; the *Harman* town hall (1891) now serves as a Masonic lodge.
PO: *August 16, 1887–January 15, 1904*

Harold D. Roberts Tunnel *(West Central Colorado)*

Denver water attorney Harold D. Roberts, who was instrumental in concluding an agreement to divert Blue River water to the capital, was honored when this transmountain diversion tunnel was dedicated in 1956.

Hartman *(Prowers)*

Hartman would have been Bristol, and vice versa, save for an error in the Chicago office of the Atchison, Topeka, and Santa Fe. George Hartman, a Santa Fe superintendent in Kansas before coming to Colorado, owned land near present Bristol; C. H. Bristol, a Santa Fe manager in La Junta, owned land near present *Hartman.* Instead of honoring each man with the name of the townsite closest to his own property, a Santa Fe clerk mistakenly reversed the names.
PO: *March 2, 1908–; Pop. 108*

Hartsel *(Park)* [HART-s'l]

Early South Park rancher Samuel Hartsel established a trading post, blacksmith shop, and other businesses; built a hotel that capitalized on the nearby hot springs; and gave his name to the community that grew up around his enterprises.
PO: March 16, 1875–; Pop. 75

Hastings *(Las Animas)*

A coal-mining town northwest of Trinidad, *Hastings* honored Alonzo Hastings, the father-in-law of Victor Coal Company president Delos A. Chappell. In 1917, a disastrous underground explosion claimed the lives of 121 miners, resulting in the closing of the Hastings Mine a few years later and the eventual decline of the community.
PO: September 12, 1889–February 15, 1939

Hasty *(Bent)*

Hasty, named for a pioneer family, benefited from the construction of the nearby John Martin Reservoir, built between 1939 and 1948.
PO: December 7, 1910–

Haswell *(Kiowa)* [HAS-w'l]

Haswell was selected as the *h* station between Galatea and Inman on the Pueblo and State Line Railway. The reason for choosing the name is lost—was it because the site on the dry eastern Colorado plains "had a well?"
PO: March 31, 1903–; Pop. 62

Hawley *(Otero)*

Named for Floyd Hawley, a long-time employee of the American Beet Sugar Company of Rocky Ford, *Hawley* grew up around a beet dump on the Atchison, Topeka, and Santa Fe.

Haxtun *(Phillips)*

At least three stories account for the naming of *Haxtun,* which has been spelled also as *Haxtum* and *Haxton.* Laid out by the Lincoln Land Company, a subsidiary of the Burlington Railroad, the town may have been named either for a contractor or for a large shipper on the line. Another version states that a Lincoln Land Company employee named the community for his home in New York.
PO: April 25, 1888–January 17, 1922, as Haxtum; January 17, 1922–; Pop. 952

Heartstrong

Hayden *(Routt)* [HAY-d'n]

Ferdinand V. Hayden, whose surveying parties christened many Colorado summits and other natural features, was himself honored with the naming of this community.
PO: November 15, 1875–September 30, 1880; November 22, 1880–August 1, 1881; October 24, 1881–;Pop. 1,444

Heartstrong *(Yuma)*

Following a disagreement between Happyville store owner Cleve Mason and other Happyville businessmen, Mason moved some buildings about two miles west to *Heartstrong.* According to local tradition, Mason wanted to name the post office Headstrong, but federal postal officials instead suggested *Heartstrong.*
PO: May 31, 1921–January 31, 1940

Heeney *(Summit)*

In recent years, *Heeney* has gained fame for its annual "Tick Festival," started in 1981 by a resident celebrating her recovery from Rocky Mountain Spotted Fever. Situated near the Green Mountain Reservoir, the community took its name from a local family.
PO: June 20, 1939–October 31, 1959; May 15, 1960–April 26, 1974; Pop. 30

Henderson *(Adams)*

Along with gold-rush prospectors came freighters such as John D. "Jack" Henderson, who brought supplies to the Cherry Creek settlements from Kansas in late 1858. Observing that his oxen survived until spring on the prairie grasses, he established a ranch on an island in the South Platte River, advertising in December 1859 that the place was "well timbered and watered" and that "with stabling for two hundred head of horses or mules, it offers extra inducements to persons having stock to winter." Henderson's Island, now home to the Adams County Regional Park, gave its name to the community that developed nearby.
PO: August 29, 1872–March 1, 1894, as Island Station; March 1, 1894–; Pop. 500

Henson *(Hinsdale)*

Henry Henson, a discoverer of the Ute and Ulay mines, gave his name to Henson Creek and the settlement of *Henson.* A Kentucky native who came to present-day Colorado in 1860, Henson was elected to the Senate of the first state General Assembly in 1876.
PO: May 17, 1883–April 22, 1884; November 12, 1892–November 30, 1913

Hereford *(Weld)* [HER-ferd]

Large numbers of Hereford cattle were shipped from this community, on the Burlington Railroad near the Wyoming border.
PO: May 8, 1909–; Pop. 50

Hermosa *(La Plata)* [her-MOH-suh]

The name of this community on the Las Animas River between Durango and Silverton means "beautiful" in Spanish. In his 1885 *Grip-Sack Guide of Colorado,* George A. Crofutt reported that the place had "a population of about 150, all of whom are engaged in stock-raising, putting up hay and raising vegetables in the summer."
PO: July 27, 1876–December 21, 1895; March 10, 1896–November 10, 1896; December 23, 1896–September 29, 1900; Pop. 100

Hesperus *(La Plata)* [HES-puh-ruhs]

Hesperus took its name from the nearby mountain named by the Hayden Survey. Proving that survey members, like other educated Victorians, had an easy familiarity with the classics, they christened the summit *Hesperus*—the Greek name for Venus as the Evening Star. Meaning "western," *Hesperus* was an apt choice for the southwestern Colorado peak.
PO: October 10, 1891–; Pop. 100

Hiawatha *(Moffat)*

Hiawatha was a company town of the Mountain Fuel Supply Company of Salt Lake City, which closed its Hiawatha Oil Field camp in 1968. Seven other states also have communities named *Hiawatha,* one of the approximately one hundred place names taken from Henry Wadsworth Longfellow's *Song of Hiawatha* (1855).
Pop. 10

Highland *(City and County of Denver)*

In 1859, a guide to Denver and Auraria noted that "a third town" was emerging on the South Platte River opposite the fledgling gold rush settlements. "It is being called Highland from the steady gradual rise of its area from the bank of the river towards the bluffs that form its outer limits." Staked out and named by William H. Larimer, Jr., and D. C. Collier, *Highland* soon became part of Denver.

Highlands *(City and County of Denver)*

Incorporated in 1875, *Highlands* was situated on high, hilly land northwest across the South Platte River from Denver. "True to her name and nature, she stands high and sightly," proclaimed the town's report in 1891. Indeed, with ordinances against drinking, fighting, and even kite flying, Highlands residents contrived to keep aloof from their sinful neighbor until economic reality induced them to vote for annexation in 1896.
PO: June 29, 1883–October 15, 1884, as Highlandtown; October 15, 1884–November 13, 1897

Highlands Ranch *(Douglas)*

After Lawrence C. Phipps II died in 1976, his *Highlands Ranch* property was bought by Mission Viejo of California and turned into a housing development that is now the largest community in Douglas County. The historic *Highlands Ranch* mansion, the main portion of which was built by a previous ranch owner in the 1890s, became the "Venneford Ranch" when the television miniseries of James Michener's 1974 novel *Centennial* was filmed.
PO: 1983– (branch of Littleton); Pop. 10,181 (CDP)

Hillrose *(Morgan)*

After the State Historical Society published information on the naming of *Hillrose* in its series on place names (1941), Charles W. Emerson wrote to correct the record. His mother, Kate Emerson, who had deeded an interest in the townsite land, named the community not for her sister, as stated, but

for her daughter, Rose Hill Emerson, by reversing and combining the first names.
PO: November 26, 1900–; Pop. 169

Hillside *(Fremont)*

Known earlier as *Texas Creek* and *Texas,* this Fremont County post office was renamed *Hillside* for the family farm of Mrs. Seth Brown after she was appointed postmistress.
PO: August 27, 1872–March 31, 1882, as Texas Creek; May 12, 1882–January 21, 1884, as Texas; January 24, 1884–; Pop. 20

Hinsdale County *(Established February 10, 1874)*

One month after the death of George A. Hinsdale, the territorial legislature created the county named in his honor. In 1865, Hinsdale, a lawyer active in southern Colorado politics, had been elected lieutenant governor following voter approval of a state constitution drafted under an 1864 congressional enabling act. President Andrew Johnson, however, reasoning that the legislation was invalid a year later, did not proclaim statehood. The appointed territorial officers thus continued to serve, and Colorado waited eleven more years to join the Union.
Pop. 467

Hoehne *(Las Animas)* [HOH-nee]

Hoehne was named for German settler William Hoehne, who dug one of the first irrigation ditches in the region. Hoehne is also credited with building the first mill, introducing the first threshing machine, and planting apple and cherry orchards.
PO: November 2, 1886–; Pop. 200

Holly *(Prowers)*

Holly was named for Hiram S. Holly, who came to Colorado after the Civil War and started the SS (Double S) ranch.
PO: November 26, 1880–; Pop. 877

Holyoke *(Phillips)* [HOLY-ohk]

Early settlers remembered Holyoke, Massachusetts, when naming this plains community. The Massachusetts town was named for nearby Mount Holyoke, which in turn honored Connecticut Valley pioneer Elizur Holyoke.
PO: November 9, 1887–; Pop. 1,931; CS

Homelake *(Rio Grande)*

In 1891, the Colorado State Soldiers and Sailors Home, now the Colorado State Veterans Center, opened east of Monte

Vista near Sherman Lake. When the post office was established in 1919 the words "home" and "lake" were combined to make *Homelake*.
PO: February 11, 1919–; Pop. 150

Hooper *(Alamosa)* [HOO-p'r]

Hooper first was named *Garrison*, for William Garrison, a partner in the general merchandise firm of Garrison and Howard. Mail intended for *Garrison* was often routed to Gunnison, however, and after residents briefly considered *Canton*, they decided to call the place *Hooper*, for Denver and Rio Grande passenger agent S. K. Hooper.
PO: January 26, 1891–July 17, 1896, as Garrison; July 17, 1896–; Pop. 112

Hoosier Pass *(Park, Summit)*

Prospectors from Indiana apparently named this pass for their home state.
Elevation: 11,541 feet

Hotchkiss *(Delta)*

Western Slope pioneer Enos Hotchkiss gave his name to *Hotchkiss*. In 1874, a few years before he settled in the North Fork Valley, Hotchkiss had discovered the Golden Fleece Mine near Lake City.
PO: October 3, 1882–; Pop. 744

Hot Sulphur Springs *(Grand)*

Hot Sulphur Springs grew up around the mineral springs that gave the town its name. From the mid-1860s to the turn of the century, *Rocky Mountain News* editor William N. Byers, who acquired and surveyed the townsite, promoted its virtues as a fashionable spa and resort. Byers Peak (which Byers climbed in 1901 at the age of seventy) perpetuates his name in the region.
PO: September 10, 1874–June 26, 1894; June 26, 1894–February 15, 1912, as Sulphur Springs; February 15, 1912–; Pop. 347; CS

Hovenweep National Monument *(Southwest Colorado, Southeast Utah)*

Pueblos, cliff dwellings, and towers—square, round, and circular—remain in *Hovenweep National Monument* as a legacy of the prehistoric Pueblo Indians, who lived in the Four Corners area until about A.D. 1300. Photographer William Henry Jackson is credited with first using the word "hovenweep" (Ute for "deserted valley") when visiting the region in 1874; the monument was established in 1923.

Howard *(Fremont)*

In 1876, John J. Howard brought his family from Tennessee to the Pleasant Valley and soon opened a store known as Howard's Place. When the Denver and Rio Grande Railway came through in 1880 the station and soon the Pleasant Valley post office became *Howard.*
PO: *March 19, 1877–July 26, 1882, as Pleasant Valley; July 26, 1882–; Pop. 160*

Howardsville *(San Juan)*

In August 1874, Hayden Survey topographer Franklin Rhoda noted that *Howardsville* "can boast of a store, a butcher-shop, assay-office, shoemaker-shop and post-office." Briefly the seat of undivided La Plata County—the first county seat in western Colorado—*Howardsville* took its name from George W. Howard, "equally well known as a miner and prospector" said the *Ouray Times* on July 6, 1878.
PO: *June 24, 1874–September 30, 1922; January 18, 1923–October 31, 1939*

Hoyt *(Morgan)*

Hoyt developed on land homesteaded by Mrs. Sidney Hoyt, who is credited with naming the place for her son, Dr. James Hoyt.
PO: *June 9, 1906–; Pop. 20*

Hudson *(Weld)*

In 1883, a Hudson post office was opened at the station on the Burlington Railroad. A few years later the Hudson City Land and Improvement Company of Denver bought property around the depot and began townsite development. "Hudson City lies in the most attractive and fertile part of Eastern Colorado," the company told potential investors in 1888. "The country is rapidly settling up, thriving farms taking the place of cattle ranches." How *Hudson* came to be named *Hudson,* however, is uncertain.
PO: *March 27, 1883–; Pop. 918*

Huerfano County *(Established November 1, 1861)*
[WAIR-fuh-noh]

The county took its name from the Huerfano River.
Pop. 6,009

Huerfano River *(Huerfano, Pueblo)*

In 1706, the Spaniard Juan de Ulibarri led an expedition into present-day Colorado and called this river the *Río de San Juan Baptista,* while his compatriot Don Antonio Valverde in 1719 christened it the *San Antonio*. By the early nineteenth century the term *Huerfano* was in use, referring to the nearby solitary volcanic cone the Spanish called *el huérfano,* or "the orphan."

Hugo *(Lincoln)* [HYOO-goh]

Hugo more likely was named for early settler Richard Hugo than for French author Victor Hugo, as some stories hold.
PO: December 1, 1871–; Pop. 660; CS

Humboldt Peak *(Custer)*

Germans who settled in the Wet Mountain Valley in the 1870s honored the great German scientist, traveler, and mountaineer Alexander von Humboldt (1769–1859) when they named this Fourteener. "He was the most famous man of his age, with the exception of Napoleon," said the noted Swiss naturalist Louis Agassiz of Humboldt in 1869.
Elevation: 14,064 feet

Huron Peak *(Chaffee)*

In 1956, the United States Geological Survey reported that *Huron Peak*, at 14,005 feet, had joined the ranks of the Fourteeners. (Later figures revised the figure downward to just 14,003 feet.) "Huron must have got its name from the nearby Huron mine," commented John L. J. Hart, author of *Fourteen Thousand Feet.*
Elevation: 14,003 feet

Hygiene *(Boulder)* [HIGH-jeen]

During the 1870s, members of the Church of the Brethren settled in the St. Vrain Valley. Popularly known as Dunkards, for their baptismal practice of immersing a person three times, they soon erected a church and the Hygiene Home, a sanitarium that gave its name to the surrounding community.
PO: June 25, 1883–; Pop. 450

Idaho Springs *(Clear Creek)*

A few months after George A. Jackson struck paydirt in January 1859, eager goldseekers poured into Clear Creek Canyon hoping to find their own bonanzas. They called the camp that sprang up *Jackson's Diggings, Sacramento Flats, Sacramento City,* and *Idaho* (or *Idahoe*) before settling on *Idaho Springs*. While the "springs" clearly referred to the hot springs in the area, the word Idaho, long thought to be Indian, is a different matter. In *Idaho Place Names* (1988), Lalia Boone sets the record straight: "Idaho is a coined word. It has no origin in any known Indian language, despite the popular belief that it was originally Ea-da-how—'Light on the Mountain.' "

PO: March 22, 1862–April 7, 1876, as Idaho; April 7, 1876–; Pop. 1,834

Idalia *(Yuma)* [igh-DAYL-yuh]

Idalia took the name of Idaleah (or Edaliah) Helmick, whose husband, John Helmick, joined other settlers in platting the townsite.
PO: August 6, 1887–September 18, 1888, as Alva; September 18, 1888–; Pop. 110

Idledale *(Jefferson)*

John C. Starbuck, an early settler, established a guest ranch in this mountain resort community west of Denver, and for a time the place was known as *Starbuck.* In 1930, however, residents voted to adopt *Idledale,* "the name it was formerly known by" said one newspaper report.
PO: January 28, 1918–July 7, 1920, as Joylan; July 7, 1920–September 1, 1930, as Starbuck; September 1, 1930–; Pop. 400

Ignacio *(La Plata)* [ig-NASH-i-oh]

This town within the boundaries of the Southern Ute Indian Reservation honored Chief Ignacio.
PO: January 31, 1882–; Pop. 720

Iliff *(Logan)* [IGH-lif]

"He was the squarest man that ever rode over these plains," said fellow cattle baron Alexander Swan after John Wesley Iliff died in 1878. The town commemorating this pioneer stockman developed around a Union Pacific siding in the heart of his South Platte River domain; in Denver, the Iliff School of Theology established by his widow also serves as a memorial.

PO: March 21, 1882–November 27, 1895; April 23, 1896–; Pop. 174

Independence *(Pitkin)*

Independence took its name (at least one of them) from the nearby Independence Mine, discovered on July 4, 1879. Residents also called the place, which combined several camps, by such names as *Sparkill, Farwell,* and *Chipeta.* "This is about the fourth change," commented the *Rocky Mountain News* after one switch. "It is expected to hold good for a week or ten days."
PO: February 1, 1882–October 18, 1887, as Sparkill; April 25, 1888–September 18, 1888, as Farwell; April 20, 1899–October 17, 1899, as Chipeta

Independence Pass *(Lake, Pitkin)*

In 1941, the WPA guide to Colorado called *Independence Pass* "probably the most impressive automobile pass in the State" and issued a warning to prospective travelers: *"altitude comparatively great; avoid overexertion."* Named for the Independence mining camp to the west, the pass is passable only in summer.
Elevation: 12,095 feet

Indian Hills *(Jefferson)*

Denver mortuary executive George Olinger and other businessmen launched the *Indian Hills* mountain housing development west of the city in the 1920s. "The pulsing finger of the Great Spirit traced the majestic lines and curves of beauty in the rolling verdure of Indian Hills," ran a typical brochure of the Indian Hills Mountain Home and Land Company. "The most superlatively beautiful mountain retreat in all the Rockies—the spot chosen, with unerring instinct, by primitive tribes of nomadic red men for their homing place." Pursuing this theme, the company imported Indians from New Mexico in the summertime to entice prospective residents with a bit of local color.
PO: June 2, 1925–; Pop. 2,000

Ione *(Weld)* [IGH-ohn]

Preparing to establish a station, a Union Pacific Railroad official asked W. A. Davis who owned the land to the north. "I own it," answered Davis. And to the south, east, and west? "I own it," Davis repeated, and thus, so the story goes, did *Ione* receive its name. Near *Ione* is the site of Fort Jackson, an 1830s fur-trading post.
PO: June 16, 1927–March 21, 1958; Pop. 10

Ironton *(Ouray)*

Ironton took its name from the iron ore prevalent in the Red Mountain mining district. Platted in 1884, the town prospered and declined with the fortunes of the Yankee Girl and other famed nearby mines.
PO: May 2, 1883–April 11, 1893; January 18, 1894–August 7, 1920

Irwin *(Gunnison)*

Several camps grew up in Ruby Gulch after ruby, wire, and native silver ores were discovered in 1879. Promoters soon platted *Irwin,* named for Canadian-born prospector Richard Irwin, and *Ruby City,* which became part of *Irwin.* By August 1880, the *Gunnison Review* could report that "the only brass band in the whole Gunnison country, is at Irwin, and the sweet music discoursed by it every evening has a charming effect, echoing through the gulches and over the distant hills and peaks."
PO: September 12, 1879–April 29, 1895; July 16, 1895–June 5, 1900

Jack's Cabin *(Gunnison)*

Jack's Cabin once flourished as a crossroads settlement and railroad station on the Crested Butte branch of the Denver and Rio Grande. The place was named for Jack Howe, variously described as a "picturesque character" and a "prince of good fellows in his way," who kept a tavern and hotel. "At one time, the Rio Grande was going to be real stylish and changed the name to Howeville," recalled a Gunnison newspaper columnist in 1929. " 'How come?' said everybody and kept right on calling it 'Jack's Cabin.' "
PO: June 26, 1879–March 11, 1880, and December 28, 1900–May 14, 1904, as Howeville; January 25, 1909–March 30, 1918

Jackson County *(Established May 5, 1909)*

Along with Presidents George Washington, Thomas Jefferson, and Abraham Lincoln, Andrew Jackson was honored with the name of a Colorado county.
Pop. 1,605

James Peak *(Clear Creek, Grand)*

When Long expedition naturalist Edwin James, with two companions, made the first recorded ascent of Pikes Peak in 1820, he also became the first botanist in North America to collect alpine flora above timberline. Afterward, the mountain was called *James Peak,* as well as *Pikes Peak* for earlier explorer Zebulon Pike, although by the 1859 "Pikes Peak or Bust" gold

rush it was clear that *James Peak* was the loser. This *James Peak,* situated to the north and about 800 feet lower in elevation, serves as some consolation. *(See also* Pikes Peak.)
Elevation: 13,294 feet

Jamestown *(Boulder)*

"Its scenic attractions are so striking that the first beholders called the place Elysian Park," wrote Amos Bixby in his 1880 history of Boulder County. Nonetheless, the post office for the mining camp on James Creek was called *Jamestown,* although many residents then (and later) preferred *Jimtown.* Who James was remains uncertain.
PO: January 8, 1867–July 15, 1930; June 19, 1934–; Pop. 251

Jansen *(Las Animas)*

In 1933, State Senator J. M. Madrid told an interviewer that *Jansen* was formerly called *Chimayoses.* As for the later name, a Colorado Writers' Project researcher concluded in 1940 that the "source of the name Jansen is not apparent."
PO: June 23, 1902–May 31, 1911; September 2, 1911–June 15, 1913; March 15, 1932–May 24, 1974; Pop. 300

Jaroso *(Costilla)* [hah-ROH-suh]

Spanish-English dictionaries define *jaroso* as meaning "full of brambles"; however, the word *jara,* from which it is derived, is "sandbar willow" in southern Colorado and northern New Mexico. Occasionally shown on maps with the feminine spelling of *Jarosa,* the town grew up around a San Luis Southern Railway depot just north of the Colorado–New Mexico state line. *(See also* La Jara.)
PO: March 10, 1911–; Pop. 40

Jefferson *(Park)*

Originating as a trading center for nearby mining camps, *Jefferson* took its name from Jefferson Territory, the extralegal government honoring President Thomas Jefferson created before the Territory of Colorado. "Many families are coming in," a *Jefferson* correspondent told the *Rocky Mountain News* on March 5, 1861. "One large store house and one for a public house are nearly completed; many more are in process of erection, and more still under contract. To those who have not seen this town site, I would say it was originally laid out as two separate towns, and called Palestine and Jefferson, and the two companies have since united their interests." Although the boom was short-lived, *Jefferson* later became a station on the Denver, South Park, and Pacific Railroad.
PO: September 3, 1861–April 4, 1863; October 3, 1879–; Pop. 100

Jefferson County *(Established November 1, 1861)*

Jefferson County was named for Jefferson Territory, which honored President Thomas Jefferson. An extralegal entity, Jefferson Territory was organized in 1859 by residents of the gold regions frustrated by the distances between their settlements and the governmental seats of the four territories—Kansas, Nebraska, New Mexico, and Utah—that encompassed the area. They adopted a constitution, elected legislators, and chose a governor. Unrecognized by Congress, Jefferson Territory ceased to exist after Colorado Territory was formed in 1861.
Pop. 438,430

Joes *(Yuma)* [JOHS]

Most accounts state that three men named Joe lived in the area; thus the town became *Three Joes,* later shortened to *Joes.* Another version traces the name to a cream station called "Joe's Place." The small plains settlement gained fame in 1929 when the high school basketball team won the state championship and placed third in the national playoffs at the University of Chicago.
PO: October 22, 1912–; Pop. 75

John Martin Reservoir *(Bent)*

Built between 1939 and 1948 and first called the *Caddoa Reservoir,* this Arkansas River project was renamed in 1940 to honor John A. Martin, a longtime congressman from Pueblo who had died in late 1939.

Johnson Village *(Chaffee)*

Opened shortly after the end of World War II, John Johnson's service station and restaurant formed the nucleus of *Johnson Village.*
Pop. 300

Johnstown *(Weld)*

As the Great Western Railway laid tracks through the area, H. J. Parish built a lumberyard and platted a townsite, which he named for his son John.
PO: April 17, 1903–; Pop. 1,579

Julesburg *(Sedgwick)*

Station manager Jules Beni gave his name to the settlement that grew up around his stage stop–trading post. Unfortunately, Beni ran afoul of Jack Slade, the division agent, characterized by Mark Twain in *Roughing It* as "at once the most bloody, the most dangerous and the most valuable citizen that inhabited the savage fastnesses of the mountains." During an altercation the notorious Slade shot Beni dead and, so the story goes, cut off both his ears, nailing one to a post and carrying the other on his watch chain. As for the community, residents moved twice before ending up at the fourth *Julesburg*, a few miles from the first location. Briefly called *Denver Junction*, the townsite marked the spot where the Denver cutoff joined the main Union Pacific Railroad in the early 1880s.
PO: May 29, 1860–January 7, 1885, as Julesburgh (with numerous interruptions and intervening moves); January 7, 1885–May 26, 1886, as Denver Junction; May 26, 1886–; Pop. 1,295; CS

Karval *(Lincoln)* [KAHR-v'l]

Local accounts agree that G. K. Kravig, a Norwegian immigrant, was the first postmaster. Here the versions diverge; some state that Kravig derived the post office name from either a valley or a settlement in Norway, while others relate that the federal Post Office coined the word *Karval* from Kravig.
PO: March 2, 1911–; Pop. 100

Kassler *(Jefferson)*

Kassler and the Denver Water Department's Kassler Treatment Plant perpetuate the name of Edwin S. Kassler, termed the "oldest Denver-born citizen, business and civic leader" by the *Rocky Mountain News* when he died at age ninety-six in 1962. Prominent in banking, Kassler was serving as president of the Denver Union Water Company when the city bought the firm in 1918. *Kassler* was preceded by a nearby Denver, South Park, and Pacific railroad station called first *Platte Canon* and then *Waterton.*

Kebler Pass *(Gunnison)*

Kebler Pass, in an important coal-mining region, took the name of Colorado Fuel and Iron Company official J. A. Kebler.
Elevation: 9,980 feet

Keenesburg *(Weld)*

Keenesburg, first known as *Keene,* was named for homesteader Les Keene. The "burg" was added when the post office was established so mail would not be sent to Keene, Nebraska.
PO: April 10, 1907–; Pop. 570

Kelim *(Larimer)*

Lee Kelim, whose business interests included a flour mill and a power plant, platted the townsite of *Kelim* east of Loveland.
PO: March 2, 1915–March 15, 1923; April 16, 1923–October 31, 1925; Pop. 50

Ken Caryl *(Jefferson)*

During the mid-1970s the Johns Manville Corporation began developing a new, planned community on the historic *Ken Caryl Ranch* southwest of Denver. Assembled in 1914 by newspaper owner John C. Shaffer, the ranch was named for Shaffer's two sons, Kent and Carroll.
Pop. 24,391 (CDP)

Kenosha Pass *(Park)* [ken-OH-shuh]

A stagecoach driver from Kenosha, Wisconsin, is credited with naming *Kenosha Pass*; the word *kenosha* means "pike" in the Potawatomi language. "I jot these lines literally at Kenosha summit, where we return, afternoon, and take a long rest, 10,000 feet above sea level," wrote Walt Whitman during his 1879 Colorado travels. "At this immense height the South Park stretches fifty miles before me. Mountainous chains and peaks in every variety of perspective, every hue of vista, fringe the view, in nearer, or middle, or far-dim distance, or fade on the horizon."
Elevation: 10,001 feet

Keota *(Weld)* [kee-OH-tuh]

Although several sources relate that *Keota* is an Indian word meaning "gone to visit" or "the fire is gone out," historian Virgil J. Vogel has convincingly shown in *Iowa Place Names of Indian Origin* (1983) that the Rock Island Railroad coined the name in Iowa by taking the first three letters of Keokuk County and the last three of Washington County; the resulting word, "Keoton," later became the easier-to-pronounce *Keota*. Missouri, Oklahoma, Nebraska, and New Mexico, in addition to Colorado, have also had places named for Keota, Iowa.
PO: September 11, 1888–January 8, 1890; January 22, 1909–December 21, 1973; Pop. 5

Kersey *(Weld)* [KER-see]

Kersey grew up around a Union Pacific station first called *Orr* for James Orr, a member of the Union Colony that founded nearby Greeley. A *Kersey* resident told the State Historical Society in 1935 that because *Orr* was sometimes confused with Carr, roadmaster John Kersey Painter, whose mother's maiden name was Kersey, renamed the station in her honor.
PO: March 16, 1884–December 20, 1894, as Orr; December 20, 1894–; Pop. 980

Keystone *(Summit)*

Opened in 1970, the *Keystone* ski resort took its name from a Denver, South Park, and Pacific railroad station established almost a century earlier. The station in turn probably was named for Keystone Gulch, shown on the 1877 Hayden Survey *Atlas of Colorado*.
PO: June 1, 1979– (branch of Dillon); Pop. 300

Kim *(Las Animas)*

Rudyard Kipling's 1901 novel *Kim* inspired the naming of this plains settlement established by Olin D. Simpson. According

Kim

to one account, Mrs. Simpson suggested naming the townsite either *Dexter*, for her husband's middle name, or *Kim*; when residents voted they opted for literature.
PO: January 30, 1917–; Pop. 76

Kiowa *(Elbert)* [KIGH-oh-wuh]

Kiowa grew up around the Kiowa Creek stage station, which like the nearby stream and the plains county to the east took its name from the Kiowa Indians.
PO: February 14, 1868–; Pop. 275; CS

Kiowa County *(Established April 11, 1889)*

Along with Cheyenne County and Arapahoe County, *Kiowa County* commemorates the Indians that once roamed the plains. During the early to mid-nineteenth century, the Kiowa and their allies, the Comanche, generally occupied the area south of the Arkansas River, while the Cheyenne and Arapaho stayed to the north.
Pop. 1,688

Kirk *(Yuma)*

An early settler named Niekirk or Neikirk gave part of his name to the town.
PO: November 18, 1887–; Pop. 110

Kit Carson *(Cheyenne)*

Established as a terminus by the Kansas Pacific Railway in 1869 a few miles from the present site, *Kit Carson* took the name of the legendary Mountain Man, scout, and Indian agent. Carson, famed for guiding John C. Frémont on his first three western expeditions during the 1840s, had died in 1868

at Fort Lyon, Colorado. Initially as wild an end-of-track town as any on the plains, *Kit Carson* survived after the riffraff cleared out to become a stable, permanent community.
PO: December 29, 1869–May 17, 1881; February 14, 1882–; Pop. 305

Kit Carson County *(Established April 11, 1889)*

Created twenty years after the community of Kit Carson was born, this county also honored the famed frontiersman.
Pop. 7,140

Kit Carson Peak *(Saguache)*

Kit Carson was remembered as well when this Fourteener was named. Other Carson-inspired names on the United States map include the Fort Carson army post near Colorado Springs and Nevada's capital, Carson City.
Elevation: 14,165 feet

Kittredge *(Jefferson)* [KIT-ridge]

Denver businessman Charles M. Kittredge, who developed this mountain community, suggested *Bear Creek* and several other post office names, but the federal Post Office chose *Kittredge*. Kittredge is also remembered for erecting the 1890 Kittredge Building, now a historic landmark, in downtown Denver.
PO: April 2, 1923–; Pop. 750

Kline *(La Plata)*

Settled by Mormons and presumably named for a church official or member, *Kline* had a post office between 1904 and 1953. That is, it had a post office name—for during much of that period the facility was actually situated in nearby Marvel. Thus Marvel residents received mail at *Kline*, while persons in *Kline* were served by a star route. (*See also* Marvel.)
PO: April 22, 1904–March 31, 1953; Pop. 100

Kokomo *(Summit)* [koh-KOH-moh]

Established by town promoter–miner Amos Smith and others north of Leadville in 1879, *Kokomo* was probably named for Smith's Indiana home town. Next door, the prospecting Recen brothers—Andrew, Henry, and Daniel—platted their town of Recen. After fire swept through Kokomo in 1881, the burned-out residents soon rebuilt in Recen, bringing with them the post office name of *Kokomo*. Much to the dismay of the Recens, the town became known as *Kokomo-Recen* or just *Kokomo*, even though it was actually on the site of Recen. Today the

controversy is moot, for the entire area is now covered with tailings from the molybdenum mine at Climax.
PO: May 5, 1879–October 8, 1965

Kornman *(Prowers)*

Landowner Charles Kornman gave his name to *Kornman.*

Kremmling *(Grand)*

About 1884, Rudolph Kremmling established a store in the area; when he became postmaster a year later, the new post office took his name. Superseded by *Kinsey* or *Kinsey City,* proposed by ranchers John and Aaron Kinsey when the townsite was platted, the original name was in place again by 1895.
PO: February 12, 1885–October 24, 1891; October 24, 1891–June 19, 1895, as Kinsey; June 19, 1895–; Pop. 1,166

Kuner *(Weld)*

Kuner took its name from the Kuner Pickle Company, which shipped cucumbers from a railroad receiving station. Now known as the Kuner-Empson Company and headquartered in Brighton, the firm still produces a variety of food products, but the *Kuner* townsite has disappeared beneath a huge cattle feedlot.
PO: July 22, 1908–September 30, 1920

Kutch *(Elbert)* [KUHT-sh]

Early cattleman and first postmaster Ira Kutch gave his name to *Kutch.*
PO: July 17, 1899–October 9, 1899; June 3, 1905–January 31, 1971

La Garita

Lafayette *(Boulder)* [lah-fay-ET]

When Lafayette (actually DeLafayette) Miller died in 1878, he left his widow Mary with six children, the youngest only six months old. Ten years later, Mary Miller gave the name *Lafayette* to the new townsite she had platted on her farmland; her son, Thomas, became the first mayor in 1890.
PO: February 4, 1889–; Pop. 14,548

La Garita *(Saguache)* [lah-guh-REE-tuh]

La garita is Spanish for "watchtower" or "lookout." Most accounts tell of Indians using a nearby hill as a lookout, thus inspiring the naming of La Garita Creek, the La Garita Mountains, and the Hispanic settlement of *La Garita*.
PO: June 24, 1874–May 18, 1875; November 13, 1886–December 7, 1894; April 7, 1897–November 11, 1972

Laird *(Yuma)*

Laid out by the See Bar See Land and Cattle Company, *Laird* honored Nebraska Congressman James Laird, who served in the United States House of Representatives during the 1880s.
PO: July 12, 1887–February 17, 1892; February 17, 1892–January 25, 1899, as Seebarsee; January 25, 1899–; Pop. 110

La Jara *(Conejos)* [lah-HAIR-uh]

La Jara, which took its name from nearby La Jara Creek, developed around a Denver and Rio Grande railroad station built a short distance from an older Hispanic settlement also called La Jara. Defined as "rock rose," the Spanish word specifically

came to mean "sandbar willow" in present-day southern Colorado and northern New Mexico. The name was in use for the stream by 1779, when New Mexico Governor Juan Bautista de Anza led his troops across the *Las Jaras* in pursuit of the Comanche.
PO: July 15, 1884–; Pop. 725

La Junta *(Otero)* [lah-HUHN-tuh]

On December 17, 1875, the *Las Animas Leader* proclaimed that the new town founded as the Kansas Pacific and Santa Fe railroads built west along the Arkansas River would be "officially known and hailed as La Junta," meaning "the junction" in Spanish. For a short time in mid-1878 the Santa Fe station was called *Otero* for Miguel Antonio Otero, who had opened a warehouse of his firm Otero, Sellar, and Company at the place; Otero was later remembered when Otero County was created in 1889.
PO: January 26, 1876–July 27, 1877; September 20, 1878–; Pop. 7,637; CS

Lake City *(Hinsdale)*

The "lake" in *Lake City* refers to Lake San Cristobal (St. Christopher) to the south. Nearby is Cannibal Plateau, where prospector Alferd Packer allegedly dined on five companions during the winter of 1873-1874. Tried in Lake City in 1883, he was convicted of murder and sentenced to hang. "They was sivin dimmycrats in Hinsdale County and ye eat five of them," shouted the judge in a widely reported but wholly apocryphal outburst. Nonetheless, Packer was granted a new trial, given a prison term, and later paroled.
PO: June 18, 1875–; Pop. 223; CS

Lake County *(Established November 1, 1861)*

Once covering more than one-third of western Colorado, *Lake County* took its name from the Twin Lakes south of Leadville. (*See also* Twin Lakes.)
Pop. 6,007

Lake George *(Park)*

Lake George took its name from the nearby body of water created when rancher George Frost dammed the South Platte River. The settlement was situated on the Colorado Midland Railway, which carried Lake George ice to customers in Colorado Springs and Cripple Creek.
PO: May 15, 1891–September 30, 1905; September 27, 1910–

Lakeside *(Jefferson)*

Lakeside has a few houses, a shopping center, and the Lakeside Amusement Park built around Lake Rhoda, named for the daughter of a longtime park owner.
PO: October 1, 1959– (branch of Denver); Pop. 11

Lakewood *(Jefferson)*

Platted in 1889, *Lakewood* took its name from Lakewood, New Jersey, the home of an investor in an early hardware manufacturing firm. During the next eighty years, *Lakewood* remained one of several neighboring Jefferson County communities until June 1969, when voters approved incorporation of these entities as one large municipality called *Jefferson City*. The following November, however, they overwhelmingly rejected *Jefferson City* in favor of *Lakewood,* although some five hundred residents did cast their ballots for other choices ranging from *Jackass Junction, Dog Town,* and *Tax Bug* to *Laugh In, Peyton Place,* and *Lunar City.*
PO: April 21, 1892–September 15, 1900; June 7, 1937–March 31, 1942; April 4, 1942– (branch of Denver); Pop. 126,481

Lamar *(Prowers)* [lah-MAWR]

Lucius Quintus Cincinnatus Lamar, then serving as secretary of the interior, was honored when this town on the Atchison, Topeka, and Santa Fe Railroad was founded in 1886. Formerly a representative and a senator from Mississippi, Lamar was an associate justice of the Supreme Court from 1888 to his death in 1893.
PO: July 16, 1886–; Pop. 8,343; CS

La Plata *(La Plata)* [lah-PLAT-uh]

Little remains today of *La Plata,* sometimes called *La Plata City,* a one-time mining camp on the La Plata ("silver") River. *Parrott City,* sometimes said to be the former name of *La Plata,* was instead a separate settlement a few miles to the southwest.
PO: July 24, 1882–December 23, 1885

La Plata County *(Established February 10, 1874)*

La Plata County took its name from the La Plata river and mountains, christened by eighteenth-century Spaniards for the silver ore found in the vicinity.
Pop. 32,284

La Plata Mountains *(Southwest Colorado)*

When the Franciscan priests Domínguez and Escalante traveled near *La Sierra de la Plata* in August 1776, they noted that

Lamar

these "silver mountains" were reported to contain "veins and outcroppings of metallic ore." Earlier, they continued, Spanish parties had obtained "metal-bearing rocks" from the area. "The opinion which some formed previously, from the accounts of various Indians and from some citizens of the kingdom, that they were silver ore, furnished the sierra with this name."

La Plata Peak (Chaffee)

Members of the Hayden Survey climbed and named _La Plata Peak_ in 1873.
Elevation: 14,361 feet

La Plata River (Southwest Colorado)

On August 9, 1776, the Franciscan priests Domínguez and Escalante came to "El Río de San Joaquin—de La Plata by another name," shown on maps today as the _La Plata River._

Laporte (Larimer) [lah-PORT]

Laporte, which means "the gateway" or "the door" in French, "is properly named," remarked Ansel Watrous in his 1911

History of Larimer County, being "the gateway to all that mountainous region lying north of the South Platte river and extending from the Plains to the Continental Divide." Settled in 1858 by trappers and gold seekers and known briefly as *Colona,* the community was the first county seat of Larimer County before losing the honor to Fort Collins in 1868.
PO: July 15, 1862–December 12, 1864, and October 5, 1866–December 21, 1894, as La Porte; December 21, 1894–; Pop. 1,300

Laramie River *(Larimer)* [LAIR-uh-mee]

Little is known of fur trapper Jacques (or Joseph, or Baptiste) LaRamee, remembered by this river and by many other Colorado and Wyoming place names.

Larimer County *(Established November 1, 1861)*

When William H. Larimer, Jr., organized the Denver City Town Company in 1858, he named one of the streets for himself; the block where his cabin stood is today the Larimer Square historic district of shops and restaurants. The first territorial legislature also honored this "founding father" with the name of a northern county.
Pop. 186,136

Larkspur *(Douglas)*

Centered around a Denver and Rio Grande railroad station, *Larkspur* most likely took its name from the many larkspur flowers growing in the vicinity. In his 1885 *Grip-Sack Guide of Colorado,* however, George A. Crofutt offered a different explanation. "Although this is Larkspur," he wrote, "you will not see the 'lark' or the 'spur,' unless the latter is a 'cowboy,' and the 'cattle on a thousand hills' are larks; but one thing is certain, when the cattle get on a *lark* it requires a great deal of spur to overtake them. Hence the name."
PO: March 24, 1860–July 9, 1861, January 22, 1862–August 29, 1867, and April 8, 1869–December 13, 1871, as Huntsville; December 13, 1871–July 27, 1892; August 26, 1892–; Pop. 232

La Salle *(Weld)*

Seventeenth-century French explorer Robert Cavelier, Sieur de La Salle, inspired many place names on the United States map. *La Salle,* Colorado, was perhaps named either for La Salle, Illinois, or for the La Salle Street railroad station in Chicago.
PO: May 6, 1886–; Pop. 1,783

Las Animas *(Bent)* [lahs-AN-i-muhs]

Founded as *West Las Animas* in 1873 with the arrival of the Kansas Pacific Railway, this community soon supplanted an earlier settlement a few miles to the east called *Las Animas City* but later known as *Old Las Animas*. Like Las Animas County, both old and new *Las Animas* took their names from the *Río de las Ánimas Perdidas en Purgatorio,* "River of Souls Lost in Purgatory," the Spanish designation for the Purgatoire River.
PO: November 3, 1873–September 4, 1886, as West Las Animas; September 4, 1886–; Pop. 2,481; CS

Las Animas County *(Established February 9, 1866)*

Las Animas County took its name from the stream that mid-nineteenth-century travelers and settlers called the *Río de Las Ánimas Perdidas en Purgatorio,* "River of Souls Lost in Purgatory," the Las Animas River, the Purgatory, or, as on current maps, the Purgatoire. The river flows through the county on its way to join the Arkansas River near Las Animas. (*See also* Purgatoire River.)
Pop. 13,765

Last Chance *(Washington)*

In 1926, two local entrepreneurs, Essa Harbert and Archie Chapman, opened a gas station and store at the crossroads of U.S. Highway 36 and Colorado Highway 71, some thirty-five miles equidistant from Brush, Strasburg, and Limon. "So they put up a sign that this was the last chance you had to get gas and water for all that distance," Mrs. Harbert remembered in 1977. "That's how Last Chance got its name."
Pop. 25

Latham *(Weld)*

First called *Cherokee City,* this busy stage station northeast of Denver was renamed to honor Milton S. Latham, a senator from California between 1860 and 1863. Frank Root, who was a mail agent at *Latham,* recalled later that frequently "as many as three stages coming from Atchison, California, and Denver—stood in front of Latham station. I have seen as many as forty passengers there at one time, going to Salt Lake and California, to Atchison and Denver, all having arrived within a period of fifteen minutes."
PO: November 25, 1862–November 25, 1863, as Cherokee City; November 25, 1863–October 22, 1864; March 14, 1867–May 16, 1870

La Veta *(Huerfano)* [luh-VEE-tuh]

La Veta was born in 1876 with the arrival of the narrow-gauge Denver and Rio Grande Railway. The meaning of the Spanish

word, "the vein," is clear; less clear is the reason why the town company, headed by D&RG founder William Jackson Palmer, chose it, although some say that either coal veins or stone dikes in the area served as the inspiration. *La Veta* was laid out where Virginia-born Colonel John M. Francisco, a well-known merchant on the Colorado–New Mexico frontier, had some years earlier established an adobe complex called *Francisco Fort* or *Francisco Plaza*.
PO: August 17, 1876–; Pop. 726

La Veta Pass. *See* North La Veta Pass.

Lawson *(Clear Creek)*

In his 1880 history of Clear Creek County, Aaron Frost reported that before the Red Elephant mines were discovered in 1876, the site was merely the location of the Six-Mile House (six miles below Georgetown), "which was well patronized by the numerous teamsters that plied a lively and profitable business before the advent of the railroad. This was kept by Alex. Lawson, to whom the village is indebted for its name."
PO: June 29, 1877–August 31, 1966; Pop. 175

Lay *(Moffat)*

A. G. Wallihan, a noted wildlife photographer and longtime *Lay* postmaster, told an interviewer in 1935 that the place had been named for a nearby army camp established in the wake of the 1879 Meeker Massacre. "Lieutenant McCulloch," he said, had christened the camp for his sweetheart, Miss Lay of Chicago, whom he later married.
PO: August 1, 1881–January 7, 1892; September 29, 1892–June 30, 1976

Lazear *(Delta)* [luh-ZEER]

Early settler J. B. Lazear gave his name to this community.
PO: January 29, 1912–; Pop. 80

Leadville *(Lake)* [LED-v'l]

Gold discoveries in 1860 brought the first prospectors to the area, where Oro City in California Gulch sprang up to meet their needs. But it was silver, found in lead carbonate, that created *Leadville* a few miles away and made it one of the richest, wildest, and most storied camps in the West. When miners met in 1877 to name the post office they considered *Carbonate* and *Cerrusite* before settling on *Leadville*, for the silver-bearing ore. A few months later, at a meeting to orga-

nize a government, town founders kept the name after discarding additional candidates including *Carbonateville*; *Agassiz*, for Swiss naturalist Louis Agassiz; and *Harrison*, for Edwin Harrison, smelting company president.
PO: July 16, 1877–; Pop. 2,629; CS

Leavick *(Park)*

Leavick took its name from Felix Leavick, who had acquired mining interests in the Mosquito Range after moving to Colorado in 1878. His namesake town, once a prosperous milling center, has largely disappeared, although several buildings were moved to the South Park City museum complex in Fairplay.
PO: December 29, 1896–August 31, 1899

Lebanon *(Montezuma)* [LEB-uh-n'n]

Early settlers called the area *Hardscrabble* before a Pueblo-based land company platted a townsite. Apparently inspired by the cedar trees in the vicinity, the founders named it *Lebanon* for the "cedars of Lebanon" in the Bible.
PO: September 29, 1908–April 15, 1939

Lewis *(Montezuma)* [LOO-is]

W. R. Lewis, one of many settlers who arrived after an irrigation system brought water to the area, opened a post office and store and gave his name to the community.
PO: September 7, 1911–; Pop. 100

Limon *(Lincoln)* [LIGH-m'n]

In 1888, while the Chicago, Rock Island, and Pacific was laying track from the Kansas border to Colorado Springs, John Limon (or Lymon) was credited with running the work camp where the railroad crossed the Union Pacific line. The town that grew up at this junction thus became *Limon*.
PO: August 6, 1889–November 14, 1903, as Limon Station; November 14, 1903–; Pop. 1,831

Lincoln County *(Established April 11, 1889)*

Thirteen counties were created during the 1889 "county-making" General Assembly. Colorado joined twenty-one other states in naming one after the sixteenth president, Abraham Lincoln.
Pop. 4,529

Lindon *(Washington)*

Pioneer L. J. Lindbeck inspired the naming of *Lindon*.
PO: February 19, 1887–September 21, 1888, as Harrisburg; September 21, 1888–; Pop. 50

Little Bear Peak *(Alamosa, Costilla)*

Franklin Rhoda of the Hayden Survey wrote in 1875 that the east face of this summit was "so steep and rugged that snow can no where find a resting-place till it reaches the bottom of the amphitheater." Once known as *West Peak, Little Bear Peak* was renamed in the early twentieth century. Nearby Little Bear Lake also commemorates this furry mountain resident.
Elevation: 14,037 feet

Littleton *(Arapahoe, Douglas)* [LITTLE-t'n]

Little happened in early *Littleton* that did not involve engineer and farmer Richard Sullivan Little. Little, who first came to the area in 1860, brought his wife Angeline from Chicago to his South Platte River land in 1862. Ten years later, after spearheading the construction of the Rough and Ready flour mill and serving as first postmaster, Little platted the townsite of *Littleton*.
PO: April 8, 1869–; Pop. 33,685; CS

Livermore *(Larimer)*

Adolphus Livernash and Stephen Moore joined forces to build a cabin in the early 1860s as a center for their prospecting ventures. They also gave their combined names to the community that later developed near their claim.
PO: December 1, 1871–; Pop. 60

Lizard Head Pass *(Dolores, San Miguel)*

Lizard Head Pass took its name from nearby 13,113-foot Lizard Head Peak, "a peculiar pinnacle," as Hayden Survey topographer Franklin Rhoda termed it in 1874. Almost a half-century later, in 1920, technical climber Albert R. Ellingwood led the first recorded ascent. "Only when seen from either side (necessarily from a distance) does it to any degree justify its name," he noted afterward, "and the writer must confess that even then he thinks its resemblance to a saurian's head not over-strong."
Elevation: 10,222 feet

Lochbuie *(Weld)*

Consisting predominantly of mobile homes, *Lochbuie* was founded in the early 1960s as *Spacious Living*. The name later

was shortened to *Space City* and then changed to *Lochbuie*, honoring the Scottish ancestry of a community leader.
Pop. 1,168

Logan County *(Established February 25, 1887)*

Logan County, which first extended eastward to the Kansas border, was created in 1887 just after the death of John Alexander Logan, a Union general in the Civil War. Logan also served as United States Representative (1859-1862 and 1867-1871) and Senator (1871-1877 and 1879-1886) from Illinois and was the unsuccessful 1884 vice-presidential nominee on the Republican ticket headed by James G. Blaine.
Pop. 17,567

Log Lane Village *(Morgan)*

Situated near Fort Morgan, *Log Lane Village* once had an ordinance that required all buildings to feature log construction.
Pop. 667

Loma *(Mesa)* [LOH-muh]

An agricultural community, *Loma* took as its name the Spanish word for "little hill" or "hillock."
PO: May 24, 1901–October 15, 1902, and January 6, 1905–August 2, 1905, as Mainard; August 2, 1905–; Pop. 200

Lonetree *(Archuleta)*

Colorado has many places named for "lone trees" as well as for lone rocks, lone pines, lone springs, and other such solitary features.

Longmont *(Boulder)* [LAHNG-mahnt]

"The Executive Council have been careful to select a name for the new town which should embrace or suggest some leading and permanent feature of interest. Among all the imposing objects that help to make up that picture of unrivaled beauty and grandeur which will forever greet the eye, first and foremost stands Long's Peak, and the name LONGMONT has therefore been decided as most appropriate." Thus did idealistic Chicago–Colorado Colony members embark on their communal venture in 1871. Residents of nearby Burlington, settled around 1860 and probably named for Burlington, Iowa, soon bowed to the inevitable and moved to the new settlement.
PO: April 14, 1873–; Pop. 51,555

Longs Peak *(Boulder)*

French trappers called this peak and its lower companion *Les Deux Oreilles,* "the two ears," before Stephen H. Long and his expedition sighted the landmarks in 1820. By 1842, John C. Frémont found that "among the traders and voyageurs the name of 'Long's peak' had been adopted and become familiar in the country." The 13,911-foot east peak later took the name *Mount Meeker,* for Greeley founder Nathan Meeker. (*See also* Meeker.)
Elevation: 14,255 feet

Los Pinos River *(Southwest Colorado)* [lahs-PEE-nuhs]

On August 7, 1776, the Franciscan priests Domínguez and Escalante led their expedition to "the western edge of the river called Los Pinos because some grow along its edges" and camped south of present Ignacio. Today this "river of the pine trees" still bears the Spanish name on many Colorado maps but is shown as the *Pine River* on others.

Louisville *(Boulder)* [LOO-is-v'l]

When Golden businessman Charles C. Welch wanted to find coal in 1877 he hired Polish-born Louis Nawatny to do the boring. Nawatny not only succeeded but the next year platted a townsite called *Louisville.*
PO: May 21, 1878–; Pop. 12,361

Louviers *(Douglas)* [LOO-v'rs]

Louviers developed around the Louviers Works, a branch explosives factory of E. I. du Pont de Nemours & Company in Douglas County. That name came from the Louviers woolen mill in Delaware, named for the center of the French wool industry and established by the du Ponts early in the nineteenth century near their Brandywine Creek powder works.
PO: June 25, 1907–; Pop. 600

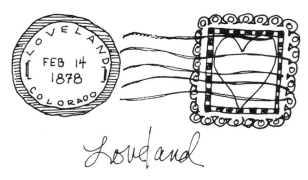

Loveland *(Larimer)* [LUV-land]

Loveland, where the postmarking of valentines is big business, took its name not from romance but from William A. H. Loveland, president of the Colorado Central Railroad. In 1877, while building between Golden and Cheyenne, the line established a station on the Big Thompson River near an existing settlement called *Old St. Louis.* Soon residents of the bypassed community moved themselves, their businesses, and their buildings to the new townsite.
PO: January 10, 1878–; Pop. 37,352

Loveland Pass *(Clear Creek, Summit)*

Entrepreneur and Golden booster William A. H. Loveland spanned this Continental Divide gateway in 1879 with his Bakerville and Leadville Wagon Road Company. Today, travelers bound for Summit County ski resorts use U.S. Highway 6 over *Loveland Pass,* although many opt for nearby Interstate 70 and the Eisenhower Memorial Tunnel that goes under the divide.
Elevation: 11,992 feet

Lowry Air Force Base *(Arapahoe, City and County of Denver)*

Lieutenant Francis Brown Lowry, a Denver native killed in France during World War I, was honored when the Colorado National Guard dedicated a Lowry Field in 1924. Fourteen years later, in 1938, the Guard deactivated that field, and the name was taken over for the facility of the new Denver Branch of the Air Corps Technical School. This second *Lowry Field,* which became *Lowry Air Force Base* in 1948, gained fame as the Summer White House during President Dwight D. Eisenhower's 1953–1955 Colorado vacations.

Lucerne *(Weld)* [loo-SERN]

Lucerne, an alternate name for alfalfa, was appropriate for this railroad siding and townsite in an alfalfa-growing region.
PO: June 23, 1892–; Pop. 150

Ludlow *(Las Animas)*

In 1913, the *Colorado Business Directory* described *Ludlow,* situated on the Colorado and Southern Railway, as "a growing small town in Las Animas County." The next year the name was known nationwide after a battle on April 20, 1914, at the tent colony that striking coal miners, evicted from company housing, had erected nearby. Two women and eleven children, victims in the struggle between the miners and state militia troops, died when fire swept through the camp during the fighting. Although much has been written about the event immediately termed the Ludlow Massacre, little information exists on the source of one of the most infamous names in Colorado history. In 1940, when place name researcher Ruth Matthews queried the postmaster, she was told only that *Ludlow* was thought to be the name of a railroad official.
PO: February 8, 1896–May 31, 1954

Lulu City *(Grand)*

Little remains of *Lulu City,* a short-lived mining camp in present-day Rocky Mountain National Park. Most early residents believed that "Lulu" was Lulu Burnett, daughter of a town founder, although Lulu Stewart, whose father carried mail, also had her supporters.
PO: July 26, 1880–November 26, 1883 as Lulu

Lycan *(Baca)* [LIGH-k'n]

Mabel Lycan told the State Historical Society in 1935 that area settlers named the post office for her "as they did like me and believed I was doing all I could for the advancement of the community." No wonder—over the years Mrs. Lycan, who was the first postmistress and the first teacher, was also active in everything from establishing the telephone company, the voting district, and the school district to building a "nice little church" and a two-room schoolhouse.
PO: June 27, 1913–September 12, 1975

Lyons *(Boulder)* [LIGH-uns]

Edward S. Lyon, who settled in the area about 1880 with his wife Adeline, helped organize the town and served as postmaster. Many buildings on the University of Colorado campus in Boulder were constructed with "Lyons sandstone" from nearby quarries.
PO: May 18, 1882–; Pop. 1,227

Mack *(Mesa)*

Mack honored President John M. Mack of the Barber Asphalt Paving Company, which built the Uintah Railway connecting the settlement on the Denver and Rio Grande with gilsonite mines in Utah.
PO: April 21, 1904–; Pop. 180

Magnolia *(Boulder)*

In 1875, Boulder County pioneer Hiram Fullen discovered and named the Magnolia Mine, which in turn gave its name to the camp.
PO: May 16, 1876–December 31, 1920

Maher *(Montrose)* [MAY-er]

According to local tradition, stagecoach driver Caleb Maher walked some seventy miles to Gunnison to submit a post office application for this ranching area.
PO: April 7, 1884–February 26, 1988; Pop. 100

Malta *(Lake)* [MAHL-tuh]

Little remains of *Malta,* even though at one time, as George A. Crofutt noted in his 1885 *Grip-Sack Guide of Colorado,* "The Maltese are trying to persuade themselves that *this,* and not

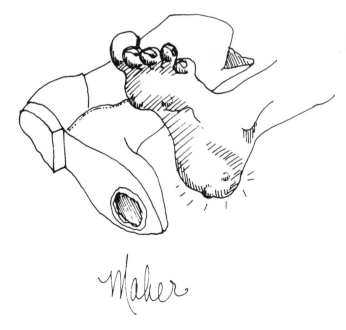

Leadville, will be the carbonate city of the future." Growing up near smelters that processed ore from its booming neighbor, *Malta* perhaps was named for the island in the Mediterranean Sea now part of the Republic of Malta.
PO: October 26, 1875–September 13, 1887; May 2, 1890–July 31, 1955

Manassa *(Conejos)* [muh-NAS-uh]

Mormons settled the town in 1879; one of the leaders suggested the name of the elder son of the biblical Joseph. *Manassa* won fame in the early twentieth century as the hometown of the "Manassa Mauler," world heavyweight champion Jack Dempsey.
PO: February 3, 1879–; Pop. 988

Mancos *(Montezuma)* [MANG-kuhs]

Mancos took its name from the nearby Mancos River. In 1885, George A. Crofutt's *Grip-Sack Guide of Colorado* described *Mancos* as "a small agricultural town where grain, except corn, and all kinds of vegetables grow to perfection" and noted that "along the Mancos river are many old ruins of cliff houses."
PO: February 19, 1877–; Pop. 842

Mancos River *(Southwest Colorado)*

In August 1776, Franciscan fathers Domínguez and Escalante camped near the confluence of the East Mancos and Mancos rivers, describing the site as being "at the edge of the first rivulet of the two which make up the San Lázaro—of the Mancos by another name." Today the river still retains the plural form of the Spanish word *manco,* which means "handless" or "maimed, faulty, imperfect."

Manitou Springs *(El Paso)* [MAN-i-too]

In his *Adventures in Mexico and the Rocky Mountains* (1848), the young English adventurer George F. Ruxton wrote of visiting springs where the Arapaho Indians "never fail to bestow their votive offerings upon the water sprite, in order to propitiate the 'Manitou' of the fountain, and ensure a fortunate issue to their 'path of war.'" Half a century later, Dr. William A. Bell, a longtime associate of William Jackson Palmer in his railroad and town-building enterprises, told the Village Improvement Society of Colorado Springs that *Manitou Springs* was first given the name *La Font,* but "finding that the name was not satisfactory and becoming better acquainted with the writings of Ruxton we chose the name which he told us the Indians had given to the 'Spirit of the Spring' Manitou." Others assert that English investor William Blackmore suggested the Algonquin word for "spirit" from one of his favorite poems, Henry Wadsworth Longfellow's *Song of Hiawatha,* which inspired many place names after its 1855 publication.
PO: October 3, 1872–February 27, 1885, as Manitou; February 27, 1885–May 20, 1892, as Manitou Springs; May 20, 1892–January 1, 1936, as Manitou; January 1, 1936–; Pop. 4,535

Manti–La Sal National Forest *(Western Colorado, Eastern Utah)* [MAHN-tee-luh-SAL]

A small part of the *Manti–La Sal National Forest* extends from southeastern Utah into western Colorado. Manti is a city in the Book of Mormon that also inspired the naming of a Utah community, while the La Sal Mountains were named for nearby salt beds (*sal* is Spanish for "salt").

Manzanola *(Otero)* [man-zan-OH-lah]

Apple and cherry orchards once abounded near this community, leading residents to change the name from the original *Catlin* to *Manzanola,* probably derived from the Spanish *manzano,* "apple tree," or *manzana,* "apple."
PO: November 6, 1879–November 4, 1895, as Catlin; November 4, 1895–; Pop. 437

Marble *(Gunnison)*

Nearby quarries on Yule Creek in the Crystal River valley furnished marble for the Colorado State Capitol, the Lincoln Memorial, and the Tomb of the Unknown Soldier.
PO: March 19, 1890–February 4, 1892; March 2, 1892–October 31, 1942; Pop. 64

Manzanola

Maroon Peak *(Gunnison, Pitkin)*

"This peak is so named from its peculiar color, that of the sandstones of which it is composed." So wrote Henry Gannett of the summit the Hayden Survey called *Maroon Mountain*. Today the two peaks of *Maroon Mountain* are considered separate Fourteeners, *Maroon* (also *South Maroon*) and *North Maroon*, and together are popularly known as the "Maroon Bells."
Elevation: 14,156 feet

Marshall *(Boulder)*

In the early 1860s, Joseph Marshall built a blast furnace named Belle Monte on South Boulder Creek, and soon the place was shown on maps as *Bellemonte* or *Belmont*. Before long, however, Marshall was concentrating on coal mining, and the community that developed around his ventures became known as *Marshall*. Although the area post office was later renamed both *Langford* (for Augustine Langford, who later managed the mines) and *Gorham* (for the Gorham Mine), residents seldom called the settlement anything but *Marshall*.
PO: August 2, 1878–October 5, 1880, and May 19, 1892–April 10, 1893, as Marshall; August 5, 1881–May 19, 1892, and May 1,

1895–August 31, 1899, as Langford; August 31, 1899–January 31, 1901, and August 5, 1901–January 15, 1942, as Gorham

Marshall Pass *(Saguache)*

Lieutenant William L. Marshall was working with the Wheeler Survey near Silverton in 1873 when he was suddenly afflicted with a bad toothache. Deciding to seek medical help in Denver, he and a companion set out across the mountains. "It was arranged in advance that the party should follow the beaten path through Cochetopa Pass," he recalled later, "but my jumping tooth rendered that route too circuitous for me, and I concluded to make an effort to find a more direct way." Marshall's shortcut, which he estimated saved 125 miles on the journey, was named *Marshall Pass* in his honor.
Elevation: 10,846 feet

Marvel *(La Plata)*

A mill called the "Marvel Midget" at the farmers' co-op suggested the name for this community. Nearby Kline, settled by Mormons, had the first area post office, which was soon moved to a store that formed the nucleus of *Marvel*. The name did not change, however, and thus the post office in *Marvel* remained Kline until 1953.
PO: April 1, 1953–; Pop. 100

Masonville *(Larimer)*

Masonville took the name of early settler J. R. Mason, who operated the Masonville Hotel around the turn of the century.
PO: September 1, 1896–; Pop. 500

Masters *(Weld)*

Ranch foreman John Masters gave his name to *Masters*.
PO: February 15, 1900–December 29, 1967

Matheson *(Elbert)* [MATH-i-s'n]

Sheepman Duncan Matheson was honored when the townsite was platted on his land, although initially both the Rock Island railroad station and the post office misspelled his name as *Mattison*.
PO: February 13, 1889–September 19, 1895, and May 12, 1906–February 17, 1915, as Mattison; February 17, 1915–; Pop. 100

Maybell *(Moffat)*

Maybell honored either May Bell or Maybell Banks when the first area post office was established at Bell and Banks's Ranch.
PO: October 14, 1884–; Pop. 100

Mayday *(La Plata)*

Mayday took its name from the nearby May Day Mine.
PO: September 4, 1913–December 31, 1914

Maysville *(Chaffee)*

Engineer William L. Marshall, who discovered nearby Marshall Pass while serving with the Wheeler Survey in 1873, recalled years later that *Maysville* was named for his "native town" of Maysville, Kentucky. Platted on William Feathers's ranch, *Maysville* was "formerly called 'Crazy Camp,' (and is thought by many to be the most appropriate name of the two)," reported the *Rocky Mountain News* on September 5, 1879.
PO: July 28, 1879–December 23, 1893; Pop. 120

May Valley *(Prowers)*

Residents in a valley north of Lamar decided in 1891 to honor May Swadley, the first child born to settlers in the area, with the community name.

McClave (Bent)

A station named for rancher and businessman Bayard T. Mc-Clave formed the nucleus of this townsite on the Atchison, Topeka, and Santa Fe Railway.
PO: October 20, 1908–; Pop. 150

McCoy (Eagle)

Charles H. McCoy, who came to the area with his family from Missouri, ran the McCoy Hotel, served as postmaster, and gave his name to the community.
PO: May 23, 1891–; Pop. 150

McPhee (Montezuma)

Named for Denver businessman William McPhee, who with a partner began a lumbering enterprise in 1924, *McPhee* housed workers until the mid-1940s, when the company ceased operations and most of the buildings were moved. Today the site is submerged beneath the waters of the McPhee Recreation Area, part of the Dolores River project.
PO: September 17, 1924–March 31, 1948

Mead (Weld)

A longtime resident told the State Historical Society that Dr. Martin L. Mead was remembered when a townsite was established on land he had homesteaded in the 1880s.
PO: March 1, 1907–; Pop. 456

Medano Pass (Huerfano, Saguache)

On January 27, 1807, Zebulon Pike led his men over *Medano Pass*, recording that their "bad days march" took them "through snows, some places three feet deep." Descending westward, the expedition soon came upon the "sand hills" now encompassed in the Great Sand Dunes National Monument; appropriately, *médano* is the Spanish word for "dune" or "sand hill."
Elevation: 9,900 feet

Meeker (Rio Blanco)

Nathan W. Meeker, former agricultural editor of the *New York Tribune* and a founder of Greeley, was named agent to the White River Ute in 1878. Visionary but unrealistic, he introduced farming and prohibited the Indians' favorite sport of pony racing. Meeker and several agency employees were killed in the subsequent Ute uprising in 1879. As a result, a military post, the *Camp on White River*, was established near the agency in October. After the camp was abandoned in

1883, valley residents bought the buildings and platted the community of *Meeker*.
PO: August 23, 1880–; Pop. 2,098; CS

Meeker Park *(Boulder)*

Meeker Park took the name of nearby Mount Meeker, which also honored Nathan W. Meeker. (*See also* Longs Peak.)
Pop. 200

Meredith *(Pitkin)*

In 1935, the *Meredith* postmaster told the State Historical Society that the community had been named for a friend of A. E. Beard, who had operated a lime kiln and quarry in the area.
PO: January 25, 1893–; Pop. 25

Merino *(Logan)* [muh-REE-noh]

Buffalo lost out to sheep when a railroad worker changed the name of *Buffalo* to *Merino* for some nearby grazing sheep that may or may not have been of that breed. "The settlers were indignant that their cattle country should have such a name," notes local historian Nell Brown Propst. *Merino* is, however, proud of native son Ralph Edwards, who gained fame on radio and television for the programs *Truth or Consequences* and *This Is Your Life.*

PO: June 24, 1874–February 21, 1883, as Buffalo; February 21, 1883–; Pop. 238

Mesa *(Mesa)* [MAY-suh]

Like the county in which it is situated, *Mesa* took the Spanish word meaning "table" or "plateau" for its name.
PO: April 29, 1887–; Pop. 150

Mesa County *(Established February 14, 1883)*

Western Colorado is a land of plateaus and mesas (the word *mesa* is Spanish for "table" or "plateau"). *Mesa County* took its name from these large, flat-topped mountains, particularly the 10,000-foot-high Grand Mesa east of Grand Junction.
Pop. 93,145

Mesa Verde National Park *(Montezuma)*

Mesa Verde National Park might have been *Colorado Cliff Dwellings National Park* if one suggestion had been accepted. Created in 1906 to protect prehistoric Indian remains, the park instead was named for the "green tableland," christened long ago by unknown Spanish-speaking peoples.

Mesita *(Costilla)* [muh-SEE-tuh]

On March 17, 1909, the *Denver Republican* heralded the birth of *Hamburg* in the San Luis Valley. "It is peopled chiefly by people from Hamburg, Ia.," the paper reported, "and the town is named after the old home of those who have moved to Colorado." A year later, however, *Hamburg* took the Spanish name of *Mesita,* meaning "small mesa," while such German street names as Goethe and Schiller became Santa Maria and San Isidro.
PO: May 27, 1910–; Pop. 25

Middle Park *(Grand)*

Fur trappers and hunters knew this mountain valley, situated between North Park (New Park) and South Park, as *Old Park.* In his classic 1902 work, *The American Fur Trade of the Far West,* Hiram M. Chittenden suggested that perhaps the name *Old Park* originated because the Mountain Men were acquainted earlier with the middle valley; later, when they discovered abundant game to the north, they called that region New Park to distinguish it from the more familiar area. John C. Frémont passed through *Middle Park* with his second expedition in June 1844. "The appearance of the country in the Old Park is interesting, though of a different character from the New;" he wrote, "instead of being a comparative plain, it is more or less broken into hills, and surrounded by the high mountains, timbered on the lower parts with quaking asp and pines."

Milliken *(Weld)*

On January 6, 1910, ceremonies were held to mark the opening of *Milliken* and the inauguration of train service by the Denver, Laramie, and Northwestern Railway. The new community honored lawyer John D. Milliken, the general counsel of the railroad and president of the subsidiary Northwestern Land and Iron Company.
PO: November 10, 1909–; Pop. 1,605

Milner *(Routt)* [MILL-n′r]

F. E. Milner, banker and merchant, gave his name to *Milner*.
PO: March 17, 1900–January 22, 1920, as Pool; January 22, 1920–November 18, 1920; January 27, 1921–October 31, 1988; Pop. 150

Milner Pass *(Grand, Larimer)*

Milner Pass, which spans the Continental Divide on Trail Ridge Road in Rocky Mountain National Park, honors T. J. Milner. An engineer and railroad organizer, Milner surveyed the crossing as part of the proposed route of the never-built Denver and Salt Lake Western Railroad.
Elevation: 10,758 feet

Mineral County *(Established March 27, 1893)*

Silver ores, discovered around Creede, and other minerals abound in this southwestern county.
Pop. 558

Mineral Hot Springs *(Saguache)*

Mineral Hot Springs was one of several resorts built around natural springs in the northern San Luis Valley. An early settler is credited with bestowing the descriptive name.
PO: May 9, 1911–December 15, 1947; Pop. 10

Minturn *(Eagle)* [MIN-tern]

Briefly called *Bocco,* for a local family, the Denver and Rio Grande station was renamed to honor Robert B. Minturn, an officer of the railroad between 1886 and 1889.
PO: September 17, 1889–; Pop. 1,066

Missouri Mountain *(Chaffee)*

Along with Huron Peak, *Missouri Mountain* became a Fourteener when the United States Geological Survey added it to

the official roster in 1956. "There is a Missouri Creek in the area and either the mountain was named after the creek or the creek after the mountain," said John L. J. Hart, author of *Fourteen Thousand Feet*, when the announcement was made. "But by whom no one knows."
Elevation: 14,067 feet

Model *(Las Animas)*

Model City was developed by the Model Land and Irrigation Company, which began work in 1909 on a dam and canal project to irrigate land northeast of Trinidad.
PO: November 6, 1911–October 26, 1912, as Roby; October 26, 1912–; Pop. 120

Moffat *(Saguache)* [MAH-f't]

David H. Moffat was serving as president when the Denver and Rio Grande Railroad laid track from Villa Grove to Alamosa in 1890. Along the line the new town of *Moffat* honored the prominent Colorado businessman who also gave his name to Moffat County.
PO: August 20, 1890–; Pop. 99

Moffat County *(Established February 27, 1911)*

Banker, mining magnate, and railroad entrepreneur David H. Moffat, who died in the year the county was created, sank his fortune into the Denver, Northwestern, and Pacific (later the Denver and Salt Lake) Railway, envisioning a route that would open up northwestern Colorado. Although high grades and snow-clogged mountain passes mired the line in red ink, the famous Moffat Tunnel, completed in 1928 under the Continental Divide, made it an all-weather route.
Pop. 11,357

Molina *(Mesa)* [moh-LEE-nuh]

Residents of *Molina*, which had a flour mill on Cottonwood Creek, settled on a Spanish name for their community after an interim period when the post office was called *Snipes*, for postmaster John Snipes. Spanish-English dictionaries define *molina* as an "oil mill of large capacity," while *molino* refers particularly to a mill that grinds corn.
PO: April 25, 1895–September 1, 1896; January 9, 1897–May 3, 1906, as Snipes; May 3, 1906-; Pop. 10

Monarch *(Chaffee)*

Monarch is both an old and a new name in Chaffee County. The first *Monarch* or *Monarch City*, a short distance southwest

of Garfield (Junction City), took its name from the nearby Monarch Mine, which was discovered in 1878. Between 1879 and 1883, however, the place was called *Chaffee City* for Colorado Senator Jerome B. Chaffee. As the mining camp declined, Monarch Pass and the Monarch ski area perpetuated the name; after the *Garfield* post office was renamed *Monarch* in 1990, *Monarch* also took over the *Garfield* spot on the state highway map. (*See also* Chaffee County and Garfield.)
PO: (1) June 6, 1879–May 14, 1883, as Chaffee; May 14, 1883–November 30, 1903; (2) January 1990–

Monarch Pass *(Chaffee, Gunnison)*

Monarch Pass took its name from the historic Monarch mining camp. Today's crossing is actually the third *Monarch Pass*, succeeding the first *"Old Old Monarch Pass"* wagon road and the 1922 *"Old Monarch Pass"* automobile route. Opened in 1939, the present highway pass was briefly called *Vail Pass*, for state highway engineer Charles D. Vail; local boosters, however, soon protested. So *Monarch Pass* it was, while Vail was honored the next year with another, and permanent, Vail Pass. (*See also* Vail Pass.)
Elevation: 11,312 feet

Montana City *(City and County of Denver)*

In September 1858, prospectors from Lawrence, Kansas Territory, founded *Montana City*, the first townsite in the gold regions, naming it for the adjective that means "mountainous" in both Latin and Spanish. Although a Lawrence newspaper reported in December that it was a "fine settlement, and contains already some thirty houses," *Montana City* soon lost out to Auraria and Denver City, which were better situated a few miles to the north at the confluence of Cherry Creek and the South Platte River. The name Montana, however, first used here as a place name, reappeared when Montana Territory was created in 1864.
PO: January 18, 1859–October 1, 1859, as Montana

Montclair *(City and County of Denver)*

With a name inspired by its magnificent mountain view, *Montclair,* now part of Denver, began as a suburb for "health seekers and pleasure lovers" promoted by Baron Walter von Richthofen (uncle of the famed World War I aviator "the Red Baron"). The Baron's *Montclair* castle, built in the mid-1880s, is a Denver landmark.
PO: July 3, 1888–March 31, 1912

Monte Vista *(Rio Grande)* [mahn-tuh-VIS-tuh]

Monte Vista grew up around a spot on the Denver and Rio Grande first called *Lariat Siding*. In 1884, the Colorado Loan and Investment Company headed by T. C. Henry acquired the land and platted the *Henry* townsite. Promoter Henry had grand plans for irrigation, farming, and town development in the San Luis Valley, backed by funds from the Travelers Insurance Company. When he couldn't repay his debts, the firm took over most of his endeavors, and the community discarded his name in favor of *Monte Vista*, "mountain view" in Spanish.
PO: August 5, 1881–April 16, 1884, as Lariat; April 16, 1884–February 18, 1886, as Henry; February 18, 1886–; Pop. 4,324

Montezuma *(Summit)* [mahn-ti-ZOO-muh]

Prospectors who founded this 1860s silver-mining camp honored the Aztec emperor of Mexico, known to well-read Victorians from William H. Prescott's *History of the Conquest of Mexico* (1843).
PO: June 15, 1871–June 30, 1972; Pop. 60

Montezuma County *(Established April 16, 1889)*

In the late nineteenth century, Americans thought that the ancient southwestern Colorado ruins, first photographed by William Henry Jackson in 1874, must have been built by the Aztecs. *Montezuma County,* home of Mesa Verde National Park and some distance from the town of Montezuma, also took the name of the Aztec ruler.
Pop. 18,672

141

Montrose *(Montrose)* [mahnt-ROZ]

Few authors were more popular among nineteenth-century readers than Sir Walter Scott. His influence reached even to western Colorado, where *Montrose* took its name from Scott's 1819 novel *The Legend of Montrose*.
PO: February 14, 1882–; Pop. 8,854; CS

Montrose County *(Established February 11, 1883)*

Montrose County was named for the town of Montrose.
Pop. 24,423

Monument *(El Paso)*

Originally, the post office was called *Monument*, while the Denver and Rio Grande Railway station was named *Henry Station* for early settler Henry Limbach. In 1874, the station took the post office name, while to the south the D&RG's Monument Station was renamed Edgerton for *its* post office. "Monument station was originally so named from its proximity to the Monument park," wrote a *Monument* correspondent to the *Rocky Mountain News* in 1874, "but the location of this place at the head of Monument creek, with the many beautiful monument parks in this vicinity, in one of which is a garden, pronounced by all who have seen it superior in beauty to the famed Garden of the Gods, seem valid reasons for retaining the name Monument here."
PO: April 8, 1869–; Pop. 1,020

Monument Park *(Las Animas)*

Monument Park was named for Monument Lake, which "gets its name from a knobby rock formation that rears up out of the green depths," as a *Denver Post* reporter put it in 1949. The area was developed as a reservoir and recreation area by the city of Trinidad.

Morgan County *(Established February 19, 1889)*

Morgan County was named for the county seat town of Fort Morgan.
Pop. 21,939

Morley *(Las Animas)*

In 1885, George A. Crofutt's *Grip-Sack Guide of Colorado* described *Morley*, a station on the Atchison, Topeka, and Santa Fe Railroad, as "a coal mining camp and nothing else." Some two decades later the Colorado Fuel and Iron Company opened the Morley Mine, operating it until 1956 and establishing a town that the Colorado WPA guidebook called "a model coal camp." Residents offered two sources of the name

to the State Historical Society's Depression-era survey: Tom Morley, an early mine owner, or William R. Morley, the AT&SF engineer credited with laying out the railroad in the area.
PO: January 11, 1882–August 3, 1882; August 27, 1884–February 16, 1885; September 26, 1888–August 31, 1907; September 12, 1907–August 24, 1956

Morrison *(Jefferson)*

Quebec stonemason George Morrison, who came to the mountains in 1859, soon settled in the area that took his name and began exploiting the nearby limestone, gypsum, and sandstone resources. In 1872, former territorial governor John Evans and other businessmen formed the Morrison Stone, Lime, and Townsite Company, which platted the town; Evans's Denver, South Park, and Pacific Railroad arrived in 1874.
PO: March 25, 1872–December 12, 1873, as Jefferson; December 12, 1873–June 8, 1908, as Morrison; June 8, 1908–August 1, 1950, as Mount Morrison; August 1, 1950–; Pop. 465

Mosca *(Alamosa)* [MAHS-kuh]

Mosca, first called *Streator* for the Illinois home of early residents, took its name from nearby Mosca Pass.
PO: April 23, 1888–December 30, 1890, as Streator; December 30, 1890–; Pop. 90

Mosca Pass *(Alamosa, Huerfano)*

Local tradition relates that *Mosca Pass* commemorates Luis de Moscoso de Alvarado, a sixteenth-century Spanish explorer said to have crossed the Sangre de Cristo Mountains. His party, however, stayed far to the south and east of present-day Colorado. During the early nineteenth century, trader Antoine Robidoux (who established Fort Robidoux) did lead pack trains over the crossing, which for a time was thus called *Robidoux Pass*. In 1853, the Gunnison Expedition described it as "Robideau's or Musca pass"; today it is simply *Mosca,* meaning "fly" in Spanish.
Elevation: 9,713 feet

Mosquito *(Park)* [mus-KEE-toh]

Methodist minister John L. Dyer recalled that when the miners were organizing a district in 1861, they couldn't agree on a name, and, leaving a blank space in the record book, decided to reconsider. "When they came together on appointment, the secretary opened the book, and a large mosquito was mashed right in the blank, showed it, and all agreed to call the district

Mosquito." The townsite within the district, officially called *Sterling* for the Sterling Lode, was also known as *Mosquito*.
PO: December 23, 1862–November 17, 1865, as Sterling

Mosquito Pass *(Lake, Park)*

Along with Mosquito Creek, Mosquito Peak, and the Mosquito Range, *Mosquito Pass* took its name from the Mosquito mining camp. Henry Gannett of the Hayden Survey accurately described the treacherous route in 1873. "The ascent is steep, and difficult for pack-animals on both sides;" he wrote, "and except in mid-summer, there is a great deal of snow on the trail." In 1879, the Mosquito Pass Toll Road Company connected Fairplay and Leadville; seventy years later the World Championship Pack Burro Race began an annual tradition. Motorists with four-wheel-drive vehicles can also enjoy a summer trip over this highest pass in the North American Rockies.
Elevation: 13,186 feet

Mountain City *(Gilpin)*

"I doubt whether there is another city west of the Missouri river, which is growing as fast as Mountain City," wrote one enthusiastic resident to the *Rocky Mountain News* on April 5, 1860. Despite such optimism, the descriptively named camp that grew up around John H. Gregory's 1859 gold discovery soon was absorbed by its rival and neighbor, Central City.
PO: January 17, 1860–October 8, 1869

Mountain View *(Jefferson)*

Situated on the western edge of Denver, this small community—six blocks long and two blocks wide—does indeed have a good view of the Colorado Rockies.
Pop. 550

Mount Antero *(Chaffee)* [an-TEH-roh]

Aquamarine, quartz, and topaz have been mined in great quantities on *Mount Antero,* named for the Uintah Ute chief Antero.
Elevation: 14,269 feet

Mount Audubon *(Boulder)* [AH-doo-bahn]

Mount Audubon honors John J. Audubon, the noted naturalist and artist.
Elevation: 13,223 feet

Mount Audubon

Mount Belford *(Chaffee)* [BEL-f'rd]

Mount Belford was named for James B. Belford, a territorial supreme court justice who was elected the first representative to Congress after Colorado achieved statehood in 1876. Belford served only about a year, however, before Thomas M. Patterson took over the seat, having successfully contested the election; Belford later served three subsequent terms in the United States House of Representatives (1879-1885).
Elevation: 14,197 feet

Mount Bierstadt *(Clear Creek)* [BEER-stahd]

During his 1863 Colorado visit, Albert Bierstadt climbed present Mount Evans (which he named Mount Rosa for his future wife). This Fourteener, situated to the west of Mount Evans, honors the artist whose 1876–1877 Colorado tour produced *Long's Peak, Estes Park, Colorado,* commissioned by the Earl of Dunraven and now owned by the Western History Department, Denver Public Library. (*See also* Mount Evans.)
Elevation: 14,060 feet.

Mount Bross *(Park)* [BRAHS]

Mount Bross took its name from Chicago journalist and politician William Bross, lieutenant governor of Illinois (1865-1869) and a frequent visitor to Colorado, where he owned mines around Alma. One one occasion Bross climbed Mount Lincoln

with a party that included the famed Methodist minister John L. Dyer. "One large company of climbers had put their names in a box which they had elevated on a tall 'liberty pole,'" wrote Dyer in *The Snow-Shoe Itinerant* (1890). "Governor Bross was so enthused that he sang the doxology. Thenceforth the boys called one peak of Lincoln, Mount Bross."
Elevation: 14,172 feet

Mount Cameron *(Park)* [KAM-ehr-uhn]

Mount Cameron is included in the United States Geological Survey listing of "Elevations of Named Summits over 14,000 Feet above Sea Level." Most Colorado mountain climbers, however, agree with the position stated by John L. J. Hart in *Fourteen Thousand Feet* (1925). "In my opinion," he wrote, "Cameron does not deserve to be called a separate mountain, as there is only about a hundred feet difference in altitude between it and the saddle [with Mount Lincoln]." The name probably honors Simon Cameron (1799-1889), Pennsylvania senator and briefly secretary of war in the Lincoln administration.
Elevation: 14,238 feet

Mount Columbia *(Chaffee)*

Columbia University graduate Roger W. Toll named this mountain in the Collegiate Peaks about 1916 while placing Colorado Mountain Club climbing registers on summits in the Sawatch range. Toll later served as superintendent of Mount Rainier, Rocky Mountain, and Yellowstone national parks.
Elevation: 14,073 feet

Mount Crested Butte *(Gunnison)*

Like its lower neighbor, Crested Butte, *Mount Crested Butte* took its name from the nearby peak. Incorporated almost a century after Crested Butte, *Mount Crested Butte* is in the center of the ski resort area.
PO: December 1981– (branch of Crested Butte); Pop. 264

Mount Democrat *(Lake, Park)*

In the 1877 Hayden Survey *Atlas of Colorado, Mount Democrat* appeared as *Buckskin,* for the nearby Buckskin Joe camp. The reason for the later change is unknown, although some have sought a connection between the name of this peak and that of neighboring Mount Lincoln, which honored a Republican president.
Elevation: 14,148 feet

Mount Elbert *(Lake)*

Territorial secretary and governor Samuel Hitt Elbert's political career was not as illustrious as that of his father-in-law, second territorial governor John Evans—physician, railroad entrepreneur, and a founder of Northwestern University and the University of Denver. His Fourteener, however, is the highest in Colorado at 14,433 feet, compared to 14,264-foot Mount Evans. In fact, the peak is a mere 61 feet shorter than Mount Whitney, the highest point in the "Lower Forty-Eight." (*See also* Elbert County.)
Elevation: 14,433 feet

Mount Eolus *(La Plata)* [EE-oh-lis]

"We even now held those peaks in awe, as there seemed to be established somewhere in their midst a regular 'manufactory of storms,'" wrote Franklin Rhoda, a member of the Hayden party that surveyed the region in 1874. *Mount Eolus* (originally *Aeolus*), commemorating the Greek god of wind, thus seemed an appropriate name for this Fourteener.
Elevation: 14,083 feet

Mount Evans *(Clear Creek)*

In 1863, the artist Albert Bierstadt and his companion, New York writer Fitz-Hugh Ludlow, traveled west to Colorado and beyond. Near Denver, Bierstadt and *Rocky Mountain News* editor William N. Byers climbed to "the summit of the highest snowy peak in the group, which Bierstadt named 'Mount Rosa,' after one of the loftiest summits of the Alps." Contrary

Mount Eolus

to Byers's account, Bierstadt was not thinking of European mountains; his "Mount Rosa" was a tribute to the lovely Rosalie, who became his wife in November 1866. At the time, Rosalie was actually Ludlow's wife; in due course the Ludlows divorced, Rosalie and Albert were married, and the new Mrs. Bierstadt took great pride in her husband's panoramic *A Storm in the Rocky Mountains—Mount Rosalie,* which had been exhibited in New York early in 1866. As for the "highest snowy peak," it was later renamed in honor of second territorial governor John Evans. "Rosalie" was given to a nearby 13,575-foot peak, while Bierstadt ended up with his own Fourteener west of *Mount Evans. (See also* Evans.)
Elevation: 14,264 feet

Mount Guyot *(Park, Summit)* [GEE-oh]

Mount Guyot honors Arnold H. Guyot, geographer and geologist and longtime professor at Princeton University. Guyot is also commemorated by the geologic term "guyot," which describes a flat-topped seamount, or underwater mountain.
Elevation: 13,370 feet

Mount Harvard *(Chaffee)*

In 1869, Harvard professor Josiah Dwight Whitney led a group of students from the school of mines to the Colorado Rockies. "One summit, which we climbed and measured, seemed to surpass in height all those so far measured in the Rockies," he reported. "We gave to it the name of Mt. Harvard in honor of the university to which most of the members belonged as students or teachers." Mount Whitney in California honors the professor himself, who also directed the California Geological Survey during his career.
Elevation: 14,420 feet

Mount Lincoln *(Park)*

When miner Wilbur F. Stone, later a Colorado Supreme Court justice, climbed this peak in 1861, he estimated the height as 17,000 feet above sea level. Afterward, Stone called upon the residents of nearby Montgomery to select a name for such a lofty eminence. Washington, Adams, and Jefferson all were mentioned when, so the story goes, "as by a common inspiration, all shouted the name of Abraham Lincoln, which signified unanimous adoption."
Elevation: 14,286 feet

Mount Lindsey *(Costilla)* [LIN-zee]

Noted lawyer and Colorado Mountain Club leader Malcolm Lindsey, who died in 1951, was honored when *Old Baldy* was rededicated in 1954 as *Mount Lindsey.*
Elevation: 14,042 feet

Mount Massive *(Lake)*

Henry Gannett of the Hayden Survey wrote that the "broad heavy outlines" of *Mount Massive* suggested the name, retained through the years despite attempts to call this second-highest Colorado Fourteener *Mount McKinley, Gannett Peak,* or *Mount Churchill.*
Elevation: 14,421 feet

Mount of the Holy Cross *(Eagle)*

Indians, trappers, and prospectors told of this mountain and its cross of snow before William Henry Jackson took the first photographs on the Hayden Survey in 1873. The storied peak also inspired paintings and sketches by Thomas Moran and an 1879 poem, "The Cross of Snow," by Henry Wadsworth Longfellow, which includes these lines:

> There is a mountain in the distant West
> That, sun-defying, in its deep ravines
> Displays a cross of snow upon its side.

Elevation: 14,005 feet

Mount Oso *(La Plata)*

"When we had nearly reached the summit, and at an elevation of 13,600 feet, a small grizzly bear suddenly jumped up a few yards in front of us and rushed down the steep slide on the south face of the peak," wrote Hayden Survey member Franklin Rhoda after his party had climbed this mountain in 1874. "After this experience we named the peak Mount Oso, from the Spanish word for bear."
Elevation: 13,684 feet

Mount Oxford *(Chaffee)*

This summit in the Collegiate Peaks was still unnamed when John L. J. Hart began writing his classic *Fourteen Thousand Feet: A History of the Naming and Early Ascents of the High Colorado Peaks.* Because Hart's brother Stephen and noted technical climber Albert R. Ellingwood had taken transit sightings on the peak from Mounts Harvard and Columbia in 1925, Hart decided to "designate it herein as Mount Oxford in honor of the University attended by the above climbers who first directed attention to this peak." (Hart did not add that he, too, had been a Rhodes Scholar at Oxford.)
Elevation: 14,153 feet

Mount Powell *(Summit)*

Soon to gain fame with his voyage through the Grand Canyon, John Wesley Powell and a companion, Ned Farrell, made

the first recorded ascent of this peak in 1868. More than sixty years later, in 1935, a Colorado Mountain Club party retrieved the tin can containing the records of Powell's climb—probably the oldest existing summit register in Colorado—and gave it to the State Historical Society.
Elevation: 13,534 feet

Mount Princeton *(Chaffee)*

Henry Gannett, a member of the 1869 expedition to the Colorado Rockies led by Harvard professor Josiah Dwight Whitney, probably named this member of the Collegiate Peaks, called *Chalk Mountain* by the Wheeler Survey. Gannett, who served with the Hayden Survey during the 1870s, subsequently joined the United States Geological Survey and headed the United States Board on Geographic Names; Gannett Peak, the highest in Wyoming, honors his contributions.
Elevation: 14,197 feet

Mount Princeton Hot Springs *(Chaffee)*

This resort area near Mount Princeton features hot mineral springs that have long attracted vacationers.
PO: September 17, 1889–June 19, 1899, as Mount Princeton; August 21, 1926–May 15, 1936

Mount Richthofen *(Grand, Jackson)* [RIKT-hoh-f'n]

Clarence King, director of the Fortieth Parallel Survey, honored German geographer and geologist Ferdinand von Richthofen with the naming of this peak. Richthofen, noted for his reports on China, was related to Baron Walter von Richthofen, founder of Montclair.
Elevation: 12,940 feet

Mount Shavano *(Chaffee)* [SHAHV-uh-noh]

Mount Shavano took the name of the Tabeguache Ute chief Shavano, "blue flower." Many legends are told about "the Angel of Shavano," a snow formation on the eastern face of the peak.
Elevation: 14,229 feet

Mount Sherman *(Lake, Park)*

Mount Sherman probably honored General William Tecumseh Sherman, who commanded troops on the frontier after the Civil War.
Elevation: 14,036 feet

Mount Silverheels *(Park)*

Once upon a time, so the story goes, a young girl with silver heels on her slippers is said to have danced in the saloons around Alma and Buckskin Joe. During a smallpox epidemic, when most of the other women fled, Silverheels stayed on to nurse the sick, then abruptly disappeared. Many years later a veiled figure visited the graves of the victims—Silverheels, some said, concealing the marks of the illness that had also destroyed her beauty. *Mount Silverheels* now honors her memory.
Elevation: 13,822 feet

Mount Sneffels *(Ouray)* [SNEF-els]

When a Hayden Survey party first climbed this peak in 1874, one member apparently thought that the Blue Lakes Basin looked like the crater in Jules Verne's *A Journey to the Centre of the Earth*. Continuing the analogy, geologist Fred Endlich thereupon christened the summit above for Sneffels, the peak described in the 1864 novel and patterned after the Icelandic Snaefellsjökull.
Elevation: 14,150 feet

Mount Sniktau *(Clear Creek)* [SNIK-tow]

Mount Sniktau took the pen name of Georgetown journalist E. H. N. Patterson. Before arriving in Colorado in 1859, Patterson had spent some time in the California gold regions and had worked briefly on a Sacramento paper. "Sniktau," sometimes spelled "Sniktaw," is often said to be an Indian word meaning "equal to any emergency." It is interesting to note, however, that Sniktaw meadow and creek in California were reportedly christened by reversing the name Watkins, probably for William Watkins, an early Sacramento newspaperman who also used the pseudonym Sniktaw.
Elevation: 13,234 feet

Mount Wilson *(Dolores)*

This Fourteener honors A. D. Wilson, topographer with the Hayden Survey party that explored southwestern Colorado. In 1874, Wilson and others made the first ascent; a few months earlier J. C. Spiller of the Wheeler Survey had tried and failed to reach the top. The Wheeler Survey names of *Glacier Point* or *Glacier Peak* lost out to *Mount Wilson*.
Elevation: 14,246 feet

Mount Yale *(Chaffee)*

Mount Yale, directly south of Mount Columbia, was named for the alma mater of Harvard professor Josiah Dwight Whitney,

who led an 1869 expedition into the area now known as the Collegiate Peaks.
Elevation: 14,196 feet

Mount Zirkel *(Jackson, Routt)*

Clarence King, director of the Fortieth Parallel Survey, named this peak for German geologist Ferdinand Zirkel, whose work on the survey's rock specimens, *Microscopical Petrography*, appeared in 1876.
Elevation: 12,180 feet

Muddy Pass *(Grand, Jackson)*

In the late spring of 1844, John C. Frémont led his second expedition across a mountain gateway now called *Muddy Pass*, "one of the most beautiful we had ever seen," he wrote on June 17. "The trail led among the aspens, through open grounds, richly covered with grass, and carried us over an elevation of about 9,000 feet above the level of the sea." That evening the men camped on Muddy Creek, a Grand (Colorado) River tributary in Middle Park.
Elevation: 8,772 feet

Namaqua *(Larimer)*

In his 1911 *History of Larimer County*, Ansel Watrous confessed that he had "searched high and low for the origin and signification of the word 'Namaqua' without success" and speculated that it was a "Pawnee proper noun." Most later accounts credit first postmaster Hiram Tadder with choosing the name but differ on what inspired him. Zethyl Gates, biographer of first settler Mariano Medina (Modena), has suggested that former Illinois resident Tadder honored Namequa, a daughter of Chief Black Hawk. Others trace the name to Namaqualand, on the west coast of Africa.
PO: January 28, 1868–January 3, 1879

Nathrop *(Chaffee)* [NAY-thrup]

Born in Germany, Charles Nachtrieb came to Denver with the Fifty-Niners before moving on to California Gulch and opening a store. Eventually he settled on a ranch on Chalk Creek and gave a version of his name to the town he helped found at the junction of the Denver and Rio Grande and Denver, South Park, and Pacific railroads. Described by a contemporary as active and energetic but brusque and outspoken, Nachtrieb built a hotel near the depot in 1881, the same year an angry cowhand gunned him down in his *Nathrop* store.
PO: August 29, 1879–September 8, 1880, as Chalk Creek; September 8, 1880–; Pop. 150

Naturita *(Montrose)* [nat-yoo-REE-tuh]

John Blake credited his father, early settler R. H. Blake, with christening the town of *Naturita.* The name, shared by nearby Naturita Creek, stems from the word "nature," *natura* in Spanish. In August 1776, Franciscan friars Domínguez and Escalante camped northwest of *Naturita* in a small meadow they called *El Paraje de San Luis.*
PO: October 21, 1881–September 15, 1882, as Chipeta; September 15, 1882–; Pop. 434

Nederland *(Boulder)* [NEH-der-l'nd]

First called *Dayton* or *Brownsville,* for early settler Nathan Brown, this mining and milling community on Middle Boulder Creek later became known as *Middle Boulder.* After Dutch investors organized the Mining Company Nederland in 1873 and bought the Caribou Mine in nearby Caribou and the Caribou Mill in *Middle Boulder,* the settlement took the name of *Nederland.*
PO: September 13, 1871–March 2, 1874, as Middle Boulder; March 2, 1874–; Pop. 1,099

Nepesta *(Pueblo)*

Indians called the Arkansas River Napeste or Napestle, inspiring the later name of this often-flooded settlement. (*See also* Arkansas River.)
PO: June 7, 1876–December 31, 1929

Nevadaville *(Gilpin)*

Nevadaville, situated about two miles west of Central City, was among the mining camps that grew up after John H. Gregory discovered gold in 1859. The post office was established in 1861 as *Nevada* (a Spanish word meaning "white as snow" or "snowfall"); in 1869, the government changed the designation to *Bald Mountain,* for the nearby peak, but residents continued

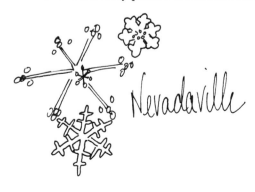

to use *Nevada, Nevada City,* or *Nevadaville.* The name perhaps
came from the California mining town of Nevada City.
*PO: January 12, 1861–December 16, 1869, as Nevada; December
16, 1869–October 15, 1921, as Bald Mountain*

New Castle *(Garfield)*

First called *Chapman* and *Grand Butte*, this town on the Colorado River took the name of the noted English coal-mining
community of *Newcastle* after coal was discovered in the area.
*PO: May 19, 1884–April 23, 1888, as Chapman; April 23, 1888–,
as Newcastle; Pop. 679*

Ninaview *(Bent)* [NIGH-nuh-vyoo]

Ninaview resident Mary Warner told the State Historical Society in 1935 that "Nina" was Nina Jones, whose husband, T. B.
Jones, served as the first postmaster when the post office was
established in their home. "The department added the View
to it," she recalled.
PO: September 20, 1915–July 30, 1965

Niwot *(Boulder)* [NIGH-waht]

According to several early accounts, when the first gold seekers entered the Boulder Valley in 1858 they came upon a
Southern Arapaho encampment led by Chief Left Hand. Al-

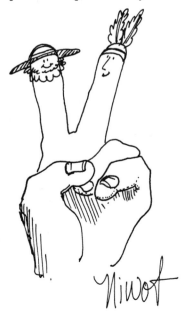

though the argonauts were trespassing on Indian land, Left Hand promised peace; today the town of *Niwot* (Left Hand's Arapaho name) honors his memory.
PO: April 2, 1873–October 2, 1879, and October 31, 1879–May 2, 1895, as Ni Wot; May 2, 1895–; Pop. 2,666 (CDP)

North Avondale *(Pueblo)*

North Avondale is situated on the north side of the Arkansas River, directly across from its namesake, Avondale. (*See also* Avondale.)
PO: August 17, 1917–May 31, 1976; Pop. 80

Northglenn *(Adams)*

Beginning in the late 1950s the Perl-Mack company planned and named the new community of *Northglenn* (first *North Glenn*), situated north of Thornton in the Denver metropolitan area. Centered around the Northglenn Mall, the city was incorporated in 1968.
PO: November 1, 1962– (branch of Denver); Pop. 27,195

North La Veta Pass *(Costilla, Huerfano)* [VEE-tuh]

Three routes form the *La Veta Pass* crossing complex west of La Veta. In 1876-1877, the Denver and Rio Grande Railway laid its tracks over the first *La Veta Pass,* later relocating the route to another crossing named Veta some eight miles south. The first automobile road followed the initial railroad line, and a 1960s realignment created the third and current highway pass called *North La Veta.* (*See also* La Veta.)
Elevation: 9,413 feet

North Maroon Peak *(Pitkin)*

Earlier considered part of Maroon Mountain, so named by the Hayden Survey, *North Maroon Peak* today enjoys distinct Fourteener status, as does its neighbor, Maroon Peak. (*See also* Maroon Peak.)
Elevation: 14,014 feet

North Park *(Jackson)*

Mountain Men called this lush valley, the most northerly of Colorado's four mountain parks, *New Park,* thus distinguishing it from Old Park (present Middle Park); they also used the term "bull pen." John C. Frémont described it as "a paradise to all grazing animals" when he and members of his second expedition visited the "beautiful circular valley" in 1844. "The Indian name for it signifies *'cow lodge,'* of which our own may be considered a translation; the enclosure, the grass, the wa-

ter, and the herds of buffalo roaming over it, naturally presenting the idea of a park." (*See also* Middle Park.)

North Pass. *See* Cochetopa Pass.

North Platte River *(Jackson)*

Rising in North Park, the *North Platte River,* which eighteenth-century Spanish explorers knew as the *Río de San Lorenzo,* flows into Wyoming before meeting the South Platte River near North Platte, Nebraska. (*See also* South Platte River.)

North Pole *(El Paso)*

With magic shows, amusement park rides, and plenty of shops, Santa's Workshop at Colorado's *North Pole* offers something for every Christmas wish. Opened in 1956, the village was patterned after a similar enterprise in New York.
PO: August 1, 1956–; Pop. 5

Norwood *(San Miguel)*

Residents of *Norwood* remembered Norwood, Missouri, the home of an early settler.
PO: December 22, 1887–; Pop. 429

Nucla *(Montrose)* [NOO-kluh]

Organized in 1894, the Colorado Co-operative Company established a utopian community first called *Cottonwood Camp* and then *Pinon.* Some ten years later the buildings were moved a short distance to a townsite that took the name *Nucla.* Former resident C. E. Williams told the State Historical Society that *Nucla* was one of several names considered. " 'Nucla' is derived from, or rather is an adaptation of the word nucleus—a center which grows by attrition, or by attracting surrounding objects," he wrote in 1935.
PO: December 12, 1904–; Pop. 656

Nunn *(Weld)* [NUN]

"Watch Nunn Grow" proclaims the *Nunn* watertower, a famous beacon along the highway between Greeley and Cheyenne. Developed around a Union Pacific railroad siding, the town honors homesteader Tom Nunn, who flagged down a train headed straight for a burning bridge.
PO: September 28, 1905–; Pop. 324

Oak Creek *(Routt)*

Named for the scrub oak growing along its banks, Oak Creek flows through this Routt County community built on coal mining.
PO: February 5, 1907–; Pop. 673

Ohio *(Gunnison)*

Gold and silver fueled the boom that gave birth to this community, briefly called *Eagle City* but known thereafter to everyone except mapmakers and postal officials as *Ohio City.* The town took its name from the nearby creek christened by early Ohio prospectors, which later became Gold Creek to avoid confusion with another Ohio Creek near Gunnison.
PO: June 15, 1880–; Pop. 70

Ohio Pass *(Gunnison)*

Ohio Creek, Ohio Peak, and *Ohio Pass* all recall the presence of "Buckeye State" pioneers in western Gunnison County.
Elevation: 10,033 feet

Oklarado *(Baca)* [ohk-luh-RAD-oh]

Situated near the Oklahoma-Colorado border, this settlement combined portions of both names to make *Oklarado.*
PO: May 12, 1916–June 29, 1935

Olathe *(Montrose)* [oh-LAY-thuh]

Olathe grew up around a Denver and Rio Grande section house named Colorow for a Ute Indian chief. The town initially also was called *Colorow,* although the post office was known as *Brown* for the first postmaster. Eventually both were renamed *Olathe* at the suggestion of a depot agent who had worked in Olathe, Kansas.

PO: *April 2, 1883–October 1, 1891, and June 2, 1892–June 4, 1896, as Brown; June 4, 1896–; Pop. 1,263*

Olney Springs *(Crowley)* [AWL-nee]

Founded with the 1887 arrival of the Pueblo and State Line Railway, a subsidiary of the Missouri Pacific, *Olney Springs* is said to honor a railroad official.

PO: *June 28, 1890–March 24, 1909, as Olney; March 24, 1909–; Pop. 340*

Ophir *(San Miguel)* [OH-fer]

Perhaps hopeful that the nearby mines would be as productive as King Solomon's, early residents named *Ophir* for the biblical site described in 1 Kings 9:28: "And they came to

Ophir, and fetched from thence gold, four hundred and twenty talents, and brought it to King Solomon." *Ophir*—actually two adjacent settlements known as *Old Ophir* and *New Ophir*—declined so dramatically after its boom days that the 1960 census showed a population of zero. (The single resident, Mayor James Noyes, was in Grand Junction and thus missed the enumerator.) Thirty years later, however, *Ophir's* fortunes were again on the upswing, with sixty-nine residents tallied in the 1990 head count.
PO: May 17, 1878–October 31, 1918, and June 12, 1920–January 31, 1921 (Old Ophir); June 3, 1922– (New Ophir); Pop. 69

Orchard *(Morgan)*

Orchard took its name from a cottonwood grove some five miles to the east on the south side of the South Platte River. Called *Fremont's Orchard* for explorer John C. Frémont, who traveled westward along the river in 1842 and 1843, the grove became a noted landmark for overland travelers. For a time a stage station and post office were operated at "the Orchard," as Frank A. Root remembered. "There was quite a cluster of stunted cottonwood trees in the bottom that looked much like an old Eastern apple orchard; hence the name of the station," he wrote in *The Overland Stage to California* (1901). "For years the trees furnished the station keepers and ranchmen in the vicinity all the fuel needed." A century later, the town played a different role in history when false-fronted buildings transformed *Orchard* into "Centennial" for the television miniseries based on James Michener's 1974 novel.
PO: March 6, 1882–; Pop. 100

Orchard City *(Delta)*

Orchard City took its name from the many orchards in this fruit-growing region of western Colorado.
Pop. 2,218

Orchard Mesa *(Mesa)*

On the Colorado map, *Orchard Mesa* is the name of both a settled area south of Grand Junction and a geographical feature. *Mesa* is the Spanish word for "table" or "plateau," and *orchard* reflects the importance of fruit cultivation on the Western Slope.
Pop: 5,977 (CDP)

Ordway *(Crowley)*

Ordway honored Denver businessman George N. Ordway, who bought land in the area and took the lead in townsite development. One local story relates that slips of paper bearing

the names of Ordway and two other promoters were placed in a hat, and with the luck of the draw, the town was named *Ordway.*
PO: June 25, 1890–; Pop. 1,025; CS

Orestod *(Eagle)*

Opened in 1934, the Dotsero Cutoff connected Dotsero on the Denver and Rio Grande Western Railroad and *Orestod* (Dotsero reversed) on the Denver and Salt Lake Railway (the Moffat Road). (*See also* Dotsero.)

Oro City *(Lake)*

Known first by such names as *Sacramento, Sacramento City,* and *Boughtown, Oro City* in California Gulch soon took the Spanish word for gold, the source of its early wealth. One visitor in July 1860 reported that "the mining portion of the Gulch is about six miles long"; *Oro City* itself occupied two successive sites a short distance apart. By the 1870s, however, the camp was in decline, and before long it was eclipsed altogether by silver-booming Leadville, built at about the location of the first *Oro City.*
PO: February 16, 1861–September 19, 1895

Otero County *(Established March 25, 1889)*

Otero County honors Miguel Antonio Otero, who played a prominent role in the development of southern Colorado. Born in New Mexico and educated in St. Louis and New York State, Otero practiced law in New Mexico and served as territorial delegate to the United States Congress (1856–1861) before he and John P. Sellar formed the wholesale merchandising firm of Otero, Sellar and Company in 1869. Moving westward with the Kansas Pacific and Atchison, Topeka, and Santa Fe railroads, the company opened warehouses in Kansas, Colorado, and New Mexico. Otero's son Miguel Antonio Otero, who later was governor of New Mexico Territory, wrote about his youthful experiences as the family traveled from town to town in *My Life on the Frontier, 1864-1882* (1935).
Pop. 20,185

Otis *(Washington)*

Otis grew up around a Burlington and Missouri River railroad siding established in 1882. Although the origin of the name *Otis* has been lost, the place apparently did *not* honor Dr. William D. Otis, who came to *Otis* some five years later.
PO: January 11, 1886–; Pop. 451

Ouray *(Ouray)* [YOO-ray]

After prospectors discovered a number of rich mines in the area, they founded a townsite in 1875 and named it for Chief Ouray. A respected Ute spokesman, Ouray died in 1880, the same year the Ute concluded an agreement with the United States government that resulted in their near total departure from western Colorado for Utah; all that remained was a small reservation. "He had evidently pondered much over the condition and future of the Indians of North America," wrote then Secretary of the Interior Carl Schurz, "and expressed his mature conclusions with the simple eloquence of a statesman."
PO: October 28, 1875–March 20, 1876; May 9, 1876–; Pop. 644; CS

Ouray County *(Established January 18, 1877)*

In 1877, the Colorado legislature established the first *Ouray County*, naming it after the Ute chief. When the present-day, smaller county was created in 1883, lawmakers briefly called it *Uncompahgre* before changing the designation to *Ouray.*
Pop. 2,295

Ovid *(Sedgwick)* [OH-v'd]

Ovid developed near the Union Pacific siding of Ovid Junction, which some residents said was named for Newton Ovid, described by one old-timer as a bachelor "whose total disregard for cleanliness was a by-word throughout the community." Compilers of a 1982

county history, however, determined that the name honored the Ovid, Michigan, birthplace of a railroad official.
PO: December 12, 1907–; Pop. 349

Oxford *(La Plata)*

Margaret A. Grommet was the first postmistress of this community, which was thus called *Grommet*. Why the place became *Oxford* is unknown, although the name could have been inspired by any one of several American Oxfords—in Maryland, Maine, Mississippi, Connecticut, Ohio, and Texas, for example—as well as by the British university and town.
PO: May 3, 1904–January 13, 1908, as Grommet; January 13, 1908–November 30, 1954

Padroni *(Logan)* [puh-DROH-nee]

Farmers Tom and George Padroni gave their last name to this community.
PO: November 10, 1909–; Pop. 100

Pagoda *(Routt)* [puh-GOH-duh]

Pagoda took its name from Pagoda Peak, said to look like an oriental pagoda or temple.
PO: February 15, 1890–March 31, 1947

Pagosa Junction *(Archuleta)* [puh-GOH-suh]

To the Denver and Rio Grande, this spot on Cat Creek has been known successively as *Gato Watertank, Gato, Pagosa Junction,* and *Gato. Pagosa* is the Ute word for hot springs; *junction* refers to the point where the Rio Grande, Pagosa, and Northern joined the D&RG line; and *gato* is Spanish for "cat." On Colorado maps, the site remains *Pagosa Junction*.
PO: July 25, 1899–November 30, 1954; Pop. 10

Pagosa Springs *(Archuleta)*

This community grew up around the celebrated hot springs the Ute called *pagosa*. As an 1878 visitor explained, "the Utes gave the name Pah-gosa (Pah signifying water, and gosa, boiling) which name, with corrupted orthography, it still retains." In 1859, an expedition led by Captain J. N. Macomb of the Topographical Engineers first visited and described the area, predicting that "in future years it will become a celebrated place of resort." By 1885, as George A. Crofutt reported in his *Grip-Sack Guide of Colorado*, that forecast was rapidly coming true. "We approached, and politely requested to know what was the principal occupation of the people of Pagosa," Crofutt wrote. "Quick as thought, while casting an eye at the scores of bath houses, came the reply, 'Bathing! by _____ sir.' "
PO: June 7, 1878–; Pop. 1,207; CS

Palisade *(Mesa)*

"Just before entering Palisade we turned off the main road to make a trip to the cliffs which gave the town its name," wrote a touring *Denver Times* reporter in 1911. "These are sheer walls of crumbling rock, with talus slopes at the bottom and sheer cliffs at the top. They rise about 500 feet above the valley." Thus protected, the *Palisade* area developed into a prime fruit-growing region noted especially for its peaches.
PO: January 26, 1891–November 1, 1924, as Palisades; November 1, 1924–; Pop. 1,871

Palmer Lake *(El Paso)*

Many towns were founded as the narrow-gauge Denver and Rio Grande Railway built south from Denver beginning in 1871. *Palmer Lake* (the name refers both to the community and to the body of water) commemorates D&RG President William Jackson Palmer, although at first the station was known as *Divide* because the area marks the division between the South Platte and the Arkansas river drainages. Near *Palmer Lake*, in July 1820, botanist Edwin James with the Stephen H. Long expedition collected the first specimens of the blue-and-white columbine (*Aquilegia coerulea*) that is now Colorado's state flower.
PO: March 22, 1887–April 26, 1887, as Palmer; April 26, 1887–September 11, 1894, as Palmer Lake; September 11, 1894–June 17, 1912, as Palmer; June 17, 1912–; Pop. 1,480

Pandora *(San Miguel)*

Named for the Pandora Mine, this community was originally and briefly called *Newport*. "The name of the new town of Newport, on San Miguel has been changed to that of Pandora, it being discovered there was another Newport in this state; hence the change," reported the *Ouray Times* on August 20, 1881. "At the present writing Telluride still holds its name. For changes the towns of the San Miguel take the cake."
PO: August 5, 1881–November 12, 1885; March 28, 1902–October 15, 1902

Paoli *(Phillips)* [pay-OH-lee]

Paoli, Colorado, took its name from Paoli, Pennsylvania, which in turn honored Pasquale Paoli, the eighteenth-century Corsican leader. Paoli, who fought against Genoese and French control of the island, was much admired in England, where he spent some time in exile, and in revolutionary America.
PO: June 8, 1888–February 11, 1890; March 9, 1910–; Pop. 29

Paonia *(Delta)* [pay-OH-nee-yah]

"The question has often been asked, How did the name 'Paonia' originate?" recalled early settler Ezra G. Wade. "The name Peona, from the peony flower, was sent to the Postoffice department. The department saw fit to change the name to Paonia." In fact, the Latin genus name for the plant is *Paeonia,* derived from Paeon, the physician of the Greek gods.
PO: June 7, 1882–; Pop. 1,403

Parachute *(Garfield)*

Parachute, which developed near the confluence of Parachute Creek and the Colorado (formerly Grand) River, resumed its historic name in 1980 following some seventy-five years as *Grand Valley.* In 1877, the name *Parachute Creek* appeared on the Hayden Survey *Atlas of Colorado,* about a century after French aeronauts had made the first successful parachute descents. Most early *Parachute* residents believed that the name had been given because the creek patterns or land contours at the head of the stream looked like an open parachute. Another story is told of hunters on the cliffs above who exclaimed, "We need a parachute to get down there!"
PO: July 27, 1885–August 19, 1904; August 19, 1904–July 4, 1980, as Grand Valley; July 4, 1980–; Pop. 658

Paradox *(Montrose)*

"A paradox? A paradox. A most ingenious paradox!" sing the characters in Gilbert and Sullivan's *The Pirates of Penzance.* The paradox here is that a south-to-north river, the Dolores, flows across a valley that is situated in a northwest-to-southeast direction. Paradox Creek and the town of *Paradox* in turn took their names from this "Paradox Valley."
PO: January 9, 1882–; Pop. 100

Park County *(Established November 1, 1861)*

Park County took its name from South Park, the mountain valley situated to the south of North and Middle parks. (*See* South Park.)
Pop. 7,174

Parkdale *(Fremont)*

Situated on the Arkansas River, *Parkdale* was probably named because the surrounding country resembled a park. The settlement claimed to have the smallest postal building in the country—seven feet by eight feet—before the office was closed in 1970.
PO: August 16, 1880–November 28, 1881; February 1, 1882–July

3, 1883; September 3, 1883–January 1, 1889; February 5, 1889–July
31, 1970

Parker *(Douglas)*

Parker grew up around the Twenty Mile House stage stop, so
called because of its distance from Denver on the Smoky Hill
South Trail. Dating from 1864, the establishment was later
bought by James S. Parker, who served for many years as
postmaster. After the Denver and New Orleans Railroad arrived in 1881, the post office name of *Pine Grove* became
Parker, to match the station name, although Postmaster Parker
had hoped to honor his daughter with the name *Edithville.*
*PO: December 8, 1873–November 7, 1877, and December 18,
1877–March 17, 1882, as Pine Grove; March 17, 1882–; Pop. 5,450*

Parlin *(Gunnison)*

Parlin took the name of rancher John Parlin, who had emi-
grated from the East to California before settling in Colorado
in the 1870s. "This place was formerly known as Tomichi," reported George A. Crofutt in his 1885 *Grip-Sack Guide of Colorado.* "It consists of a hotel, grocery, saloon, and blacksmith
shop."
*PO: October 24, 1879–August 23, 1880, as Tumichi; August 23,
1880–; Pop. 40*

Parrott City *(La Plata)*

Prospectors from California backed by Parrott and Company
honored the San Francisco banking firm with the naming of
Parrott City, briefly the county seat of La Plata County.
*PO: May 5, 1876–November 12, 1885, and January 6, 1887–Octo-
ber 31, 1898, as Parrott*

Parshall *(Grand)*

Alonzo Franklin Polhamus, who spearheaded irrigation development in the Williams Fork basin, probably named the town
he laid out for his friend Ralph L. Parshall. A 1904 graduate of
the State Agricultural College (now Colorado State University), Parshall later joined the faculty and developed the
Parshall flume to measure water flow.
PO: November 17, 1906–; Pop. 100

Pawnee National Grassland *(Northeast Colorado)* [PAH-nee]

Pawnee Indians often ranged into present-day Colorado from
their Nebraska and Kansas villages. Today the *Pawnee National
Grassland* carries the name of this important Plains tribe.

Peckham *(Weld)* [PEHK-'m]

First postmaster Ulysses B. Peckham gave his name to *Peckham*.
PO: August 11, 1898–June 15, 1911; June 19, 1916–December 31, 1931

Peetz *(Logan)*

Peetz was first known as *Mercer* to the Burlington Railroad, but it later took the name of homesteader Peter Peetz.
PO: November 20, 1908–; Pop. 179

Pella *(Boulder)*

Settlers from Pella, Iowa, named *Pella* and its companion, North Pella. Both *Pella*s declined after the Denver, Utah, and Pacific Railroad built through Hygiene, situated between the two communities, in 1885.
PO: April 5, 1871–November 12, 1885

Penrose *(Fremont)*

Early in the twentieth century, as one of his many business ventures, Spencer Penrose of Colorado Springs headed the Beaver Land and Irrigation Company, which organized the townsite of *Penrose* as part of a plan to develop the area around Beaver Creek. "Mr. Penrose has been for years connected with many large enterprises in the up-building of the West," the sales brochure informed prospective buyers, "and this new town, with a very bright future ahead, is certainly honored in having a man such as Mr. Penrose allowing it to carry his name." Penrose, whose fortune came from Cripple Creek gold and Utah copper, later built the Broadmoor Hotel in Colorado Springs.
PO: May 8, 1909–; Pop. 2,235 (CDP)

Peterson Air Force Base *(El Paso)*

In 1942, soon after the government took over part of the Colorado Springs airport for an air base, the facility was named *Peterson Field* for Lieutenant Edward J. Peterson, the first pilot killed while on duty there. Now the headquarters for the United States Space Command, the installation became *Peterson Air Force Base* in 1976.
PO: April 16, 1961–August 31, 1977, as Peterson Field; August 31, 1977—(station of Colorado Springs)

Peyton *(El Paso)* [PAY-t'n]

George Peyton, who had preempted land on which the townsite was platted, gave his name to the post office after federal

officials said that the first choice of *Mayfield* might be confused with Mayfield, California.
PO: February 14, 1889–; Pop. 140

Phillips County *(Established March 27, 1889)*

The Lincoln Land Company, a subsidiary of the Burlington Railroad, developed many communities in eastern Colorado. *Phillips County* took the name of company secretary R. O. Phillips.
Pop. 4,189

Phippsburg *(Routt)*

Named for Lawrence C. Phipps, this community grew up around a division point on the Denver, Northwestern, and Pacific (later the Denver and Salt Lake) Railway. Phipps, who had made a fortune through his association with Andrew Carnegie's Pittsburgh steel enterprises, had invested in the railroad and other ventures after moving to Denver at the turn of the century. Phipps later was active in Republican politics and served two terms in the United States Senate (1919-1931).
PO: March 3, 1909–; Pop. 175

Pieplant *(Gunnison)*

"Peel with care the tender stalks of the pie plant," began an 1856 rhubarb pie recipe, which then recommended alternating layers of the plant with "thickly scattered good brown sugar and very thin slices of fresh lemon until the dish is filled." Probably many such delicacies were baked in *Pieplant,* a short-

Pieplant

lived Gunnison County mining town named for the wild rhubarb growing nearby.
PO: August 24, 1904–May 14, 1906

Pierce *(Weld)*

Pierce grew up around a railroad switch on the Denver Pacific (later Union Pacific) named for John Pierce, who served as president of the Denver Pacific after a stint as surveyor general of Colorado.
PO: November 4, 1903–; Pop. 823

Pike National Forest *(Central Colorado)*

Zebulon Pike's famous peak is a landmark in this national forest, formed in 1907 from the Pikes Peak, Plum Creek, and South Platte timberland reserves.

Pikes Peak *(El Paso)*

Although explorer Zebulon Pike sighted this Fourteener in November 1806, he neither named it nor reached its summit. "No human being could have ascended to its pinical," Pike wrote later after he and his men, dressed only in summer uniforms, tried to climb the "Grand Peak" or the "blue mountain." Just fourteen years later, however, in July 1820, naturalist Edwin James and two companions with the Stephen H. Long expedition made it to the top. Saying that he thought it "proper to call the peak after his name," Long thereupon placed *James Peak* on the official maps. In the following decades, the trappers, travelers, and army officers who came into the region referred both to *James Peak* and *Pikes Peak,* but by 1859 the winner was clear—"Pikes Peak or Bust" read the banners on countless wagons headed for the gold fields. (*See also* James Peak.)
Elevation: 14,110 feet

Pine *(Jefferson)*

Pine developed around the Pine Grove station on the Denver, South Park, and Pacific Railroad named for the pine trees in the vicinity. "Near the station is a 'hermit's cabin,' occupied by a very aged man, whose history 'no fellah can find out,'" wrote George A. Crofutt in his 1885 *Grip-Sack Guide of Colorado.*
PO: March 28, 1882–December 14, 1918; April 11, 1919–; Pop. 500

Pinecliffe *(Boulder)*

Pinecliffe took its name from the "pines" and "cliffs" of South Boulder Creek. Situated along the famed Moffat Road, the re-

sort community also has had railroad station names of *Gato* ("cat" in Spanish) and *Cliff*.
PO: March 8, 1909–; Pop. 75

Pine Junction *(Jefferson)*

Listed in the 1993 Colorado state map index but, for reasons of space, not actually shown on the map, *Pine Junction* is situated in western Jefferson County.

Pinewood Springs *(Larimer)*

Pinewood, with a schoolhouse built in 1873 and a post office that operated from 1879 to 1921, was an early settlement in southern Larimer County. Nearby is the more recent community of Pinewood Springs.

Pitkin *(Gunnison)*

Situated on Quartz Creek, *Pitkin* was first called *Quartzville* before taking the name of Governor Frederick W. Pitkin, said to have been a friend of the first postmaster. "Pitkin, Colorado, has three women, seven children, 180 dogs, one cat, two burros and three fiddlers; and they are not happy," reported the *Ouray Times* on January 31, 1880. "They want a saw mill and a newspaper."
PO: June 9, 1879–September 1, 1879, as Quartzville; September 1, 1879–; Pop. 53

Pitkin County *(Established February 23, 1881)*

Legislators honored Republican governor Frederick W. Pitkin, who served from 1879 to 1883, when the county was created in 1881.
Pop. 12,661

Placerville *(San Miguel)* [PLAS-er-v'l]

"Population, about 100, most of whom are engaged in placer mining in the vicinity," reported George A. Crofutt's 1885 *Grip-Sack Guide of Colorado* about the aptly named camp of *Placerville*. Cattle and sheep ranching later kept the community alive after the placer gold deposits were exhausted.
PO: April 22, 1878–; Pop. 100

Platoro *(Conejos)*

Because both silver and gold were mined nearby, the camp name combined the Spanish words *plata*, "silver," and *oro*, "gold." The boom days are long gone, although summer visitors have helped keep *Platoro* on the map.

PO: March 12, 1888–May 15, 1895; April 9, 1898–April 30, 1919; Pop. 100

Platteville *(Weld)*

Established in 1871 when the Platte River Land Company bought land from the Denver Pacific Railroad, the town took its name from its location on the east bank of the South Platte River.
PO: February 11, 1875–; Pop. 1,515

Pleasant View *(Montezuma)*

Bypassed when the road between Cortez and the Colorado-Utah state line was realigned and improved, residents of Ackman, a few miles to the southwest, established the new town of *Pleasant View* closer to the highway.
PO: June 23, 1939–; Pop. 250

Poncha Pass *(Chaffee, Saguache)* [PAHN-chah]

Indians and Spaniards early crossed *Poncha Pass,* and speculation on the origin of the word "poncha"—also spelled punche, poncho, and puncho—has centered on both the Ute and the Spanish languages. George A. Crofutt wrote in his 1885 *Grip-Sack Guide of Colorado* that *poncho* was "an Indian word"; some accounts have reported that it came from a Ute word for tobacco and that a weed used as a tobacco substitute grew in the pass. *Pancho,* the colloquial Spanish word for "paunch" or "belly," supposedly referring to the low altitude of the pass, has also been offered as a source. Another suggestion is the Spanish word *poncho, -cha* meaning "mild." George R. Stewart, in *American Place Names* (1970) perhaps best summed up the problem. *Poncha* and *punche,* he wrote, probably went back "to some undetermined Indian original, having been attracted by folk-etymology to the semblance of Spanish words."
Elevation: 9,010 feet

Poncha Springs *(Chaffee)*

In its name, *Poncha Springs* (first *Poncho Springs*) combined references to nearby Poncha Pass and to the springs that one 1880s promotional brochure claimed were "the only hot springs that are similar to the celebrated Hot Springs in Arkansas."
PO: April 22, 1868–March 13, 1877, as South Arkansas; March 13, 1877–September 30, 1922, and March 16, 1923–November 22, 1924, as Poncho Springs; November 22, 1924–; Pop. 244

Portland *(Fremont)*

Portland had its origins as a company town for workers in the cement industry, which utilized the Portland manufacturing process developed in England and named because the cement resembled limestone quarried on the Isle of Portland. In 1901, noted Colorado industrialist Charles Boettcher organized the Portland Cement Company, which absorbed an earlier firm and became the nucleus of the Ideal Cement Company, later Ideal Basic Industries, which merged in 1990 with Switzerland-based Holnam, Inc.
PO: March 20, 1900–August 31, 1952

Poudre Park *(Larimer)*

Poudre Park took its name from the Cache la Poudre River, which residents often call simply "the Poudre." (*See also* Cache la Poudre River.)
Pop. 150

Powderhorn *(Gunnison)*

Pioneers in the Powderhorn Valley gave two versions of the source of the name. A few said that the first settlers had found a powderhorn filled with gunpowder in the area. Most, however, agreed with the *Gunnison Daily Review,* which reported in 1882 that an "old-timer" had given the name *Powderhorn* to a ridge "which runs down from the divide" between Cebolla Creek and the Lake Fork of the Gunnison River. "This wonderful powderhorn is ten or eleven miles long," the paper continued. "Commencing at the divide, it gradually enlarges, twists and seems so much like a cow's horn that it is easily identified and cannot be mistaken." The creek and later this post office settlement also took the distinctive name.
PO: January 12, 1880–April 22, 1881; May 18, 1881–; Pop. 50

Powder Wash *(Moffat)*

Several explanations have been offered for the origin of the name *Powder Wash,* shared by this settlement, Powder Wash Creek, and the Powder Wash oil and gas field. One account credits the president of the Mountain Fuel Supply Company, which drilled the first wells in the early 1930s, with coining the name after he noted that water from the Powder Springs had carved a "wash," or dry creek bed. Another version traces the name to the appearance of the ground in the area. When dry, "it resembles old type gunpowder," said a local informant. "When wet it washes away easily and sticks to everything."
Pop. 60

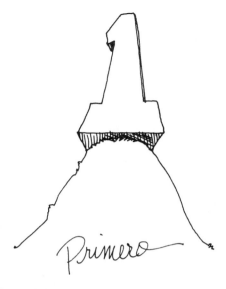

Primero

Primero *(Las Animas)* [prim-AIR-oh]

Primero was the first mining camp developed after the Colorado Fuel and Iron Company gained control of long-contested Maxwell Grant lands in Colorado, originally awarded by the New Mexican governor to Guadalupe Miranda and Carlos Beaubien in 1841. First called *Smith's Canon* and later *Purgatory Mine,* the town ultimately took the name *Primero,* meaning "first" in Spanish.
PO: December 11, 1901–April 29, 1933

Pritchett *(Baca)* [PRIT-ch't]

Named for Henry S. Pritchett, a director of the Atchison, Topeka, and Santa Fe, *Pritchett* was born when the AT&SF subsidiary Dodge City and Cimarron Valley Railway came through Baca County in 1926–1927.
PO: March 15, 1927–; Pop. 153

Proctor *(Logan)*

Although some local sources state that *Proctor* was named for an Indian-fighting "General Proctor," the town more likely commemorated Redfield Proctor, a former Vermont governor who served as secretary of war under President Benjamin Harrison. Proctor was elected to three terms in the United States Senate before he died in 1908, the same year the *Proctor* post office was established.
PO: November 21, 1908–December 30, 1963

Prospect Heights *(Fremont)*

Prospect Heights was incorporated in 1905 to provide thirsty mine and smelter workers with liquor that was unavailable in nearby "dry" Canon City.
Pop. 19

Prospect Valley *(Weld)*

An early settler thought that the "prospects" were favorable in this area.
Pop. 40

Prowers County *(Established April 11, 1889)* [PROW-ers]

The name of cattleman John Wesley Prowers was honored when *Prowers County* was created in 1889. Born near Westport, Missouri, in 1838, Prowers went west as a teenager and soon was driving wagons of trade goods to and from Bent's New Fort. After the Civil War he grazed cattle along the Arkansas River and lived at Boggsville with his Indian wife Amache, for whom the World War II relocation center was named, and their large family. Prowers also served in the territorial and state legislatures before his death in 1884.
Pop: 13,347

Pryor *(Huerfano)*

Cattlemen Mack and Ike Pryor, who settled in the area after the Civil War, gave their last name to this community, which became a coal-mining settlement.
PO: February 26, 1898–; Pop. 25

Pueblo *(Pueblo)* [PWEB-loh]

Pueblo (Spanish for "town") took its name from the adobe trading post built in the early 1840s near the confluence of Fountain Creek and the Arkansas River. Although other names such as *Arkansas Pueblo* and *Robert Fisher's Fort* crop up in accounts of the period, those who lived there knew it as *Pueblo*. Protected by two bastions and enclosed by a wall with a single gate, the post was also called *Fort Pueblo*, especially after prospectors began settling around it in 1858, four years after all the residents were captured or killed by Ute Indians. Northeast of the confluence *Fountain City* (now part of *Pueblo*) was platted in 1859, while the town of *Pueblo* was organized in 1860.
PO: December 13, 1860–; Pop. 98,640; CS

Punkin Center

Pueblo County *(Established November 1, 1861)*

Pueblo County, created by the first territorial legislature, was named for the county seat.
Pop. 123,051

Pueblo West *(Pueblo)*

Pueblo West is a new, planned community situated west of Pueblo and north of the Pueblo Dam and Reservoir, completed in the mid-1970s as part of the Frying Pan–Arkansas Water Project.
PO: October 20, 1969–; Pop. 4,386 (CDP)

Punkin Center *(Lincoln)*

During the 1920s, the original store and service station at this plains crossroads were coated with pumpkin orange paint. "It looks just like a big punkin!" the owner's daughter exclaimed, and before long, the neighbors were calling the place *Punkin Center.*

Purcell *(Weld)*

Landowner Lawrence Purcell platted the townsite of *Purcell.*
PO: December 23, 1911–April 30, 1951

Purgatoire River *(Southeast Colorado)* [per-gah-TWAHR]

In the report of his 1806–1807 expedition, Zebulon Pike called this Arkansas River tributary the "First Fork." In 1820, however, the Stephen H. Long expedition learned from guide-interpreter Joseph Bijou that the stream was "known among the Spaniards of New Mexico, as the river of the souls in purgatory," memorializing members of a Spanish expedition who had died without the last rites of the Catholic church. Captain John R. Bell of the Long party rendered the name as "Les ammes du purgatri"; the full Spanish version was *Río de las Ánimas Perdidas en Purgatorio* ("River of Souls Lost in Purgatory"). French trappers and traders later called it the *Purgatoire,* while to Americans it was the *Purgatory* or the informal but still prevalent *Picketwire.*

Pyramid Peak *(Pitkin)*

Henry Gannett of the Hayden Survey wrote in 1874 that this summit "has been named Pyramid Peak, from its peculiar shape."
Elevation: 14,018 feet

Quandary Peak *(Summit)* [KWAHN-dree]

"Near Mount Lincoln is a peak sometimes called Quandary Peak, sometimes McCullough's Peak, sometimes Ute Peak, and one man called it Hoosier Peak," wrote William H. Brewer, a member of an 1869 surveying party led by Professor Josiah Dwight Whitney of Harvard University. Miners who could not identify ore found on the mountain apparently gave the name that survived.
Elevation: 14,265 feet

Querida *(Custer)*

In 1877, Edmund Bassick, who had once mined in Australia, struck it rich near Rosita and gave his name to *Bassickville.* Most sources credit David Livingstone, reputedly a nephew of the famous explorer, with renaming the camp *Querida,* "darling" in Spanish, although in 1881 the *Colorado Miner* reported that a "Mrs. Francklyn" had suggested the name.
PO: January 12, 1880–November 29, 1887; April 29, 1891–May 21, 1895; August 27, 1897–May 14, 1906

Rabbit Ears Pass *(Grand, Jackson)*

Rabbit Ears Pass took its name from nearby Rabbit Ears Peak, which noted traveler and author Bayard Taylor described in 1866 as "two remarkable Alpine horns on the western border of the North Park."
Elevation: 9,426 feet

Radium *(Grand)*

Harry Porter is credited with suggesting the post office name after he opened a mine that contained small amounts of radium.
PO: February 9, 1906–1974

Rabbit Ears Pass

Ramah *(El Paso)* [RAY-muh]

In November 1888, the *Denver Times* reported that the El Paso
Land and Water Company of Colorado Springs had platted a
town on the Rock Island line "and called it Ramah." Other
stories attribute the christening of the community to a railroad
official's wife who spotted the name of the city in the Bible.
PO: August 8, 1889–; Pop. 94

Rand *(Jackson)*

Rand took the name of North Park rancher Jack Rand, remembered by one old-timer as "a character of the early days, being
practically a hermit."
PO: September 3, 1883–November 13, 1886; June 2, 1887–; Pop. 15

Rangely *(Rio Blanco)* [RANGE-lee]

Rangely residents interviewed in 1940 offered two sources for
the town's name. One informant credited early settler and first
postmaster C. P. Hill with remembering his former home of
Rangeley, Maine; another said that D. B. Case named the
place for a community in Massachusetts.
*PO: August 26, 1884–September 10, 1885, as Rangley; September
10, 1885–; Pop. 2,278*

Raton Pass *(Las Animas, Colfax County, New Mexico)*

Indians and Spaniards first used this pass, which spans the
present-day Colorado–New Mexico border; the word *ratón* is
Spanish for "mouse" or "ground squirrel." Later the Mountain Branch of the Santa Fe Trail, "Uncle Dick" Wootton's toll
road, the Atchison, Topeka, and Santa Fe Railroad, and finally

Interstate 25 all crossed this historic gateway. (*See also* Wootton.)
Elevation: 7,834 feet

Raymer *(Weld)*

Laid out in 1888 on the Burlington and Missouri River line, *Raymer* took the name of railroad engineer George Andrew Raymer. Born in 1857 in Pennsylvania, Raymer had been a civil engineer on several railroads before his death in 1907, according to descendants who visited *Raymer* in 1981. Although most of the first settlers in Raymer's namesake town soon fled the dry plains, the community was revived in the early twentieth century and the post office was reestablished as *New Raymer.*
PO: June 27, 1888–May 14, 1895; November 13, 1909, as New Raymer–; Pop. 98

Raymond *(Boulder)*

Raymond is situated on land first owned by Canadian-born Charles H. Raymond, who built a hotel there in 1904.

Red Cliff *(Eagle)*

Hematite colors the nearby cliffs that gave *Red Cliff* its name.
PO: February 4, 1880–February 7, 1895, as Red Cliff; February 7, 1895–April 1, 1979, as Redcliff; April 2, 1979–; Pop. 297

Redcloud Peak *(Hinsdale)*

Topographer J. C. Spiller of the Wheeler Survey climbed and named this reddish-hued peak in 1874.
Elevation: 14,034 feet

Red Feather Lakes *(Larimer)*

Several stories are told about the naming of *Red Feather Lakes.* According to one version, the resort investors honored a Cherokee-Creek singer who toured the country as Princess Redfeather. Another account traces the name to a legendary "Chief Red Feather."
PO: July 2, 1924–January 31, 1925; August 4, 1926–; Pop. 150

Redmesa *(La Plata)* [red-MAY-suh]

With its reddish soil, the Red Mesa gave its name to the community of *Redmesa*—one word on maps but often two in local usage.
PO: April 24, 1907–November 30, 1954, as Red Mesa; Pop. 125

Red Mountain *(Ouray)*

Famed for the rich Yankee Girl and several other nearby
mines, the town of *Red Mountain* took its name from three red-
dish-colored peaks to the east. A separate settlement called
Red Mountain City also existed briefly on the south side of
Red Mountain Pass in San Juan County.
*PO: January 29, 1883–March 16, 1895; April 27, 1896–February
28, 1913*

Red Mountain Pass *(Ouray, San Juan)*

"US 550 rises in tortuous twists and turns to the top of Red
Mountain Pass," noted the WPA guide to Colorado about the
road south of Ouray. Descending past the three Red Mountains that inspired the name of both the mining camp and the
mountain crossing, the route is the famed "Million Dollar
Highway," a one-time wagon road later upgraded for automobile traffic. Many stories are told about the origin of the
name—that the road originally was built for a million dollars,
or that gold tailings were used to surface it. In alternative versions, a highway contractor is credited with coining the
phrase during the early 1920s reconstruction project.
Elevation: 11,008 feet

Redstone *(Pitkin)*

Named for towering red sandstone cliffs, *Redstone* was developed as a model town for Colorado Fuel and Iron Company employees by John Cleveland Osgood. Here married men lived with their families in comfortable cottages featuring lawns and gardens, while bachelors maintained quarters in the lodge and clubhouse. All enjoyed lectures, concerts, and theatrical events in their leisure hours. Nearby, coal baron Osgood built "Cleveholm," his turn-of-the-century mansion now operated as a bed-and-breakfast inn.
PO: May 19, 1898–September 30, 1918; May 16, 1925–February 15, 1943; June 1, 1959–August 1, 1962; Pop. 150

Redvale *(Montrose)*

Platted by the Redlands Town Company in an area of red soil, this Montrose County community took the post office name of *Redvale* so that mail would not be missent to other Redlands.
PO: December 1, 1909–; Pop. 200

Red Wing *(Huerfano)*

Residents who heard a passer-by whistling the tune "Red Wing" were so inspired, according to one account, that they called their post office *Red Wing*. Other versions trace the name to Red Wing, Minnesota, which honored several Sioux chiefs and where some settlers had lived before coming to Colorado.
PO: May 22, 1914– as Redwing; Pop. 10

Republican River, North and South Forks *(North Central Colorado)*

Two forks of the *Republican River,* the *North* and the *South,* flow through north-central Colorado before joining the parent stream in western Nebraska. So many buffalo once grazed along the *Republican* that the Pawnee called it *"Manure River,"* while to the Osage it was *"Buffalo-Dung River."* Later, the French name *Republicaine* came from the Pawnee band the French called *Pahni Republicaine* after it broke with the Grand Pawnee in 1776—a move supposedly equated with the colonists' rebellion in the East.

Rico *(Dolores)*

Carbonate City, Dolores City, Doloresville, Carbonateville, and *Lead City* were only a few of the early names for this San Juan mining camp. Others such as *Glasgow, Lovejoy, Patterson,* and *Belford* were considered when "a lot of engineers, prospectors and adventurous spirits" met to name the community. As an

"Old San Juan Resident" continued the story in the *Denver Republican* (March 13, 1882): "A big miner who had a good idea of the eternal fitness of things, turned to me and asked the Spanish for rich. I told him Rico. He said the town ought to have a Spanish name, and as it was supposed to be a rich spot he proposed the name of Rico. The idea caught and so the town was named."
PO: August 25, 1879–; Pop. 92

Ridgway *(Ouray)*

Situated at the junction of the Rio Grande Southern and Denver and Rio Grande railroad lines, *Ridgway* took the name of veteran D&RG superintendent Robert M. Ridgway, who was named to head the Rio Grande Southern Construction Company in 1890.
PO: October 1, 1890–; Pop. 423

Rifle *(Garfield)*

Local legend tells of a soldier who left his rifle on a creek bank—or perhaps he found a rifle lost by a previous traveler. Soon the stream was known as Rifle Creek, and the town that developed beside it became *Rifle*.
PO: April 23, 1884–; Pop. 4,636

Rio Blanco *(Rio Blanco)* [ree-oh-BLAHNG-koh]

Known first as *Rioblanco* to the postal department, this settlement, like the county, took the Spanish name for the White River.
PO: May 6, 1899–July 1, 1950, as Rioblanco; July 1, 1950–May 23, 1975

Rio Blanco County *(Established March 25, 1889)*

Once called the *San Clemente*, the White River gave its name in Spanish, *Río Blanco*, to the county through which it flows. In the 1930s, old-timer Thomas Baker told an interviewer that H. H. Eddy, who was serving as a senator from northwestern Colorado when the county was created, suggested the Spanish name to honor Senator Casimiro Barela for his help in passing the legislation. (*See also* White River.)
Pop: 5,972

Rio Grande *(Southern Colorado)* [ree-oh-GRAND]

Rising in the San Juan Mountains of Colorado, this "great river" flows southward through the San Luis Valley and New Mexico to Texas, where it forms the United States–Mexican border before emptying into the Gulf of Mexico. Along the way and through the centuries the *Rio Grande,* known also along its lower course as the *Río Bravo del Norte,* "Bold River of the North," acquired a number of names, including the *Río Grande del Norte,* "Great River of the North." When Don Juan de Oñate took possession of New Mexico in 1598 he called the river the *Río del Norte,* "River of the North," while another sixteenth-century Spaniard, upon seeing its mouth, named it the *Río de las Palmas,* "River of the Palms." In all, Paul Horgan found seventeen different names when he researched his *Great River: The Rio Grande in North American History* (1954).

Rio Grande County *(Established February 10, 1874)*

Rio Grande County took its name from the "great river" that flows through the county.
Pop. 10,770

Rio Grande National Forest *(Southwest Colorado)*

Encompassing the headwaters of the river, the *Rio Grande National Forest* was established in 1908.

River Bend *(Elbert)*

River Bend took its name from the nearby curve in Big Sandy Creek. Once a busy cattle shipping point, River Bend declined as Limon prospered a few miles to the east; today, little remains except the cemetery on a hill overlooking Interstate 70.
PO: January 4, 1875–January 31, 1939

Roaring Fork River *(West Central Colorado)*

Topographer Henry Gannett, who had explored the Roaring Fork Valley with the Hayden Survey in the early 1870s, noted later that this Colorado River tributary was "so named from its steep and rapid descent."

Robinson *(Summit)*

Leadville businessman George B. Robinson grubstaked prospectors in 1878 who struck paydirt north of Leadville. Soon the Robinson Mine and the nearby camp, known variously as *Ten Mile City, Summit,* and *Summit City* as well as *Robinson,* were prospering, but Robinson himself had little time to enjoy his bonanza. In November 1880, shortly after his election as lieutenant governor, Robinson was accidentally killed by one of his own men during a property dispute.
PO: May 16, 1879–February 17, 1881, as Ten Mile; February 17, 1881–January 8, 1883; January 9, 1883–February 28, 1911

Rockport *(Weld)*

A crossroads restaurant complex, Rockport was perhaps named for its rocky walls, although Rockport, Illinois, has also been suggested as the inspiration.

Rockvale *(Fremont)*

In 1919, prominent Fremont County entrepreneur B. F. Rockafellow recalled the naming of this coal-mining community on the Atchison, Topeka, and Santa Fe line. Rockafellow said that when railroad officials asked him to sell lots for the new town in 1882, they suggested naming the place in his honor. Rockafellow, who had camped with his Civil War company at Rockville, Maryland, disagreed: "I said, 'No,' name it Rockvale, being in a beautiful valley bound in by rocky walls, that is appropriate, and I urge it."
PO: March 17, 1882–April 12, 1882, as Rockdale; April 12, 1882–; Pop. 321

Rockwood *(La Plata)*

In *The Crest of the Continent* (1885), naturalist and former Hayden Survey member Ernest Ingersoll described *Rockwood* as a "lively village" in a "secluded yet picturesque" setting. The name perhaps commemorated area pioneer Thomas Rockwood. Alternatively, "rockwood" might have been suggested by the community's location amidst quarries and thick timber; Ingersoll noted that "the meadows in the small depression beside the town are fringed with trees, which are tall and imposing, and yet look more like dwarfed bushes against the massive background of towering bluffs."
PO: July 8, 1878–July 15, 1895; November 8, 1895–April 14, 1917; April 20, 1923–February 15, 1940

Rocky Ford *(Otero)*

Famed for its watermelons and cantaloupes, *Rocky Ford* took its name from a nearby Arkansas River crossing point.
PO: December 1, 1871–; Pop. 4,162

Rocky Mountain National Park *(Boulder, Grand, Larimer)*

Once called the Shining or the Stony Mountains, the Rockies stretch from Alaska to northern New Mexico, bisecting Colorado and separating the eastern plains from the Western Slope plateau country. *Rocky Mountain National Park,* proposed originally as *Estes National Park,* was created in 1915 to preserve this area rich in wildlife, alpine flora, and spectacular mountain scenery. One-third of the park is above timberline; Trail Ridge Road, opened in 1932, reaches an altitude of 12,183 feet above sea level.

Roggen *(Weld)*

Roggen apparently took the name of Edward P. Roggen, a surveyor and engineer who served as the secretary of state for Nebraska.
PO: November 15, 1883–; Pop. 150

Rollins Pass *(Boulder, Gilpin, Grand)*

Also known as *Boulder Pass* and *Corona Pass, Rollins Pass* commemorates John Quincy Adams Rollins, whose road connected Rollinsville with Middle Park in 1873. Later, David H. Moffat's Denver, Northwestern, and Pacific Railway used Rollins's route, establishing a station called Corona at the summit. Trains were no match for the high, snowy *Rollins Pass* crossing, however, and today the main line goes through the Moffat Tunnel south of the pass. (*See also* Moffat County.)
Elevation: 11,671 feet

Rollinsville *(Gilpin)*

Born in New Hampshire in 1816, John Quincy Adams Rollins arrived at the gold fields in 1860, "the perfect type of a bold, pushing, organizing, civilizing frontiersman," said one contemporary biographer. Soon he amassed an empire of mining property and farmland around his home, which became the nucleus of *Rollinsville*.
PO: January 31, 1871–; Pop. 300

Romeo *(Conejos)*

In 1935, the *Romeo* superintendent of schools told the State Historical Society that *Romeo* had first been *Romero,* for an early settler. The Romero Town Company filed the plat in 1899; two years later the post office opened as *Romeo,* apparently to avoid confusion with Romero, New Mexico.
PO: July 24, 1901–September 10, 1908; September 14, 1908–; Pop. 341

Roosevelt National Forest *(Northern Colorado)*

President Theodore H. Roosevelt, who established a number of forest reserves during his administration (1901-1909), was honored when the *Colorado National Forest* was renamed in 1932. Originally part of the Medicine Bow Forest Reserve, the area became the *Colorado National Forest* in 1910, three years after forest reserves became national forests. Roosevelt often visited Colorado in the early twentieth century seeking both votes and recreation; one memorable hunting trip inspired Silver Dollar Tabor, daughter of Horace and Baby Doe, to pen a 1908 song entitled "Our President Roosevelt's Colorado Hunt."

Rose's Cabin *(Hinsdale)*

San Juan prospector Corydon Rose built a cabin on Henson Creek that became the nucleus of *Rose's Cabin.*
PO: June 27, 1878–September 19, 1887

Rosita *(Custer)* [roh-ZEE-tuh]

As author Helen Hunt Jackson explained after she visited *Rosita* in the 1870s, the first miners had "found several fine springs of water, each spring in a thicket of wild roses. As they went to and fro from their huts to the springs they found in the dainty blossoms a certain air of greeting, as of old inhabitants welcoming new-comers." To Jackson, "it seemed no more than courteous that the town should be called after the name of the oldest and most aristocratic settler"—*Rosita,* meaning "little rose" in Spanish. "Not even a millionaire of mines," she concluded, "will ever dare to dispute this vested title of the modest little flower."
PO: July 8, 1874–December 2, 1966

Routt County *(Established January 29, 1877)* [ROWT]

Routt County, which once extended to the Utah line, honors John L. Routt, who was serving as second assistant postmaster general in the Ulysses S. Grant administration before his 1875 appointment as Colorado territorial governor. A year later, Routt was elected the first governor of the Centennial State; subsequently, he served another gubernatorial term from 1891 to 1893.
Pop. 14,088

Routt National Forest *(Northwest Colorado)*

Established in 1905, the *Park Range Forest Reserve* was renamed *Routt National Forest* three years later for former governor John L. Routt.

Roxborough Park *(Douglas)*

Roxborough Park is a recently developed residential community near Roxborough State Park, which encompasses the jagged rock formations first described by the Stephen H. Long expedition in 1820. "Our party travelled along outside the range. . .," wrote Captain John R. Bell on July 8, "where we had new and very interesting views of insolated masses of rock laying in the valley of singular colour and formation, the whole scenery truly picturesque & romantic." Some forty years later, homesteader Edward Griffith is said to have named the area *Roxborough* because it resembled a place near his English home.
Pop. 300

Royal Gorge *(Fremont)*

"Survey the breathtaking vistas of the magnificent Royal
Gorge from the world's highest suspension bridge, an amaz-
ing 1,053 feet above the rushing Arkansas River. Ride the
world's steepest incline railway to the bottom of the incredible
canyon. Soar high above the chasm in the thrilling aerial
tram." So runs a recent advertisement for *Royal Gorge Park*.
Owned by the city of Canon City, which was granted the land
by Congress in 1906, the park is operated with private funds.
Royal Gorge even has its own post office (now a branch of
Canon City) and its own ZIP code (81246). (*See also* Canon
City.)
PO: July 21, 1949–; Pop. 5

Rulison *(Garfield)*

Homesteader C. M. Rulison gave his name to *Rulison*. In 1969,
Rulison became the center of controversy as protestors sought
in vain to halt the detonation of a nuclear device near the settlement. Aimed at stimulating natural gas fields, the September 10 underground blast was part of Project Plowshare,
which also set off a similar explosion in 1973 near Rio Blanco.

Rush *(El Paso)*

Rush took its name from early settler Christian Rush, whose
combined store and post office served other homesteaders
from Missouri, Kansas, and Oklahoma.
PO: February 15, 1908–; Pop. 30

Russell Gulch *(Gilpin)*

After he and other Georgia prospectors found gold in 1858 on
the South Platte River, William Green Russell, with brothers J.
Oliver and Levi, decided to try his luck in the mountains. *Russell Gulch,* south of Central City, commemorates this pioneer
argonaut, who left the territory in 1863 to fight for the Confederacy. Russell later returned to southern Colorado during the
1870s, ultimately settling with his part-Cherokee wife in Indian Territory (present-day Oklahoma), where he died in
1877.
PO: September 29, 1879–May 31, 1943

Rustic *(Larimer)*

George A. Crofutt noted in his 1885 *Grip-Sack Guide of Colorado*
that *Rustic* was "a rustic ranche and postoffice" on the Cache
la Poudre River, "where grand scenery, fine trout and game in
great variety abound." As he told his readers, it was a "fine
resort for invalids and pleasure-seekers."
PO: October 18, 1880–October 31, 1887; Pop. 50

Rye *(Pueblo)*

Residents renamed their post office *Rye,* for the grain grown in the area, after federal postal officials asked them to discard the longer *Table Mountain.*
PO: March 7, 1881–; Pop. 168

Ryssby *(Boulder)*

Although the Boulder Valley settlement founded by Swedish immigrants from Ryssby, Småland, is gone, the Lutheran church built in 1881–1882 and modeled after one in the old parish is listed in the National Register of Historic Places. It is still the setting for traditional Midsummer Day and Christmas services as well as many weddings.

Saguache *(Saguache)* [suh-WAHCH]

A few months after Saguache County was created in December 1866, John Lawrence and other founders established the townsite of *Saguache,* which became the county seat.
PO: April 1, 1867–; Pop. 584; CS

Saguache County *(Established December 29, 1866)*

When early San Luis Valley settler John Lawrence was serving as an interpreter for Hispanic members of the 1866-1867 territorial legislature, he wrote the bill establishing *Saguache County.* As Lawrence told Frank Hall some years later for Hall's *History of the State of Colorado,* the name came from the Ute word *Sa-gua-gua-chi-pa,* "signifiying 'blue earth,' or rather the water at the blue earth, and referred to certain large springs in which blue earth was found, situated at or near the upper crossing of the Saguache river, some twenty miles above the town of Saguache." When traders and trappers came into the area who "could not or would not pronounce the long and difficult Indian name," Lawrence continued, "they abridged it to the more pronounceable 'Saguache,' and thus it has stood to the present time."
Pop. 4,619

Saints John *(Summit)*

Saints John, first called *Coleyville* for prospector John Coley, was later renamed for the patron saints of the Masons, Saint John the Baptist and Saint John the Evangelist. Early argonauts brought Masonry to Colorado; the first recorded informal meeting took place on November 3, 1858, in Auraria.
PO: August 8, 1876–February 1, 1881

Salida *(Chaffee)* [suh-LIGH-duh]

First called *South Arkansas, Salida* was established by the Denver and Rio Grande Railway in 1880. Both former territorial governor Alexander Hunt, then associated with the railroad, and his wife have been credited with suggesting the name, which means "exit" or "outlet" in Spanish. "This point is the outlet for the numerous mining camps over the range and on the South Arkansas river and our town is to be hereafter known as Salida," commented the *Salida* newspaper on July 24, 1880. "It is an appropriate name, is a very pretty name, and is much shorter and therefore more convenient than the old name of South Arkansas."
PO: June 16, 1880–March 28, 1881, as Arkansas; March 28, 1881–; Pop. 4,737; CS

Salina *(Boulder)*

Prospectors from Salina, Kansas, named this Boulder County mining camp.
PO: November 19, 1874–January 1, 1925; Pop. 10

San Acacio *(Costilla)* [san-uh-KASH-ee-oh]

Legend has it that when Hispanic settlers were attacked by Indians near their plaza, they appealed for help to San Acacio (St. Acacius). Miraculously, the Indians turned back—some say that Spanish soldiers appeared as if in a vision—and the people then decided to name the plaza in honor of San Acacio. Established by 1853, the village was later known as *Old*

Town or *Old San Acacio (Viejo San Acacio)* to distinguish it from a nearby townsite, also called San Acacio, laid out in the early twentieth century by the Costilla Estate Development Company.
PO: November 11, 1909–; Pop. 60

Sanford *(Conejos)*

Sanford, a townsite settled by Mormons in 1885, took the name of Silas Sanford Smith, then serving as president of the San Luis Stake. Settlers from nearby Ephraim and Richfield soon moved to the new community.
PO: June 2, 1888–February 6, 1889; April 9, 1889–; Pop. 750

San Francisco *(Costilla)*

Costilla, Las Animas, and Conejos counties have all had settlements named *San Francisco,* Spanish for St. Francis. Still on the state map is this San Francisco, situated on San Francisco Creek in Costilla County.
Pop. 130

Sangre de Cristo Mountains *(Southern Colorado)*
[sang-ri-day-KRIS-toh]

Lost in legend is the name of the first Spaniard who exclaimed *"sangre de Cristo!"* "blood of Christ," when viewing these rugged southern Colorado mountains. Probably, as most stories have it, he was inspired by sunlight on the snowy peaks, although other versions say that he saw red scrub oak leaves glowing in the dawn of an early fall morning.

San Isabel National Forest *(Central and Southern Colorado)*

San Isabel, Spanish for "St. Isabel," was an early mining and ranching settlement on San Isabel Creek in Saguache County. The town had a post office from 1872 to 1912. "This seems the earliest use of San Isabel as a place name in Colorado," wrote scholar James Grafton Rogers in his place name files. A later San Isabel, which had a post office between 1936 and 1938, is situated in Custer County surrounded by the present national forest.

San Juan County *(Established January 31, 1876)* [san-WAHN]

A century after the Domínguez-Escalante expedition described the San Juan River, the Colorado legislature created *San Juan County.* By that time the term "San Juan Country" was used to describe the area around the San Juan Mountains, named, like the river, by Spanish explorers.
Pop. 745

San Juan National Forest *(Southwest Colorado)*

In southwestern Colorado a river, a mountain range, a county, and this national forest all carry the Spanish name *San Juan,* used in the region for more than two centuries.

San Juan River *(Southwest Colorado)*

When the Spanish priests Domínguez and Escalante came upon this stream in 1776, they found that the name by which it is still known, *San Juan* or "St. John," was already in use. "El Río de San Juan carries more water than the Navajo," they reported, "and they say that farther north it has good and large meadows because it flows over more open country."

San Luis *(Costilla)* [san-LOO-is]

Situated near Culebra "snake" Creek and established in 1851, *San Luis* was early called *San Luis de Culebra* or *Plaza de Medio,* the "middle village" on the Culebra. "Some fifteen miles or so from Fort Garland, in the heart of the San Luis Park, lies San Luis de Culebra, a hamlet of five or six hundred people, the most considerable 'city' there," wrote an 1866 visitor, James F. Rusling, in *Across America* (1874). "Culebra was then a genuine Mexican town without an atom of the Yankee in or about it, and seemed a thousand years old, it was so sleepy, though comparatively a new settlement." *San Luis* claims to be the "oldest town in Colorado," although other Costilla County settlements such as Garcia vie for the honor. (*See also* San Luis Valley.)
PO: February 15, 1862–; Pop. 800; CS

San Luis Peak *(Saguache)*

San Luis Peak is situated to the west of the San Luis Valley. *Elevation: 14,014 feet*

San Luis Valley *(Southern Colorado)*

Southernmost of Colorado's four mountain parks—the others are North, Middle, and South—the *San Luis Valley* was named by the Spanish. One valley legend tells of missionary Francisco Torres and his companions, who came into the area from the south searching for gold to mine and Indians to convert. A native of Seville, Torres is credited with naming the valley for St. Louis, San Luis in Spanish, the patron saint of that city.

San Miguel County *(Established March 2, 1883)* [san-mih-GIL]

San Miguel County took its name from the San Miguel "St. Michael" River, which flows through the eastern part of the county. In 1776 the Domínguez-Escalante expedition wrote of

El Río de San Pedro, "the River of St. Peter," but the later Spanish name was in use when the county was formed in 1883.
Pop. 3,653

San Pablo *(Costilla)* [san-PAB-loh]

The Hispanic settlement of *San Pablo,* "St. Paul," is situated south of Culebra Creek opposite San Pedro, "St. Peter," a village on the north side.
PO: January 7, 1893–; Pop. 100

San Pedro *(Costilla)*

San Pedro, "St. Peter," a Hispanic village on the north side of Culebra Creek opposite San Pablo, "St. Paul," was known early as *Plaza Arriba* or *Upper Culebra.*
Pop. 100

Sapinero *(Gunnison)* [sap-i-NEHR-oh]

Sapinero, a member of the Tabeguache Ute band, was a brother of Chief Ouray's wife Chipeta. Ernest Ingersoll, formerly with the Hayden Survey, wrote in *The Crest of the Continent* (1885) that Sapinero "was looked upon by the whites as a man of unusual sagacity."
PO: November 23, 1882–November 24, 1988; Pop. 5

Sargents *(Saguache)*

Sargents honored merchant and first postmaster Joseph Sargent, a former employee of the Los Pinos Indian Agency, whose ranch became the nucleus of the community. Originally called *Marshalltown,* for nearby Marshall Pass, the town was renamed in 1882.
PO: July 13, 1880–January 26, 1882, as Marshalltown; January 26, 1882–; Pop. 50

Sawpit *(San Miguel)*

In 1941, the Colorado Writers' Project described *Sawpit* as "a mining community of rambling unpainted frame buildings, all of which have seen better days." The structures were products of the boom a half-century earlier, when miners sawed timber in the "saw pits" that inspired the town's name. In this process, a depression or pit was dug in the ground and a log positioned over it; two men, one above and one below, could then saw through the timber.
PO: July 13, 1892–February 21, 1896, as Seymour; February 21, 1896–March 31, 1926; Pop. 36

Schofield Pass *(Gunnison)*

Schofield, a silver mining camp platted by B. F. Schofield and others in 1879, lasted only a few years. The nearby pass, however, still retains the Schofield name.
Elevation: 10,707 feet

Security-Widefield *(El Paso)*

Two post–World War II housing developments combined to create the *Security-Widefield* area south of Colorado Springs. The builders of *Security* chose a name that would inspire confidence in prospective homeowners, whereas *Widefield* founders opted for history, taking the name of the Widefield School District which dated from 1874.
Pop. 23,822 (CDP)

Sedalia *(Douglas)* [si-DAYL-yah]

Sedalia grew up near the confluence of East Plum and West Plum creeks, where an early settler had built a circular corral known as Round Corral. The community later was called *Plum* and then *Plum Station* before adopting the name of *Sedalia,* for the Missouri home town of first postmaster Henry Clay.
PO: April 8, 1872–; Pop. 350

Sedgwick *(Sedgwick)*

Although the post office was briefly known as *Henderson,* the town ultimately took its name from Fort Sedgwick. (*See* Fort Sedgwick.)
PO: May 7, 1883–September 10, 18ᴇↄ, as Henderson; September 10, 1885–May 11, 1894; April 30, 1896–; Pop. 183

Sedgwick County *(Established April 9, 1889)*

Sedgwick County also was named for Fort Sedgwick.
Pop. 2,690

Segundo *(Las Animas)* [si-GUHN-doh]

In 1901, the Colorado Fuel and Iron Company began building coke ovens and washers to process coal mined at nearby Primero. The new CF&I town, situated across the Purgatoire River from an earlier Hispanic settlement called Varros, was first known as *Humoso* before taking the name *Segundo.* Meaning "second" in Spanish, the name denoted the camp's establishment in CF&I chronology—after Primero ("first") and before Tercio ("third"). (*See also* Primero and Tercio.)
PO: July 17, 1901–; Pop. 125

Segundo

Seibert *(Kit Carson)* [SIGH-bert]

In October 1900, the *Burlington Republican* reported that a Rock Island train had stopped at *Seibert* "to allow Mr. Henry Seibert to see the new library he has presented this town." Some two hundred volumes were on the shelves, and the railroad official who had been honored with the community name promised to fill up another section. "That will make a library of about 400 books," the paper noted with satisfaction.
PO: October 17, 1888–; Pop. 181

Severance *(Weld)*

David E. Severance, who owned part of the townsite land and submitted the post office application, gave his name to *Severance*. Early residents also called the place *Tailholt*, probably referring to "The Little Town o' Tailholt" in James Whitcomb Riley's 1879 poem.
PO: March 8, 1894–November 10, 1896; January 20, 1897–June 30, 1902; September 18, 1907–; Pop. 106

Shaffers Crossing *(Jefferson)*

Landowner Samuel Shaffer is remembered by *Shaffers Crossing.*

Shawnee *(Park)* [SHAH-nee]

First a Denver, South Park, and Pacific railroad station called *Riceville, Shawnee* later took the name of the Shawnee Lodge, which the Colorado and Southern Hotel System opened in 1899 along with the companion Kiowa Lodge at Bailey. Nearby Shawnee Peak (11,922 feet) also carries the name of the Algonquin tribe.
PO: April 19, 1900–; Pop. 250

Sheridan *(Arapahoe)*

Sheridan was organized when residents thought that the new military post nearby would be called Fort Sheridan; as it turned out, the installation became Fort Logan. Thus only the town, which incorporated several smaller communities, and Sheridan Boulevard honored Union General Philip H. Sheridan, noted for commanding troops on the plains after the Civil War. (*See* also Fort Logan.)
Pop. 4,976

Sheridan Lake *(Kiowa)*

Townsite promoters said that General Philip H. Sheridan had camped at a nearby buffalo wallow, which they called *Sheridan Lake* in the hope of enticing prospective purchasers.
PO: August 16, 1887–September 20, 1887, and October 15, 1887–October 27, 1887, as Bee; September 20, 1887–October 15, 1887; October 27, 1887–; Pop. 95

Silt *(Garfield)*

Silt grew up around a Denver and Rio Grande stop named for the fine soil or "silt" in the area. Periodic attempts to change the earthy name to something more refined have so far proved unsuccessful; in 1992, for example, residents decided to stay with *Silt* instead of opting for *Grandview* or *Pistol.*
PO: October 27, 1898–; Pop. 1,095

Silver Cliff *(Custer)*

"The discovery of horn silver in the summer of 1878, in the stained porphyry cliff thirty feet high, standing up like a wall on the side of a prairie hollow, was the cause of our metropolis coming into existence," wrote Richard Irwin in the 1881 *History of the Arkansas Valley* about the town and its namesake cliff.
PO: October 30, 1878–; Pop. 322

Silver Plume *(Clear Creek)*

According to several accounts, in 1870 "Commodore" Stephen Decatur, then editor of the Georgetown *Colorado Miner,* suggested christening the camp for the Silver Plume Mine, so named because feathery streaks of silver could be seen in the first ore discovered. When asked what to call the booming but unnamed settlement, Decatur reportedly exclaimed, "The name? You've already got the name! It was written on the ore you brought me!" He then lapsed into poetry:

> The knights today are miners bold,
> Who toil in deep mines' gloom!
> To honor men who dig for gold,
> For ladies whom their arms enfold,
> We'll name the camp Silver Plume!

Nonetheless, some maintain that *Silver Plume* honored either a miner named Plume or James G. Blaine, a prominent congressman whose nickname was the "Plumed Knight." Decatur's version is certainly the most colorful, however, worthy of an eccentric character said to have had "a talent of extemporizing verse which flowed through his mustache with the rapidity of a mountain stream."
PO: December 1, 1875–January 1896; January 1896– as Silverplume; Pop. 134

Silverthorne *(Summit)*

Marshall Silverthorn, a Pennsylvanian who came west with the gold rush and established the Silverthorn Hotel in Breckenridge, was remembered a century later when this new community, born with the construction of the Eisenhower Memorial Tunnel, took the name *Silverthorn* with an *e*.
PO: January 1, 1962–; Pop. 1,768

Silverton *(San Juan)*

Situated at an altitude of 9,300 feet, *Silverton* was first known briefly as *Quito,* for the equally high capital of Ecuador. By August 1874, however, the new community had adopted the present name; one area settler recalled voting between *Silverton* and *Greeneville*. A more colorful but apocryphal story quotes a miner who exclaimed, "We may not have much gold, but we've got silver by the ton!" In fact, residents apparently just combined "silver" with "ton," a contraction for "town," to make *Silverton*.
PO: February 1, 1875–; Pop. 716; CS

Simla *(Elbert)* [SIM-luh]

Simla took its name, so the story goes, from the Rock Island station christened by a railroad official's daughter who had read a book mentioning the city of Simla in India. *Simla* is proud of native athlete Glenn Morris, who won the decathlon

gold medal at the 1936 Berlin Olympics.
PO: August 12, 1909–; Pop. 481

Skyway *(Mesa)*

Skyway is situated along the scenic Skyway Drive across the Grand Mesa near Grand Junction.
PO: June 4, 1927–June 30, 1945; Pop. 10

Slater *(Moffat)* [SLAY-ter]

Although William Slater stayed only briefly on land he homesteaded in the Snake River Valley, he remained long enough to leave his name on this settlement, as well as on nearby Slater Creek.
PO: December 24, 1888–; Pop. 5

Slick Rock *(San Miguel)*

"Slick rock," a descriptive term for the smooth Entrada Sandstone prominent in the area, inspired the name of this community.
PO: May 1, 1941–June 30, 1946; August 10, 1957–; Pop. 60

Slumgullion Pass *(Hinsdale)*

On the west side of this pass is a slump or slide known as the Slumgullion Earth Flow, a National Natural Landmark. The word "slumgullion" can refer either to the refuse left after a whale has been cut up or to a meat-and-vegetable stew—both meanings have been suggested as the inspiration for a name to describe this colorful geological feature.
Elevation: 11,361 feet

Smoky Hill River *(East Central Colorado)*

Rising in eastern Colorado, the *Smoky Hill River* meets the Republican River in Kansas to form the Kansas River. The stream took its name from the Smoky Hills of central Kansas, which as an early trapper remarked were "landmarks widely known, to be seen from a great distance through an atmosphere frequently hazy with smoke." Many gold seekers followed the *Smoky Hill River* into present Colorado and then took one of several branch routes across the plains to Denver. More direct than the trails along the South Platte or Arkansas rivers, the Smoky Hill Trail was also more dangerous, earning the nickname "Starvation Trail" owing to the shortage of water and game.

Snowmass *(Pitkin)*

Snowmass is situated along Snowmass Creek, which derived its name from Snowmass Mountain. Settled in the 1880s, *Snowmass* is almost a century older than Snowmass Village, some seven miles distant.
PO: February 19, 1901–April 14, 1904; October 7, 1904–January 31, 1914; April 8, 1914–; Pop. 20

Snowmass Mountain *(Gunnison, Pitkin)*

As Hayden Survey topographer Henry Gannett wrote in 1874, *Snowmass Mountain* "received its name from an immense field of snow on its eastern face." Survey members did, however, briefly consider calling the peak *Whitehouse* as a logical companion to nearby Capitol Peak.
Elevation: 14,092 feet

Snowmass Village *(Pitkin)*

Opened in 1967, the Snowmass-at-Aspen ski resort gave birth to the town of *Snowmass Village*.
PO: January 1, 1967– (branch of Aspen); Pop. 1,449

Snyder *(Morgan)*

Cattlemen D. H. and J. W. Snyder, who came to Colorado from Texas, gave their name to *Snyder*.
PO: June 16, 1882–; Pop. 150

Somerset *(Gunnison)*

Situated in the coal regions of western Gunnison County, *Somerset* is thought to have been named for Somerset, Pennsylvania, also a coal-mining town.
PO: March 19, 1903–; Pop. 140

Sopris *(Las Animas)* [SOH-pris]

Established as a coal mining camp in 1887, *Sopris* took the name of Elbridge B. Sopris, Trinidad pioneer and early surveyor. Today the site of *Sopris* is submerged under the waters of Trinidad Lake, created by a dam on the Purgatoire River.
PO: July 25, 1888–January 2, 1969

South Denver *(City and County of Denver)*

Bounded by Alameda Avenue, Colorado Boulevard, Yale Avenue, and the South Platte River and incorporated in 1886, *South Denver* was an independent town before annexation by the capital city in 1894.
PO: November 20, 1889–May 13, 1896

Southern Ute Indian Reservation *(Southwest Colorado)*

Descendants of Colorado Ute who accepted individual land allotments now live on the *Southern Ute Indian Reservation* adjoining the Ute Mountain Ute Indian Reservation of nonallotted tribal land. In 1941, the WPA guide to Colorado called the narrow reservation strip across the southwestern corner of Colorado "the least attractive and desirable section of the great empire of mountains, plains, and valleys over which the powerful Ute once roamed." (*See also* Ute Mountain Ute Indian Reservation.)

South Fork *(Rio Grande)*

South Fork, a riverside resort community, developed at the junction of the Rio Grande and the South Fork of the Rio Grande.
PO: February 10, 1876–May 23, 1883; May 5, 1892–September 9, 1909; November 9, 1910–; Pop. 250

Southglenn *(Arapahoe)*

A counterpart to Northglenn, *Southglenn* began as a suburban Denver development and shopping mall planned by the Perl-Mack company in the early 1960s.
Pop. 43,087 (CDP)

South Park *(Park)*

Because of the salt marshes on the western side, the Spanish spoke of this high mountain valley as the *Valle Salado,* "Salt Valley," while to the French it was the *Bayou Salade.* Eclectic American trappers called the park the *Bayou Salado.* Zebulon Pike traveled through the region in 1806, as did John C. Frémont in 1844, observing that "the appearance of buffalo in great numbers indicated that there were Indians in the Bayou Salade, (South Park,) by whom they were driven out." Here too came gold-rush prospectors, looking for the ore that Kentucky trapper James Purcell claimed to have discovered in 1805.

South Park City *(Park)*

Between 1869 and 1874, *Fairplay* was called *South Park City* (although the post office was *Fairplay*). The present *South Park City,* an outdoor museum in Fairplay, had its origins in the 1959 Rush to the Rockies celebration. The "city" is largely made up of historic buildings moved from such South Park communities as Alma, Buckskin Joe, and Leavick.

South Platte River *(Northeast Colorado)* [PLAT]

Rising in South Park, the *South Platte River,* which the Spanish in the seventeenth and eighteenth centuries called the *Río de Jesús y Maria,* joins the main Platte near North Platte, Nebraska. In almost any language, the Platte is a "flat river"—*Río Chato* in Spanish; *Platte* in French—so termed by brothers Pierre and Paul Mallet as they crossed the plains in 1739 on a trading venture to Santa Fe; *nibthacka* and *nibraska,* the words that became Nebraska, in the Omaha and Oto tongues.

Spanish Peaks *(Huerfano, Las Animas)*

In November 1806, explorer Zebulon Pike and his party gave "three *cheers* to the *Mexican mountains*" from a vantage point on the Arkansas River near present Las Animas. Southward were the *Spanish Peaks,* then in Spanish territory, to which later travelers even applied Pike's name before Pikes Peak was established for the summit to the north. Indians called the mountains "the twins" or "the breasts of the world," rendered in many different spellings including *Huajatolla, Wahtoyah,* and *Juajatoya.* In 1898, naturalist and editor Elliott Coues wrote that *Wahtoyah* was a Ute word meaning "twins," noting as well that he had "sometimes heard the French names Les Tetons and Les Mamelles." North in present Wyoming, Frenchmen similarly called the famous Teton Range *Les Trois Tetons,* "the three breasts."
Elevation: 13,626 feet (west peak); 12,683 feet (east peak)

Spar City *(Mineral)*

Spar City was known briefly as *Fisher City,* for prospector John Fisher, before taking its name from rich silver-bearing feldspar. The camp had a newspaper entitled the *Spar City Spark* and a post office called *Spar* before declining yields and the demonitization of silver extinguished the spark in *Spar City.* Some cabins, however, still are used as summer vacation homes.
PO: August 16, 1892–August 23, 1895, as Spar; Pop. 10

Springfield *(Baca)*

Kansas promoters formed the townsite company in 1887; many of those who first purchased lots were from Springfield, Missouri, and they named the community for their former home.
PO: June 2, 1887–; Pop. 1,475; CS

Sprucewood (Douglas)

Sprucewood marks the site of the Sprucewood Inn in western Douglas County.

Starkville (Las Animas)

Albert G. Stark opened the Starkville coal mine and gave his name to the community that was first briefly known as *San Pedro.*
PO: *January 31, 1879–May 23, 1879, as San Pedro; May 23, 1879–; Pop. 104*

State Bridge (Eagle)

In 1941, the WPA guide to Colorado reported that *State Bridge* on the Colorado River had a population of 15. "This cluster of weathered buildings, named for the span across the river, lies at the northern foot of Rainbow Mountain, named for its many-hued rock formations."
PO: *November 8, 1909–April 15, 1915*

St. Charles (City and County of Denver)

With better planning and a little luck, *St. Charles* might have been Colorado's capital. On September 24, 1858, a group of prospectors, promoters, and traders formed an association to lay out the townsite near the confluence of Cherry Creek and the South Platte River. Charles Nichols, who had lived in St. Charles, Missouri, suggested the name. Some two months later, however, after most members had returned to eastern Kansas Territory for the winter, the Denver City Town Company took over the vulnerable *St. Charles* site. Although a few *St. Charles* shareholders wanted to fight, most eventually joined the usurpers. (*See also* Denver.)

Steamboat Springs (Routt)

Settled in the mid-1870s, the town took its name from the Steamboat Spring, which to early trappers sounded like a steamboat chugging down a river. Silent today—perhaps as a result of later railroad construction—Steamboat Spring is one of more than one hundred natural springs in the area. Nearby Mount Werner, famed for fine skiing, honors hometown athlete Wallace "Buddy" Werner, who won a number of major European ski titles before his death in a 1964 Swiss avalanche.
PO: *May 20, 1878–; Pop. 6,695; CS*

St. Elmo (Chaffee)

First called *Forest City,* this once-flourishing mining town was renamed for *St. Elmo,* the popular 1866 novel by southern

writer Augusta Evans Wilson.
PO: June 23, 1880–October 15, 1952; Pop. 5

Sterling *(Logan)*

Early settler David Leavitt is credited with naming *Sterling* for his hometown of Sterling, Illinois. During the early 1870s a number of Southerners fleeing Reconstruction came to the *Sterling* area upon finding the best land around Greeley already taken. With the arrival of the Union Pacific line in 1881, the residents of the first *Sterling* moved a few miles southwest to the present site on the railroad.
PO: February 24, 1874–; Pop. 10,362; CS

Stewart Peak *(Saguache)*

Once listed as a Fourteener, *Stewart Peak* now officially measures seventeen feet below the magic number. John L. J. Hart concluded in *Fourteen Thousand Feet* that the Wheeler Survey probably named the mountain for William M. Stewart, a senator from Nevada (1865-1875, 1887-1905), but suggested that Sir William Drummond Stewart of Scotland, who traveled the Mountain Man's West in the 1830s and 1840s, might also be a candidate for the honor.
Elevation: 13,983 feet

Stoneham *(Weld)* [STOH-n'm]

Named for Elenora B. Stone, owner of the townsite land, *Stoneham* continued the rocky trend with such streets as Slate, Granite, Marble, and Flint.
PO: August 2, 1888–January 12, 1892; May 27, 1907–October 15, 1908; June 8, 1910–; Pop. 35

Stoner *(Montezuma)*

Stoner is situated on Stoner Creek, which might have been named for its rocky or "stony" bed. An early settler has also been suggested as the source of the name.
PO: April 4, 1917–November 30, 1954; Pop. 25

Stonewall *(Las Animas)*

"Cattle and sheep, goats and babies, Mexicans and Americans, possess the country, together with black tail deer, elk, bear, and wild turkeys and trout in all the streams in abundance," wrote George A. Crofutt about *Stonewall* in his 1885 *Grip-Sack Guide of Colorado.* Here, in about 1867, had settled a man named James M. Stoner; thus, according to some versions, the formation behind his home was called "Stoner's Wall," condensed later to *Stonewall.*
PO: August 6, 1878–January 31, 1918; Pop. 150

Stonington *(Baca)*

Initially called *New Stonington*, this Baca County settlement was the successor to an earlier Stonington promoted nearby during the late 1880s townsite boom. The first community, which became known as Old Stonington, had acquired its name from the man who ran the ranch post office in the area.
PO: January 20, 1888–; Pop. 30

Strasburg *(Adams, Arapahoe)* [STRAHS-berg]

History books relate that on May 10, 1869, the Union Pacific and Central Pacific railroads met at Promontory Point, Utah, to complete the first transcontinental line. Not so, say the folks in *Strasburg*, pointing to the fact that until March 22, 1872, the Union Pacific had no permanent bridge across the Missouri River, thus making it necessary to ferry cars across the water. The real "joining of the rails" occurred at a point called Comanche Crossing, Colorado, when two Kansas Pacific crews met on August 15, 1870. Since the Kansas Pacific bridge across the Missouri dated from June 30, 1869, the moment marked the completion of the first "permanent, continuous, uninterrupted" railroad across the United States. In 1875, this historic juncture was renamed to honor Kansas Pacific section foreman John Strasburg.
PO: May 25, 1908–

Stratton *(Kit Carson)*

Stratton was Claremont before residents decided in 1906 to honor gold king Winfield Scott Stratton, who had died four years earlier in Colorado Springs. Once a carpenter, Stratton had struck it rich with the Independence Mine—staked out July 4, 1891—and other mining properties near Cripple Creek.
PO: September 11, 1888–March 24, 1906, as Claremont; March 24, 1906–; Pop. 649

St. Vrain Creek *(Boulder, Weld)*

In 1820, the Stephen H. Long expedition reported that this stream was "called Potera's creek, from a Frenchman of that name, who is said to have been bewildered upon it, wandering about for twenty days, almost without food." Later, the creek took the name of the fur-trading post Fort St. Vrain, built near the confluence with the South Platte River. (*See also* Fort St. Vrain.)

Sugar City *(Crowley)*

In 1899, the National Beet Sugar Company (later the National Sugar Manufacturing Company) organized the Sugar City Townsite Company to develop a community for its workers.

Although other enterprises such as a grain elevator later were built, *Sugar City*'s fortunes rose and fell with the sugar beet factory, which closed in 1967.

PO: February 26, 1900–March 27, 1900, as Wait; March 27, 1900–;
Pop. 252

Summit County *(Established November 1, 1861)*

Created by the first territorial legislature in 1861, *Summit County* originally covered the northwestern quarter of Colorado from the Continental Divide to the Wyoming and Utah borders. Later, six additional counties—Grand, Eagle, Garfield, Rio Blanco, Routt, and Moffat—were carved from this vast area, reducing *Summit County* to its present boundaries.
Pop. 12,881

Summitville *(Rio Grande)*

With a name probably inspired by its lofty elevation—more than 11,000 feet above sea level—the mining camp of *Summitville* boomed several times from the first gold discovery in 1870 to the 1930s. In 1885, George A. Crofutt reported in his *Grip-Sack Guide of Colorado* that *Summitville* was "reached by a good wagon road in summer, and saddle and snow shoes in winter."

PO: February 10, 1876–September 24, 1879, and October 16,

Sunbeam

1879–November 17, 1880, as Summit; November 17, 1880–April 30, 1912; July 12, 1935–November 25, 1947

Sunbeam *(Moffat)*

James Templeton, a long-time Yampa Valley resident, told State Historical Society researchers that early settler N. C. Bonivee had suggested the post office name. "Mr. Bonivee stated to me that, to him the sun rays or beams shone brighter on this particular spot in the valley than at any other point," Templeton wrote in 1935.
PO: October 1, 1912–June 15, 1942

Sunlight Peak *(La Plata)*

Whitman Cross of the United States Geological Survey named *Sunlight Peak* while mapping the area around the turn of the century.
Elevation: 14,059 feet

Sunset *(Boulder)*

Boulder County counted both Sunshine and *Sunset* among its mountain mining towns. At *Sunset*, first called *Pennsylvania Gulch*, the Colorado and Northwestern (later Denver, Boulder, and Western) or "Switzerland Trail" tracks diverged, one line climbing to Ward, the other to Eldora. Now, with the railroad long gone, the roadbed has been torn up and the sun has set on *Sunset*.
PO: September 25, 1883–April 30, 1917; March 11, 1918–November 15, 1921

Sunshine *(Boulder)*

In the spring of 1874, D. C. Patterson finally struck paydirt in the mountains near Boulder. "The good fortune in finding such valuable property after several years of discouraging toil, induced the owner to call the mine 'Sunshine,'" wrote T. O. Saunders in an 1876 Fourth of July oration delivered in the camp. Soon Patterson's fellow miners decided to name the place *Sunshine,* for the "early discovery and great richness" of the mine, "together with the beauty of the name and its appropriate significance with reference to the peculiarity of the location." Susie Sunshine Turner, the first baby born in the camp, arrived the following November.
PO: February 26, 1875–August 31, 1913

Sunshine Peak *(Hinsdale)*

Members of the Hayden Survey narrowly missed being hit by lightning when they climbed this peak in 1874. Called merely *"Station 12"* in the survey reports, the mountain was known both as *Niagara Peak* and *Mount Sherman.* "On the origin of Sunshine nothing is known," wrote John L. J. Hart in *Fourteen Thousand Feet,* speculating that the United States Geological Survey gave the name in the early twentieth century.
Elevation: 14,001 feet

Superior *(Boulder, Jefferson)*

Settlers from Superior, Wisconsin, named this one-time coal town, which has grown dramatically since annexing land for the Rock Creek subdivision in 1987.
PO: December 14, 1896–March 15, 1900; April 14, 1900–January 31, 1955; Pop. 255

Swink *(Otero)*

Swink honors George Washington Swink, pioneer melon grower and founder and first mayor of Rocky Ford, who served as a Colorado state senator during the 1890s.
PO: January 10, 1900–February 7, 1906, as Fairmount; February 7, 1906–; Pop. 584

Tabeguache Mountain *(Chaffee)* [tay-bih-WASH]

Tabeguache Mountain took the name of the Tabeguache Ute band, while nearby Mount Shavano honored the Tabeguache chief Shavano.
Elevation: 14,155 feet

Tabernash *(Grand)* [TAB-'r-nash]

In the late summer of 1878, as conflict escalated between Ute Indians and white settlers in Middle Park, "Big Frank" Addison killed the Ute Tabernash near the Junction Ranch, where the Rollins Pass and Berthoud Pass roads converged. The town that developed later with the coming of the Denver, Northwestern, and Pacific Railway (the Moffat Road) took the name of the fallen Ute.
PO: September 30, 1905–; Pop. 300

Tabor City *(Lake)*

In his 1881 *Grip-Sack Guide of Colorado,* George A. Crofutt noted that *Tabor City* was named for Horace Tabor, "of Leadville bonanza notoriety," and consisted of one store "and about one dozen buildings of all kinds." First called *Chalk Ranch, Tabor City* soon declined as did the fortunes of its namesake, one of Colorado's most famous "silver kings." After years of storekeeping and grubstaking, Tabor had struck it rich with the Little Pittsburg near Leadville in 1878. Bad judgment and the Panic of 1893 brought an end to his wealth, but not before he built opera houses in Leadville and Denver, won election as Colorado lieutenant governor (1878), and served a brief term as a United States senator (1883). Along the way he divorced his loyal first wife Augusta and married the beautiful Elizabeth McCourt "Baby" Doe, with whom he had two daughters. A century later, although *Tabor City* has disappeared from the map, the romantic Tabor legend lives on in countless books and articles and in the soaring music of *The Ballad of Baby Doe,* an opera that premiered in Central City in 1956.
PO: April 14, 1879–January 27, 1881, as Tabor

Tarryall *(Park)*

Tarryall boomed for a few years after prospectors discovered gold in 1859 and decided the spot was, as a correspondent told the *Rocky Mountain News* in 1867, "a good place to tarry." Disgruntled latecomers, however, nicknamed the camp "Grab-all" and soon moved on to new diggings they called Fairplay. (Another, later Tarryall, also known as Puma City and situated southeast of present Tarryall Reservoir, had a post office between 1896 and 1933.)
PO: January 4, 1860–September 29, 1863

Ted's Place *(Larimer)*

"Ted" was Edward I. Herring, and his "place" was the gas station and restaurant he opened northwest of Fort Collins in 1922. Herring served as both a representative and a senator in the Colorado legislature between 1939 and 1955, and some suggested that political influence was behind the dot marking *Ted's Place* on the state map. After Herring's death in 1963, *Ted's Place* went through a succession of owners until it was finally torn down in 1989 and replaced by a modern service station.

Teller County *(Established March 23, 1899)*

The county created after the Cripple Creek gold rush attracted thousands to the area was named for Central City mining lawyer Henry M. Teller. Long active in territorial politics, Teller became one of the first two senators from the new "Centennial State" in 1876. From 1882 to 1885 he served as secretary of the interior, continuing thereafter in the Senate until 1909. *Pop. 12,468*

Telluride *(San Miguel)* [TEL-yoo-righd]

"The upper San Miguel may properly be called the valley of the three cities," reported the *Ouray Times* in 1881. "There are three growing towns, namely, Newport, Columbia and San Miguel City." Newport was renamed Pandora, while *Columbia,* as *Telluride,* became the most prosperous of the three. The word "telluride" comes from tellurium, "the chemical element of perhaps more importance in Colorado than in any other state," writes geologist Richard M. Pearl. "Curiously, the district of Telluride does not contain the minerals for which it was named." More colorfully, *Telluride* is sometimes said to be derived from a warning given to prospective visitors: "To Hell You Ride!"
PO: July 26, 1880–August 17, 1880; December 13, 1880–; Pop. 1,309; CS

Tennessee Pass *(Eagle, Lake)*

Prospectors from Tennessee apparently named this Continental Divide gateway. John C. Frémont crossed it with his third expedition in 1845; some forty years later, naturalist and author Ernest Ingersoll traveled on the Denver and Rio Grande Railway over the summit. "Rising along a tortuous path cut at a heavy grade, as usual, into the side hills, we mount slowly into Tennessee Pass, which feeds the head of the Eagle river on one side and one source of the Arkansas on the other," he wrote in *The Crest of the Continent* (1885). "It is a comparatively low and easy pass, covered everywhere with dense timber, and a wagon-road has long been followed through it."
Elevation: 10,424 feet

Tercio *(Las Animas)* [TER-see-oh]

Tercio followed Primero, "first," and Segundo, "second," in the roster of Colorado Fuel and Iron Company Spanish-

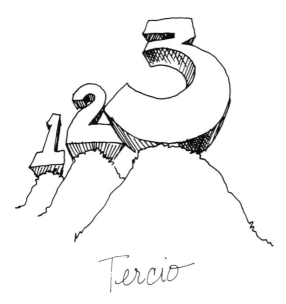

Tercio

named coal towns developed on the Maxwell Grant. First *Torres* and later *Rincon,* the camp ultimately was called *Tercio,* meaning "third" in Spanish. (*See also* Primero and Segundo.)
PO: July 5, 1902–September 30, 1949

Texas Creek *(Fremont)*

Cowboys driving Texas steers northward christened the Fremont County stream that gave *Texas Creek,* first known as *Ford,* its name. (Another Texas Creek in Fremont County is now known as Hillside.)
PO: January 4, 1881–September 10, 1885, as Ford; September 10, 1885–; Pop. 15

Thatcher *(Las Animas)*

With extensive interests in banking, merchandising, ranching, and politics, the Thatcher brothers—Mahlon D., John A., and Henry C.—made their name one of the most prominent in southern Colorado. *Thatcher* commemorated especially Mahlon, who had a large ranch near the town. In Pueblo, Mahlon Thatcher's mansion has been razed, but John Thatcher's "Rosemount" is now maintained as a Victorian house museum.
PO: November 9, 1883–December 3, 1884; January 29, 1885–October 13, 1888; December 30, 1890–May 20, 1911; August 29, 1911–July 20, 1973

The Forks *(Larimer)*

At *The Forks,* the main highway continues to Laramie, Wyoming, while another road branches off toward Red Feather Lakes. Robert O. Roberts opened The Forks Hotel in 1875, which provided a center for area settlers.

Thornton *(Adams)*

Developers who planned this community in the early 1950s named it for Dan Thornton, a Gunnison rancher who served as governor of Colorado from 1951 to 1955.
PO: April 6, 1957– (branch of Denver); Pop. 55,031

Tiger *(Summit)*

Perhaps the prospector who christened the Royal Tiger Mine knew that *tigre,* the Spanish word for "tiger," was often used as a name for mines in Spain, Mexico, and South America. Although the earliest discoveries and settlement dated from the 1860s, the company town of *Tiger* was founded in 1918 by the Royal Tiger Mines Company, which had consolidated a number of mines including the Royal Tiger.
PO: December 26, 1919–October 31, 1940

Timnath *(Larimer)* [TIM-nath]

In 1882, the Greeley, Salt Lake, and Pacific Railway reached the farming community southeast of Fort Collins called Sher-

Tiger

wood for an early settler; the town that soon grew up around the station took the name *Timnath,* from the Presbyterian church named for the biblical village where Samson found a wife (Judges 14:1–8). "In imitation of Samson's example," wrote Ansel Watrous in his 1911 *History of Larimer County,* "many a present day Samson has gone down to Timnath to take a rosy-cheeked damsel for his wife, justifying his course by liberal quotations from the Bible."
PO: July 10, 1884–; Pop. 190

Timpas *(Otero)* [TIM-p's]

In his 1850 book *Wah-to-yah and the Taos Trail,* the young Ohioan Lewis Garrard mentioned camping on *La Río Timpa* during his 1846–1847 travels along the Santa Fe Trail. "The Timpa rises in New Mexico," he wrote, "and is the beginning of a series of streams, whose names are much more euphonious than those in the American territory." Shown on current maps as Timpas Creek, the stream gave its name to the community of *Timpas.* The word *timpa* is Spanish for "tymp," defined as "the mouth of the hearth of a blast-furnace through which the molten metal descends"; it is formed by a masonry arch (tymp-arch), a stone block (tymp-stone), or both.
PO: May 27, 1891–October 23, 1970

Tincup *(Gunnison)*

First called *Virginia* or *Virginia City,* this mining camp was soon officially renamed *Tin Cup* (now *Tincup*). Many stories account for the origin of the name—that prospector Jim Taylor (or Ben Gray, or Fred Lottis) panned for gold with a tin cup; that ore samples in the assay office were weighed in tin cups; or that a tin cup was found where gold was first discovered. Although *Tin Cup*'s glory days did not last, in the early 1950s Denver broadcaster Pete Smythe set off another boom when he chose *Tincup* as the first site of his "Smythe's General Store" show

Tincup

on radio and then television. So many fans visited the town looking for the fictitious store that Smythe soon changed the location to East Tincup to placate residents of the real *Tincup*. *PO: July 22, 1879–February 28, 1880, as Virginia; February 28, 1880–May 7, 1895, as Tin Cup; May 7, 1895–January 31, 1918, as Tincup*

Tiny Town *(Jefferson)*

Tiny Town was started in 1919 by George Turner, owner of a Denver moving and storage company, both as a project to please his children and as an advertising medium (a replica of the Turner Fireproof Warehouse was one of the most prominent buildings). First called *Turnerville*, the Lilliputian community, complete with its own railroad, became *Tinytown* (later *Tiny Town*) by 1926. Turner sold *Tiny Town* in 1927, and for the next sixty years floods, fire, and general bad luck plagued a succession of owners. Today, thanks to the efforts of dedicated volunteers, *Tiny Town* is restored and again open to the public, featuring twenty-five original structures as well as many new buildings. Full-size people live in the surrounding mountain residential community.
Pop. 75

Tobe *(Las Animas)* [TOHB]

In 1940, the *Tobe* postmaster recalled that residents had suggested the last name of their neighbor, Tobe Benavidez, for the post office. Instead, the federal Post Office selected *Tobe*. *PO: December 17, 1910–January 31, 1960*

Tomichi

Tolland *(Gilpin)* [TOH-l'nd]

When the Denver, Northwestern, and Pacific Railway (the Moffat Road) built to this place in mid-1904, the station was known as *Mammoth*. By August, however, the name had become *Tolland*, in honor of townsite owner Katherine Wolcott Toll's family home of Tolland, England, as well as her married name.
PO: October 26, 1904–June 30, 1944; Pop. 5

Tomichi *(Gunnison)* [toh-MEE-chee]

First called *Argenta*, *Tomichi* was a silver-mining camp that boomed briefly on Tomichi Creek. The name was pronounced "To-mee-chee," said George A. Crofutt's 1885 *Grip-Sack Guide of Colorado*; local sources generally identify *tomichi* as a Ute word meaning "hot" or "boiling," referring to the hot springs in this part of Gunnison County.
PO: July 2, 1880–August 23, 1880, as Argenta; August 23, 1880–August 31, 1893; October 27, 1898–November 30, 1899

Toonerville *(Bent)*

Fontaine Fox's popular "Toonerville Folks" comic strip made the Toonerville Trolley famous and inspired residents in an area called *Red Rock* to rename their community. By the time the cartoon ceased publication in 1955, however, drought and depression had taken their toll on the plains settlement, and today both *Toonervilles* exist chiefly in memory.

Toponas *(Routt)* [tuh-POHN-us]

According to local tradition, *toponas* is an Indian word for "sleeping lion," referring to a nearby animal-like rock forma-

tion.
PO: July 25, 1888–; Pop. 50

Torreys Peak *(Clear Creek, Summit)* [TOHR-ees]

Torreys Peak honors botanist John Torrey, who coauthored the *Flora of North America* (1838-1843) with Asa Gray and wrote reports of specimens brought back by western expeditions. Along with Grays Peak, *Torreys Peak* was named in 1861 by the younger botanist Charles C. Parry; although prospector Richard Irwin laid claim to the mountain a few years later, *Torreys Peak* eventually triumphed over Irwin Peak. (*See also* Grays Peak.)
Elevation: 14,267 feet

Towaoc *(Montezuma)* [TOH-way-ahk]

Towaoc, the headquarters community of the Ute Mountain Ute Indian Reservation, means "just fine" or "all right" in the Ute language.
PO: April 1, 1915–; Pop. 700 (CDP)

Towner *(Kiowa)*

After the Missouri Pacific's Pueblo and State Line Railway came through Memphis in 1887, the place was renamed *Towner,* apparently for a Mr. Towner who lived in the area and worked for the railroad. *Towner* is still remembered for a 1931 school bus accident. Stranded by a fierce March blizzard, five children and the bus driver lost their lives.
PO: February 20, 1888–July 28, 1989; Pop. 55

Trail Ridge High Point *(Larimer)*

"Unlike other roads that ascend mountain ranges by way of valleys and canyons, the trail makes its way upward to Milner Pass along the ridge tops, roughly following an old Ute trail," noted the WPA Colorado guide about Trail Ridge Road, which it called "one of the finest examples of mountain highway engineering in America." Traversing Rocky Mountain National Park between Estes Park and Grand Lake, the highway reaches an elevation of 12,183 feet, some fifteen hundred feet higher than the Continental Divide crossing at Milner Pass (10,758 feet).
Elevation: 12,183 feet

Trinchera *(Las Animas)* [trin-CHAIR-uh]

In his 1882 history of Trinidad and Las Animas County, early Trinidad doctor Michael Beshoar explained that Trinchera Creek was "so-named because approach that river as you will,

the prairie will present the appearance of a slightly undulating plain for miles beyond, till you suddenly find yourself on the high bank of the narrow valley of the stream, which fact struck the early Mexican traveler as presenting the appearance of a trench. They therefore named it Trinchera, meaning Trench." Later, the nearby settlement also took the Spanish name.
PO: February 14, 1889–; Pop. 70

Trinidad *(Las Animas)* [TRIN-i-dad]

The Spanish word *Trinidad* refers to the Trinity, although the immediate source of the name for this southern Colorado community is disputed. Some accounts attribute the name to a daughter of early settler Felipe Baca, but available records do not identify a Baca daughter called Trinidad. Several pioneers related that *Trinidad* was chosen, in the words of Dr. Michael Beshoar, "to dedicate the place directly to the Holy Trinity." However, A. W. Archibald, who was present when the name was selected, later told an interviewer that Gabriel Gutierrez suggested *Trinidad* to honor "an affinity named Trinidad," a "handsome woman" (not his wife) with whom he had been enamored in New Mexico.
PO: June 17, 1862–September 19, 1864; February 6, 1866–; Pop. 8,580; CS

Trout Creek Pass *(Chaffee, Park)*

Zebulon Pike crossed Trout Creek Pass in 1806; later came a wagon road, two railroads—the Denver, South Park, and Pacific and the Colorado Midland—and a modern highway. *Trout Creek* and *Pass* honor "the pride of Colorado," as the Colorado WPA guide termed the "cutthroats, steelheads, speckled, Eastern brook, Loch Leven, and famed rainbow trout—names that bring a sparkle to every angler's eye."
Elevation: 9,346 feet

Tungsten *(Boulder)* [TUNG-sten]

Tungsten mining and milling operations fueled the growth of this settlement in the early twentieth century. Demand for the metal, used in hardening steel, peaked during World War I; as prices declined thereafter, so did the community.
PO: July 10, 1916–November 30, 1949

Turret *(Chaffee)*

A late-booming mining camp established in 1897, *Turret* took its name from Turret Mountain, "though which eminence bears the name is difficult to determine, for there is a range of low bold peaks or promontor[i]es of granite," commented the

Denver Republican on September 9, 1897. "Indeed it is the most rugged and wildly picturesque scene in all the mountains for miles around."
PO: February 28, 1898–October 31, 1939

Twin Lakes *(Lake)*

Twin Lakes took its name from the two lakes now known as the Twin Lakes Reservoir. In 1885, George A. Crofutt called *Twin Lakes* "the most charming summer resort in Colorado" in his *Grip-Sack Guide of Colorado*. "The lakes abound in trout, and boats and tackle are provided at the hotels, and those that could not be happy here, we fear will find the great hereafter an uncomfortable abiding place."
PO: December 19, 1879–; Pop. 80

Two Buttes *(Baca)* [two-BYOOTS]

Promoters of the Two Buttes Townsite Company chose the name of a nearby local landmark for their new community.
PO: March 1, 1910–; Pop. 63

Tyrone *(Las Animas)* [tuh-ROHN]

In 1941, a *Tyrone* resident told the Colorado Writers' Project that the community had first been called *Yetta*, for the postmaster's wife. She did not say, however, why the name later became *Tyrone*, and no further details have come to light.
PO: August 5, 1916–August 1, 1929, as Yetta; August 1, 1929–December 6, 1968

Uncompahgre National Forest *(Southwest Colorado)* [un-kum-PAHG-ray]

In addition to the southwestern Colorado river, a plateau, a Fourteener, and this national forest carry the Ute name *Uncompahgre*.

Uncompahgre Peak *(Hinsdale)*

In 1874, members of the Hayden Survey made the first recorded ascent of this peak, which took its name from the river.
Elevation: 14,309 feet

Uncompahgre River *(Southwest Colorado)*

On August 26, 1776, the Spanish Domínguez-Escalante expedition "came upon the banks and meadows of El Río de San Francisco—among the Yutas called Ancapagari (which, according to our interpreter, means Red Lake), because they say that near its source there is a spring of red-colored water, hot and ill-tasting." More than two centuries later the river is still known by its Ute name, rendered today as *Uncompahgre*.

Uravan *(Montrose)* [OOR-uh-van]

Uravan combined the first syllables of uranium and vanadium, minerals extracted from nearby carnotite ore deposits. Developed in the mid-1930s by the United States Vanadium Corporation on the site of an earlier community called Joe Junior Camp, *Uravan* fell victim in the 1980s to stricter environmental standards and competition from foreign imports.
PO: August 27, 1936–July 15, 1988; Pop. 350

Ute Mountain Tribal Park *(Montezuma)* [YOOT]

Back-country tours to ancient Anasazi ruins are offered in the *Ute Mountain Tribal Park*, which the Ute Mountain Ute Indians are developing adjacent to Mesa Verde National Park.

Ute Mountain Ute Indian Reservation *(Southwest Colorado, Northwest New Mexico)*

Once the Ute Indians ranged over all of present western Colorado as well as northern New Mexico and eastern Utah. Today, descendants of Colorado Ute who did not accept individual allotment of tribal land live on the *Ute Mountain Ute Indian Reservation,* which adjoins the Southern Ute Indian Reservation of allotted land. (*See also* Southern Ute Indian Reservation.)

Ute Pass *(Teller)*

Described by Edwin James of the 1820 Stephen H. Long expedition as a "large and much frequented road," this mountain gateway had been used for centuries by the Ute Indians traveling into South Park. After the gold rush brought prospectors and settlers to the Pikes Peak region, a wagon road, a railroad—the Colorado Midland—and ultimately a modern highway wound through the passage that inspired the naming of El Paso County—"the pass" in Spanish.
Elevation: 9,165 feet

Utleyville *(Baca)* [UT-lee-vil]

When Azel Utley became postmaster, he moved the area post office a few miles west to his land and changed the name from Tuck to *Utleyville.*
PO: June 9, 1917–January 5, 1973

Vail *(Eagle)*

Officially dedicated in January 1963, this ski resort town took its name from nearby Vail Pass.
PO: October 1, 1963–; Pop. 3,659

Vail Pass *(Eagle, Summit)*

When state highway engineer Charles D. Vail died in 1945, Colorado had around five thousand miles of paved roads, ten times more than had existed in 1930 when Vail was appointed to office. *Vail Pass,* crossed by U.S. Highway 6 in 1940 and later by Interstate 70, honors his contributions.
Elevation: 10,666 feet

Valdez *(Las Animas)* [val-DEZ]

Homesteader Gabriel Valdez gave his name to this coal-mining community.
PO: April 20, 1910–September 15, 1961

Valmont *(Boulder)*

Early settlers combined "valley" and "mountain" to make *Valmont*.
PO: September 15, 1865–June 29, 1901

Valverde *(City and County of Denver)*

In 1873, the Valverde Town and Improvement Company laid out *Valverde* south of Denver on the Denver, South Park, and Pacific Railroad. Named from the Spanish *valle,* "valley," and *verde,* "green," and incorporated in 1888, *Valverde* joined the capital with the 1902 creation of the City and County of Denver.
PO: October 14, 1889–February 29, 1908

Vancorum *(Montrose)*

Established by the Vanadium Corporation of America, *Vancorum* combined the first syllable of each word in the company name; over time, *am* was modified to the present *um*.
Pop. 60

Vernon *(Yuma)*

As early settlers debated a name for the townsite, John J. Vernon, a Methodist circuit-riding minister, stepped into the fray with a prayer for divine guidance. Inspired by his eloquence, so the story goes, those assembled decided to call the place *Vernon*.
PO: May 23, 1892–; Pop. 35

Vicksburg *(Chaffee)*

Storekeeper Vick Keller was honored when the mining camp of *Vicksburg* was named.
PO: May 3, 1881–July 30, 1885, as Vicksburgh

Victor *(Teller)*

"The town of Victor was named by my brother, H. E. Woods," Frank Woods told a local author in 1932. "He gave it that name partly from the Victor mine, which was then a producer, and partly from his belief that the big production of the district would come from that vicinity, which proved to be true." Almost forty years earlier, in 1893, the brothers' Woods Investment Company had established the townsite, which soon absorbed rival Lawrence. Although some later histories state that the name honored Lawrence homesteader Victor Adams, Frank Woods's account, written shortly before his death, is convincing. *Victor* was the boyhood home of noted journalist, broadcaster, and world traveler Lowell Thomas.
PO: June 7, 1894–; Pop. 258

Vilas *(Baca)* [VIGH-lus]

Organized by a group of Kansas townsite promoters in 1887, *Vilas* took the name of William F. Vilas, who was then serving as postmaster general in the Grover Cleveland administration. Vilas subsequently was secretary of the interior (1888–1889) and a United States senator from Wisconsin (1891–1897).
PO: June 20, 1887–; Pop. 105

Villa Grove *(Saguache)* [vil-lah-GROVE]

In 1935, *Villa Grove* correspondent Clifford Meister answered the State Historical Society's request for information. The name, he explained, was "applied to the town because Villa meant Village and where the town site was originally started was surrounded by groves of trees, hence Grove." The post office, briefly called *Garibaldi,* has been spelled as both one word and two.
PO: June 13, 1870–January 19, 1872, as Garibaldi; January 19, 1872–October 12, 1894, as Villa Grove; October 12, 1894–July 1, 1950, as Villagrove; July 1, 1950–; Pop. 50

Villegreen *(Las Animas)* [vil-lah-GREEN]

Villegreen resident Zelma Ballard told researcher Ruth Matthews in 1940 that the federal Post Office had combined the French word *ville* for "town" or "city" with "green" for first postmaster James Green to make *Villegreen.*
PO: April 21, 1917–November 11, 1985; Pop. 30

Vineland *(Pueblo)*

Grape vines grown by farmers on the south side of the Arkansas River inspired the naming of *Vineland.*

Virginia Dale *(Larimer)*

In *Beyond the Mississippi* (1867), journalist Albert D. Richardson wrote that *Virginia Dale* was named by "the Secession founder of the station" to honor Mrs. Jefferson Davis—her name, however, was Varina, not Virginia. Most other sources state that in 1862 the first agent, "Black Jack" Slade, named the stage station near the present-day settlement for his wife, Virginia. Slade, whose reputation was as black as his name, is remembered in Colorado history as the slayer of Jules Beni, for whom Julesburg was named; he himself met his end at the wrong end of a rope in Montana in 1864. (*See also* Julesburg.)
PO: January 9, 1868–September 28, 1868; September 14, 1871–; Pop. 20

Vineland

Vona *(Kit Carson)* [VOH-nuh]

Several old-timers said that Vona King was the daughter of
early printer and lawyer Fred N. King and the niece of Pearl S.
King, who platted the townsite; however, E. H. Haynes, who
arrived in the spring of 1888, told the State Historical Society
that Vona was Pearl King's daughter.
*PO: January 19, 1889–July 9, 1895; June 25, 1901–October 14,
1905; January 21, 1907–; Pop. 104*

Wagon Wheel Gap *(Mineral)*

Someone, sometime, abandoned wheels from broken wagons
in the "gap" or opening through which the Rio Grande flows
near this settlement. Whose wagons, what expedition, which
year are all questions that have no answers, although Charles
Baker's 1860-1861 prospecting venture is often mentioned.
Those who found the relics later contributed the distinctive
name also taken by the community. As Ernest Ingersoll explained in *The Crest of the Continent* (1885), "To distinguish it
from other gaps in the range it was spoken of as the 'gap
where the wagon wheel was found,' which soon, by natural

Wagon Wheel Gap

process of curtailment, condensation and transposition, became 'Wagon Wheel Gap,' and Wagon Wheel Gap it is, even unto this day."

PO: August 27, 1875–February 2, 1895; June 24, 1895–March 26, 1901, as Thornton; March 26, 1901–September 30, 1957

Walden *(Jackson)*

Early settler Marcus A. Walden gave his name to the *Walden* post office, first located on his claim southeast of the present-day community. *Walden* celebrated its centennial by sending the 1990 Christmas tree, cut in the Routt National Forest, to the United States Capitol.

PO: February 28, 1881–; Pop. 890; CS

Wallstreet *(Boulder)*

"Wall Street Camp is attracting considerable attention in a large amount of capital from New York and other Eastern cities," reported the *Mining Investor* on April 9, 1898. First called *Sugar Loaf* and *Delphi,* the Boulder County settlement was renamed when such "Wall Street financiers" backed various turn-of-the-century mining and milling ventures.

PO: October 31, 1895–April 18, 1898, as Delphi; April 18, 1898–September 15, 1921; Pop. 30

Walsenburg *(Huerfano)*

Walsenburg had its origins in an older Spanish settlement called *La Plaza de los Leones* for Don Miguel Antonio Leon. After Fred Walsen opened a general store in 1870 the community became *Walsenburg,* with Walsen serving as the first mayor. Despite Walsen's prominence, some promoters tried to change the name to *Tourist* or *Tourist City* in 1887; most citizens were relieved when the post office designation was rescinded. "Those few upstarts who wished to run away with an established mining town—name and all—and to merge it into a wildcat scheme of their own certainly deserved this rebuke," commented the Trinidad *Citizen* on November 30.

PO: December 14, 1870–October 20, 1887, as Walsenburgh; October 20, 1887–November 29, 1887, as Tourist; November 29, 1887–December 22, 1892, as Walsenburgh; December 22, 1892–; Pop. 3,300; CS

Walsh *(Baca)*

In 1926, the land company of the Atchison, Topeka, and Santa Fe Railway platted *Walsh* on its subsidiary Dodge City and Cimarron Valley line. Most residents and businesses from nearby Stonington moved to the new town, said to be named for a Santa Fe employee.

PO: December 23, 1926–; Pop. 692

Ward *(Boulder)*

Miner Calvin Ward found gold in 1860 and gave his name to
the camp that developed around his discovery. Almost forty
years later, Horace Tabor, his riches long gone, came to the
Ward area with his wife Baby Doe and their two daughters. Tabor briefly worked several mines in 1897 and early 1898 before
word of his appointment as Denver postmaster came through;
he died not long afterward in April 1899. (*See also* Tabor City.)
*PO: January 13, 1863–September 11, 1894, as Ward District; Sep-
tember 11, 1894–; Pop. 159*

Washington County *(Established February 9, 1887)*

When the bicentennial of George Washington's birth was cele-
brated in 1932, thirty-two counties carried his name, including
Washington County in Colorado.
Pop. 4,812

Watkins *(Adams)*

Situated on Box Elder Creek, *Watkins* grew up around a Kansas Pacific Railway station first called *Box Elder;* nearby was
the site of the Box Elder stage station. The later name honored
rancher L. R. Watkins.
*PO: January 3, 1878–October 14, 1893; November 6, 1894–; Pop.
890*

Waunita Hot Springs *(Gunnison)* [wahn-EE-tuh]

First called *Tomichi*—the word is said to mean "hot" or "boiling" in the Ute language—these hot springs later took the
name of the legendary Ute maiden Waunita, whose tears for
her dead Shoshone lover created the steaming waters. Settlement around the springs began in 1879, and soon facilities for
health-seeking visitors were being developed. Eventually the
popular resort, known for a time as *Waunita Hot Radium
Springs,* included cabins, a hotel, a sanitarium, and an enclosed swimming pool. In recent years, the place has been operated as the family-oriented *Waunita Hot Springs Ranch.*
PO: May 27, 1910–October 31, 1942

Webster *(Park)*

William and Emerson Webster, who opened a road over Webster Pass in 1878, also gave their name to this settlement on
the Denver, South Park, and Pacific Railroad. George A. Crofutt reported in his 1885 *Grip-Sack Guide of Colorado* that during the Leadville rush, at the hotel "one dollar for a blanket
and 'lay' on the floor were the best accommodations afforded.
One would suppose that this exorbitant price for a blanket
would satisfy the most rapacious landlord, yet when the de-

mand for blankets exceeded the supply, the greedy host would watch for a sleeper, and finding one, snatch away the blanket once sold for a dollar for the night, and sell it for another dollar, and so on *ad libitum.*"
PO: May 7, 1877–May 31, 1904; June 1, 1904–September 30, 1909

Welby *(Adams)*

Welby, laid out by a subsidiary of the Denver, Laramie, and Northwestern Railway, was named for that line's first vice-president, Arthur E. Welby. Born in South Africa, Welby had long been associated with the Denver and Rio Grande before joining the new road shortly before his death in 1909.
PO: December 19, 1910–March 31, 1911; Pop. 10,218 (CDP)

Weld County *(Established November 1, 1861)*

Weld County, which originally extended to the eastern border, honored 1854 Yale graduate Lewis Ledyard Weld, a nephew of abolitionist Theodore Dwight Weld. The younger Weld practiced law in Kansas before arriving in Denver in 1860. For about a year (1861–1862), he served as territorial secretary, then briefly edited a Denver newspaper before joining the Union army; he died of exposure in 1865. Weld is generally credited with having designed the territorial seal, which with slight changes became the state seal; the motto *Nil sine Numine,* "Nothing without the Deity," appears on the Weld coat of arms.
Pop. 131,821

Weldona *(Morgan)* [wel-DOH-nuh]

Weldona is situated in the Weldon Valley, named either for an early settler, a "General Weldon," or Weld County, which encompassed the area before Morgan County was created in 1889. The federal Post Office is said to have added the *a* to distinguish the place from Walden.
PO: February 15, 1883–July 18, 1907, as Deuel; July 18, 1907–; Pop. 300

Wellington *(Larimer)*

Wellington took its name from C. L. Wellington, a Colorado and Southern Railway traffic manager. Supreme Court Justice Byron R. White, nicknamed "Whizzer" during his University of Colorado football-playing days, grew up in *Wellington.*
PO: August 25, 1903–; Pop. 1,340

Westcliffe *(Custer)*

Briefly named *Clifton, Westcliffe* originated in the spring of 1881 with the arrival of the Denver and Rio Grande narrow-

gauge tracks. Its name may have stemmed simply from its location, about one mile west of Silver Cliff. Alternatively, many sources assert that Dr. William A. Bell, a longtime associate of D&RG founder William Jackson Palmer, bestowed the name in honor of his birthplace, Westcliffe-on-the-sea, England. Bell, however, was born of an English family in County Tipperary, Ireland. He did have large landholdings in the *Westcliffe* area, including the Clifton Hay Farm, but maintained his home at Manitou. "Dr. Bell, being a prominent member of the Denver & Rio Grande Railway Directory, has not paid much personal attention to his ranch in the valley, but it has been very well managed by his agents," commented the 1881 *History of the Arkansas Valley.*
PO: July 14, 1881–November 21, 1882; January 22, 1886–; Pop. 312; CS

Westcreek *(Douglas)*

Incorporated in 1896, *West Creek* (now *Westcreek*) encompassed several gold-booming townsites along West Creek, including *Pemberton,* on Walsh Pemberton's ranch, and *Tyler,* on George F. Tyler's ranch.
PO: January 23, 1896–April 14, 1902, as Pemberton; April 14, 1902–August 31, 1918; October 26, 1918–June 14, 1919; January 9, 1935–November 6, 1968

Westminster *(Adams, Jefferson)* [west-MIN-ster]

Early settler Pleasant DeSpain gave his name to the railroad station, which later became *Harris* or *Harris Park* for a real estate developer. Later, residents voted to name the community for nearby Presbyterian Westminster University. Today the landmark red sandstone building houses schools operated by the Pillar of Fire church.
PO: April 21, 1890–June 5, 1908, as Harris; June 5, 1908–; Pop. 74,625

Weston *(Las Animas)*

Blacksmith S. A. Weston gave his name to *Weston,* situated near the confluence of the north and south forks of the Purgatoire River. In the 1930s, longtime Las Animas County resident J. M. Madrid told researchers that the place had been known earlier both as *Los Sisneros,* for the Juan Sisneros family, and as *La Junta,* "the junction."
PO: September 9, 1889–; Pop. 175

Weston Pass *(Lake, Park)*

Most accounts trace the name of this pass to A. S. Weston, who came to California Gulch in 1860, ranched on the west-

Wet Mountains

ern side, and built a thriving Lake County law practice. Philo M. Weston, a rancher on the eastern side, has also been suggested as the inspiration.
Elevation: 11,900 feet

Wetmore *(Custer)*

Rancher William H. "Billy" Wetmore is credited with surveying and naming *Wetmore*.
PO: April 19, 1881–

Wet Mountains *(Southern Colorado)*

Known to the Spanish as the *Sierra Mojada* or "wet mountain range," this part of the Rocky Mountain chain was an important landmark to early travelers. In his report of the 1853-1854 John W. Gunnison expedition, Lieutenant E. G. Beckwith aptly described the "broken range of mountains [that] extends towards the Arkansas river, called the Sierra Mojada or Wet mountain, from the constant rains which fall upon it." The range also is referred to as the *Greenhorn*—12,347-foot *Greenhorn Mountain* is the highest summit—although in 1891 the United States Board on Geographic Names decreed *Wet Mountains* as the official name. (*See also* Greenhorn Mountain.)

Wetterhorn Peak *(Hinsdale, Ouray)*

Probably christened by the Wheeler Survey in the early 1870s, *Wetterhorn Peak* is some two thousand feet higher in elevation than its Swiss namesake.
Elevation: 14,015 feet

Wheat Ridge *(Jefferson)*

In the aftermath of the Pikes Peak gold rush, some erstwhile prospectors turned to farming in the area around present-day *Wheat Ridge*. Soon, "the locality became famous for its wonderful wheat production," remembered W. W. Wilmore about

the community he knew as a child in the 1880s. "I have been told by the old residents that they sometimes got a yield of as high as 60 bushels per acre. Under these circumstances the name of Wheat Ridge was an easy suggestion." Later, the production of fruits and vegetables supplanted wheat farming.
PO: July 7, 1913–; Pop. 29,419

Wheeler *(Summit)*

Wheeler or *Wheeler's Ranch* took the name of John S. Wheeler, a Massachusetts-born Fifty-Niner who ultimately found more success in agriculture and townsite development than he did in mining or politics.
PO: April 1, 1880–May 14, 1894

Wheeler Geologic Area *(Mineral)*

Wheeler Geologic Area honors Lieutenant George Wheeler, who headed the army's surveys west of the one-hundredth meridian during the 1870s. Filled with dramatic rock formations but remote and difficult to reach, the area was formerly a national monument.

White River *(Northwest Colorado)*

In September 1776, the Franciscan friars Domínguez and Escalante arrived with their party at a river they called the *San Clemente;* "we crossed it and halted on its northern edge, where there is a middle-sized meadow of good pasturage. This river is middling and flows west through here, and the terrain adjacent to it offers no prospects for a settlement." A

Wideawake

century later the name *White River* was in use, as shown on the 1877 Hayden Survey *Atlas of Colorado*.

White River National Forest *(Northwest Colorado)*

Covering large areas of northwestern Colorado, the *White River National Forest* took its name from the White River.

Whitewater *(Mesa)*

Alkali colors Whitewater Creek, which gave its name to the nearby community.
PO: October 9, 1884–

Wideawake *(Gilpin)*

A few years after Muriel Sibell Wolle published *Stampede to Timberline* (1949), a Gilpin County old-timer told her how the *Wideawake* mining camp north of Black Hawk was named. Several meetings were held, he said, but no decision was reached. "The men were then told that one more meeting would be called, 'and you'd better be wideawake.' 'Why don't we call it Wideawake?' someone shouted. And that was it."

Widefield *(El Paso)*. *See* Security-Widefield.

Wiggins *(Morgan)*

Wiggins, known earlier as *Corona,* took the name of frontiersman Oliver P. Wiggins, who told many a tall tale about his ex-

ploits with Kit Carson and John C. Frémont. A number of later writers believed and repeated his yarns, although historians have since demonstrated that very little of what Wiggins ever said was true.
PO: April 14, 1874–December 20, 1878, and November 10, 1882–December 2, 1896, as Corona; December 2, 1896–; Pop. 499

Wild Horse *(Cheyenne)*

Wild horses seen in the vicinity inspired the naming of the Kansas Pacific (later Union Pacific) railroad station around which the community developed in the early twentieth century. More recently, Wild Horse became noted as the address of the fan club for country singer Loretta Lynn. The club was run by the Johnson sisters from their nearby home before they moved to Nashville.
PO: January 5, 1877–May 25, 1877; April 13, 1904–; Pop. 25

Wiley *(Prowers)*

Situated on an Atchison, Topeka, and Santa Fe branch line, Wiley was named for William M. Wiley, who headed the Holly Sugar Company and was active in southeastern Colorado railroad and town promotion.
PO: April 22, 1907–; Pop. 406

Willard *(Logan)*

Many residents believed that *Willard* honored Daniel S. Willard, who became second vice-president of the Chicago, Burlington, and Quincy Railroad in 1904 before going on to a thirty-year tenure as president of the Baltimore and Ohio. Instead, the community, platted in 1888 by the Burlington's Lincoln Land Company subsidiary, was named for local landowner Willard House.
PO: September 26, 1888–April 10, 1894; January 26, 1897–March 30, 1900, as Arnold; March 30, 1900–February 28, 1901; April 5, 1910–July 14, 1967; Pop. 40

Williamsburg *(Fremont)*

After Morgan D. Williams died in 1903, the *Denver Times* called him "one of the most influential independent coal operators in Fremont county" and credited him with the founding of *Williamsburg*. In 1940, however, an informant told place name researcher Ruth Matthews that it was John Williams who opened the mine and inspired the naming of the community.
PO: January 10, 1882–October 31, 1916, as Williamsburgh; Pop. 253

Wilson Peak *(San Miguel)*

Only a short distance from Mount Wilson, this peak also took the name of Hayden Survey topographer A. D. Wilson, who in 1870 had climbed Mount Rainier shortly after the first ascent. *(See also* Mount Wilson.)
Elevation: 14,017 feet

Windom Peak *(La Plata)*

Like neighboring Sunlight Peak, *Windom Peak,* named for politician William Windom, was christened by Whitman Cross of the United States Geological Survey while mapping the area around the turn of the century. Elected to Congress from Minnesota in 1858, Windom later served in the Senate and as secretary of the treasury (1881; 1889-1891).
Elevation: 14,082 feet

Windsor *(Weld)* [WIN-zer]

According to tradition, the Reverend Samuel Asa Windsor, a Methodist minister from Fort Collins who held services in the community, overheard residents discussing possible town names. "Why not name it after me?" he asked, and thus the settlement became *Windsor.*
PO: January 18, 1884–August 19, 1911, as New Windsor; August 19, 1911–; Pop. 5,062

Winter Park *(Grand)*

Spearheaded by George Cranmer, manager of parks and improvements, the city of Denver developed this ski area around West Portal, which began as a construction camp at the west entrance of the Moffat Tunnel. The name was changed from *West Portal* to *Winter Park* shortly before the resort opened in 1940.
PO: October 12, 1923–December 1, 1939, as West Portal; December 1, 1939–; Pop. 528

Wolcott *(Eagle)* [wohl-KAHT]

First called *Russell,* this Eagle County community was renamed in 1889, apparently for Edward O. Wolcott, who served as a United States senator from Colorado between 1889 and 1901.
PO: September 12, 1889–; Pop. 25

Wolf Creek Pass *(Mineral)*

> Wolf Creek Pass way up on the Great Divide
> Truckin' on down the other side.

So runs the refrain in C. W. McCall's 1978 hit song "Wolf Creek Pass," which immortalized this Continental Divide

crossing known for its deep snowfalls and dangerous slides. The grey or "timber" wolf, once common in most of North America, now ranges to the north from the Canadian border area to Alaska.
Elevation: 10,850 feet

Woodland Park *(Teller)*

Lumbering and tourism both flourished among the forested hills surrounding *Woodland Park.* Situated in Ute Pass west of Colorado Springs on the Colorado Midland line, the railroad station and settlement were first called *Manitou Park* before taking the more descriptive name.
PO: March 19, 1888–February 20, 1890, as Manitou Park; February 20, 1890–; Pop. 4,610

Woodmen *(El Paso)*

From 1909 to 1947 the Modern Woodmen of America, founded in the late nineteenth century primarily to provide insurance to members, operated a tuberculosis sanitarium north of Colorado Springs. One of many in the area catering to the "lungers" who sought relief in Colorado's sunshine and dry climate, the establishment once had 180 tent cottages for patients, while in the surrounding community were stores, employee housing, and a post office. Today, such names as Woodmen Road and Woodmen Valley commemorate the society's work.
PO: January 20, 1912–January 31, 1949

Woodrow *(Washington)*

Local tradition traces the name *Woodrow* to Woodrow Wilson, who was serving as president of the United States when the community was founded.
PO: September 10, 1913–; Pop. 15

Woody Creek *(Pitkin)*

Wooded Woody Creek gave its name to this Pitkin County settlement, known in recent years as the home of "gonzo journalist" Hunter Thompson.
PO: September 4, 1920–; Pop. 450

Wootton *(Las Animas)*

From his first wagon trip over the Santa Fe Trail at age twenty in 1836 to his death in 1893, Richens Lacy "Uncle Dick" Wootton saw it all. "He has trapped beaver where Denver now stands; he owned a buffalo farm on the site of Pueblo, and he fought wild animals and Indians where other prosperous

communities now are," said the *Denver Republican* in its obituary. In 1865, Wootton began building a toll road over Raton Pass, which he operated until the Atchison, Topeka, and Santa Fe Railroad came through in 1878. The site where the toll gate and his large adobe home once stood is still shown on maps as *Wootton*, commemorating the man the *Republican* called "the pioneer of Colorado pioneers."
PO: December 4, 1908–January 14, 1922

Wray *(Yuma)* [RAY]

Although most accounts credit the naming of *Wray* to John Wray, a 1961 biography of cattleman I. P. (Print) Olive traces the name to his older brother James Thomas (Tom) Wray, who worked for the outfit in the mid-1870s.
PO: June 26, 1882–April 9, 1883; May 2, 1883–; Pop. 1,998; CS

Yampa *(Routt)* [YAM-puh]

First called *Egeria*, for a water spirit in the Roman religion, this Routt County community later took the same name as the nearby Yampa River.
PO: October 30, 1894–; Pop. 317

Yampa River *(Northwest Colorado)*

Yampa is the Ute name for a plant with roots resembling carrots or sweet potatoes. Many Indian tribes in the western United States have used this plant for food; when the Franciscan priests Domínguez and Escalante were traveling through present northwestern Colorado in 1776 they came upon a band of Comanche known as the *Yamparica* or "yampa eaters."

Yellow Jacket *(Montezuma)*

Swarming yellow-jacket wasps are said to have inspired the naming of Yellow Jacket Canyon, which in turn gave its name to this community. Some sources, however, trace the name to a Ute Indian known as Yellow Jacket.
PO: May 5, 1914–; Pop. 20

Yoder *(El Paso)* [YOH-d'r]

Yoder took the name of first postmaster A. F. Yoder.
PO: April 21, 1904–; Pop. 40

Yuma *(Yuma)* [YOO-muh]

Local tradition relates that a teamster known as Yuma died while working on the Burlington Railroad. The switch where he was buried, which thus was called Yuma, later provided

Yellow Jacket

the community name. Other versions state that the worker
was a Yuma Indian from the lower Colorado River region of
Arizona and California.
PO: November 24, 1885–; Pop. 2,719

Yuma County *(Established March 15, 1889)*

This plains county was created four years after the Yuma post
office was named.
Pop. 8,954

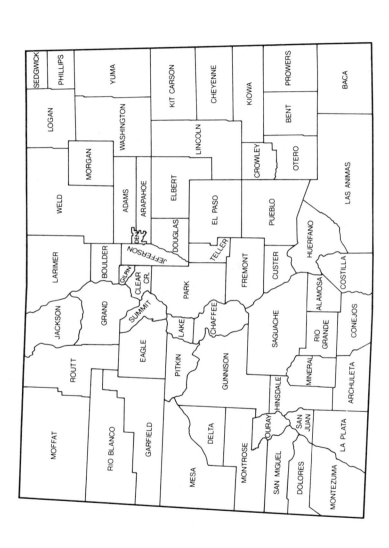

Index of Counties

ADAMS: Arvada, Aurora, Barr Lake, Bennett, Brighton, Broomfield, Commerce City, Dupont, Eastlake, Federal Heights, Fitzsimons Army Medical Center, Henderson, Northglenn, Strasburg, Thornton, Watkins, Welby, Westminster

ALAMOSA: Alamosa, Blanca Peak, Ellingwood Point, Great Sand Dunes National Monument, Hooper, Little Bear Peak, Mosca, Mosca Pass

ARAPAHOE: Aurora, Blakeland, Bow Mar, Buckley Air National Guard Base, Byers, Cherry Hills Village, Columbine Valley, Deer Trail, Englewood, Fort Logan, Glendale, Greenwood Village, Littleton, Lowry Air Force Base, Sheridan, Southglenn, Strasburg

ARCHULETA: Arboles, Chimney Rock, Chromo, Edith, Lonetree, Pagosa Junction, Pagosa Springs

BACA: Bartlett, Campo, Lycan, Oklarado, Pritchett, Springfield, Stonington, Two Buttes, Utleyville, Vilas, Walsh

BENT: Big Timbers, Boggsville, Caddoa, Fort Lyon, Hasty, John Martin Reservoir, Las Animas, McClave, Ninaview, Toonerville

BOULDER: Allenspark, Boulder, Broomfield, Caribou, Crisman, Eldora, Eldorado Springs, Erie, Gold Hill, Gunbarrel, Hygiene, Jamestown, Lafayette, Longmont, Longs Peak, Louisville, Lyons, Magnolia, Marshall, Meeker Park, Mount Audubon, Nederland, Niwot, Pella, Pinecliffe, Raymond, Rocky Mountain National Park, Rollins Pass, Ryssby, Salina, St. Vrain Creek, Sunset, Sunshine, Superior, Tungsten, Valmont, Wallstreet, Ward

CHAFFEE: Buena Vista, Cleora, Cottonwood Pass, Garfield, Granite, Grizzly Peak, Huron Peak, Johnson Village, La Plata Peak, Maysville, Missouri Mountain, Monarch, Monarch Pass, Mount Antero, Mount Belford, Mount Columbia, Mount Harvard, Mount Oxford, Mount Princeton, Mount Princeton Hot Springs, Mount Shavano, Mount Yale, Nathrop, Poncha Pass, Poncha Springs, Salida, St. Elmo, Tabeguache Mountain, Trout Creek Pass, Turret, Vicksburg

CHEYENNE: Arapahoe, Aroya, Cheyenne Wells, Firstview, Kit Carson, Wild Horse

CLEAR CREEK: Argentine Pass, Berthoud Pass, Dumont, Echo Lake, Eisenhower Memorial Tunnel, Empire, Georgetown, Grays Peak, Guanella Pass, Idaho Springs, James Peak, Lawson, Loveland Pass, Mount Bierstadt, Mount Evans, Mount Sniktau, Silver Plume, Torreys Peak

CONEJOS: Antonito, Capulin, Conejos, Cumbres Pass, Ephraim, La Jara, Manassa, Platoro, Romeo, Sanford

233

COSTILLA: Blanca, Blanca Peak, Chama, Culebra Peak, Fort Garland, Fort Massachusetts, Garcia, Garland City, Jaroso, Little Bear Peak, Mesita, Mount Lindsey, North La Veta Pass, San Acacio, San Francisco, San Luis, San Pablo, San Pedro

CROWLEY: Crowley, Olney Springs, Ordway, Sugar City

CUSTER: Colfax, Crestone Needle, Crestone Peak, Humboldt Peak, Querida, Rosita, Silver Cliff, Westcliffe, Wetmore

DELTA: Austin, Bowie, Cedaredge, Crawford, Delta, Dominguez, Escalante, Fort Robidoux, Hotchkiss, Lazear, Orchard City, Paonia

DENVER, CITY AND COUNTY OF: Argo, Auraria, Barnum, Berkeley, Camp Weld, Denver, Elyria, Globeville, Harman, Highland, Highlands, Lowry Air Force Base, Montana City, Montclair, South Denver, St. Charles, Valverde

DOLORES: Cahone, Dove Creek, Dunton, El Diente Peak, Lizard Head Pass, Mount Wilson, Rico

DOUGLAS: Castle Rock, Deckers, Franktown, Greenland, Highlands Ranch, Larkspur, Littleton, Louviers, Parker, Roxborough Park, Sedalia, Sprucewood, Westcreek

EAGLE: Avon, Basalt, Bond, Burns, Camp Hale, Dotsero, Dowd, Eagle, Edwards, Fryingpan River, Fulford, Gilman, Gypsum, McCoy, Minturn, Mount of the Holy Cross, Orestod, Red Cliff, State Bridge, Tennessee Pass, Vail, Vail Pass, Wolcott

ELBERT: Agate, Buick, Elbert, Elizabeth, Fondis, Kiowa, Kutch, Matheson, River Bend, Simla

EL PASO: Air Force Academy, Black Forest, Calhan, Cascade, Chipita Park, Colorado City, Colorado Springs, Ellicott, Ent Air Force Base, Falcon, Fort Carson, Fountain, Garden of the Gods, Green Mountain Falls, Manitou Springs, Monument, North Pole, Palmer Lake, Peterson Air Force Base, Peyton, Pikes Peak, Ramah, Rush, Security-Widefield, Woodmen, Yoder

FREMONT: Brookside, Canon City, Coal Creek, Coaldale, Cotopaxi, Florence, Hardscrabble, Hillside, Howard, Parkdale, Penrose, Portland, Prospect Heights, Rockvale, Royal Gorge, Texas Creek, Williamsburg

GARFIELD: Battlement Mesa, Carbondale, Douglas Pass, Glenwood Springs, New Castle, Parachute, Rifle, Rulison, Silt

GILPIN: Black Hawk, Central City, East Portal, Mountain City, Nevadaville, Rollins Pass, Rollinsville, Russell Gulch, Tolland, Wideawake

GRAND: Berthoud Pass, Blue River, Fraser, Gore Pass, Granby, Grand Lake, Hot Sulphur Springs, James Peak, Kremmling, Lulu City, Middle Park, Milner Pass, Mount Richthofen, Muddy Pass, Parshall, Rabbit Ears Pass, Radium, Rocky Mountain National Park, Rollins Pass, Tabernash, Winter Park

GUNNISON: Almont, Castle Peak, Coffeepot Pass, Cottonwood Pass, Crested Butte, Doyleville, Gothic, Gunnison, Irwin, Jack's Cabin, Kebler Pass, Marble, Maroon Peak, Monarch Pass, Mount Crested Butte, Ohio, Ohio Pass, Parlin, Pieplant, Pitkin, Powderhorn, Sapinero, Schofield Pass, Snowmass Mountain, Somerset, Tincup, Tomichi, Waunita Hot Springs

HINSDALE: Capitol City, Handies Peak, Henson, Lake City, Red Cloud

Peak, Rose's Cabin, Slumgullion Pass, Sunshine Peak, Uncompahgre Peak, Wetterhorn Peak

HUERFANO: Cuchara, Ellingwood Point, Farisita, Fort Stevens, Gardner, Greenhorn Mountain, Huerfano River, La Veta, Medano Pass, Mosca Pass, North La Veta Pass, Pryor, Red Wing, Spanish Peaks, Walsenburg

JACKSON: Cameron Pass, Coalmont, Cowdrey, Gould, Mount Richthofen, Mount Zirkel, Muddy Pass, North Park, North Platte River, Rabbit Ears Pass, Rand, Walden

JEFFERSON: Arvada, Bergen Park, Bow Mar, Broomfield, Buffalo Creek, Conifer, Edgewater, El Rancho, Evergreen, Foxton, Genesee, Golden, Idledale, Indian Hills, Kassler, Ken Caryl, Kittredge, Lakeside, Lakewood, Morrison, Mountain View, Pine, Pine Junction, Shaffers Crossing, Superior, Tiny Town, Westminster, Wheat Ridge

KIOWA: Arlington, Brandon, Chivington, Eads, Galatea, Haswell, Sheridan Lake, Towner

KIT CARSON: Bethune, Burlington, Flagler, Seibert, Stratton, Vona

LAKE: Climax, Fremont Pass, Hagerman Pass, Independence Pass, Leadville, Malta, Mosquito Pass, Mount Democrat, Mount Elbert, Mount Massive, Mount Sherman, Oro City, Tabor City, Tennessee Pass, Twin Lakes, Weston Pass

LA PLATA: Allison, Bayfield, Breen, Durango, Fort Lewis, Gem Village, Hermosa, Hesperus, Ignacio, Kline, La Plata, Marvel, Mayday, Mount Eolus, Mount Oso, Oxford, Parrott City, Redmesa, Rockwood, Sunlight Peak, Windom Peak

LARIMER: Bellvue, Berthoud, Big Thompson River, Cache la Poudre River, Cameron Pass, Campion, Deer Ridge, Drake, Estes Park, Fort Collins, Glendevey, Glen Haven, Kelim, Laporte, Laramie River, Livermore, Loveland, Masonville, Milner Pass, Namaqua, Pinewood Springs, Poudre Park, Red Feather Lakes, Rocky Mountain National Park, Rustic, Ted's Place, The Forks, Timnath, Trail Ridge High Point, Virginia Dale, Wellington

LAS ANIMAS: Aguilar, Barela, Berwind, Beshoar Junction, Boncarbo, Branson, Cokedale, Delhi, El Moro, Gulnare, Hastings, Hoehne, Jansen, Kim, Ludlow, Model, Monument Park, Morley, Primero, Raton Pass, Segundo, Sopris, Spanish Peaks, Starkville, Stonewall, Tercio, Thatcher, Tobe, Trinchera, Trinidad, Tyrone, Valdez, Villegreen, Weston, Wootton

LINCOLN: Arriba, Bovina, Boyero, Genoa, Hugo, Karval, Limon, Punkin Center

LOGAN: Atwood, Crook, Dailey, Fleming, Fort Wicked, Iliff, Merino, Padroni, Peetz, Proctor, Sterling, Willard

MESA: Cameo, Clifton, Collbran, Colorado National Monument, De Beque, Fruita, Gateway, Glade Park, Grand Junction, Loma, Mack, Mesa, Molina, Orchard Mesa, Palisade, Skyway, Whitewater

MINERAL: Creede, Spar City, Wagon Wheel Gap, Wheeler Geologic Area, Wolf Creek Pass

MOFFAT: Blue Mountain, Craig, Dinosaur, Elk Springs, Fort Davy Crockett, Great Divide, Green River, Greystone, Hamilton, Hiawatha, Lay, Maybell, Powder Wash, Slater, Sunbeam

MONTEZUMA: Arriola, Centennial Peak, Cortez, Dolores, Lebanon,

Lewis, Mancos, McPhee, Mesa Verde National Park, Pleasant View, Stoner, Towaoc, Ute Mountain Tribal Park, Yellow Jacket

MONTROSE: Bedrock, Black Canyon of the Gunnison National Monument, Cimarron, Fort Crawford, Maher, Montrose, Naturita, Nucla, Olathe, Paradox, Redvale, Uravan, Vancorum

MORGAN: Brush, Fort Morgan, Goodrich, Hillrose, Hoyt, Log Lane Village, Orchard, Snyder, Weldona, Wiggins

OTERO: Bent's Old Fort, Cheraw, Fowler, Hawley, La Junta, Manzanola, Rocky Ford, Swink, Timpas

OURAY: Camp Bird, Dallas, Dallas Divide, Ironton, Mount Sneffels, Ouray, Red Mountain, Red Mountain Pass, Ridgway, Wetterhorn Peak

PARK: Alma, Antero Junction, Bailey, Boreas Pass, Buckskin Joe, Como, Fairplay, Garo, Grant, Guffey, Hartsel, Hoosier Pass, Jefferson, Kenosha Pass, Lake George, Leavick, Mosquito, Mosquito Pass, Mount Bross, Mount Cameron, Mount Democrat, Mount Guyot, Mount Lincoln, Mount Sherman, Mount Silverheels, Shawnee, South Park, South Park City, Tarryall, Trout Creek Pass, Webster, Weston Pass

PHILLIPS: Amherst, Haxtun, Holyoke, Paoli

PITKIN: Ashcroft, Aspen, Basalt, Capitol Peak, Castle Peak, Coffeepot Pass, Conundrum Peak, Fryingpan River, Grizzly Peak, Hagerman Pass, Independence, Independence Pass, Maroon Peak, Meredith, North Maroon Peak, Pyramid Peak, Redstone, Snowmass, Snowmass Mountain, Snowmass Village, Woody Creek

PROWERS: Amache, Amity, Bristol, Carlton, Cheney Center, Granada, Hartman, Holly, Kornman, Lamar, May Valley, Wiley

PUEBLO: Avondale, Baxter, Beulah, Boone, Cedarwood, Colorado City, Devine, Fort Reynolds, Greenhorn Mountain, Huerfano River, Nepesta, North Avondale, Pueblo, Pueblo West, Rye, Vineland

RIO BLANCO: Buford, Meeker, Rangely, Rio Blanco

RIO GRANDE: Del Norte, Homelake, Monte Vista, South Fork, Summitville

ROUTT: Clark, Columbine, Hahn's Peak, Hayden, Milner, Mount Zirkel, Oak Creek, Pagoda, Phippsburg, Steamboat Springs, Toponas, Yampa

SAGUACHE: Bonanza City, Center, Challenger Point, Cochetopa Pass, Crestone, Crestone Needle, Crestone Peak, Great Sand Dunes National Monument, Kit Carson Peak, La Garita, Marshall Pass, Medano Pass, Mineral Hot Springs, Moffat, Poncha Pass, Saguache, San Luis Peak, Sargents, Stewart Peak, Villa Grove

SAN JUAN: Animas Forks, Gladstone, Howardsville, Red Mountain Pass, Silverton

SAN MIGUEL: Dallas Divide, Egnar, Gypsum Gap, Lizard Head Pass, Norwood, Ophir, Pandora, Placerville, Sawpit, Slick Rock, Telluride, Wilson Peak

SEDGWICK: Fort Sedgwick, Julesburg, Ovid, Sedgwick

SUMMIT: Argentine, Argentine Pass, Blue River, Blue River (town), Boreas Pass, Breckenridge, Copper Mountain, Dillon, Dyersville, Eisenhower Memorial Tunnel, Fremont Pass, Frisco, Grays Peak, Heeney, Hoosier Pass, Keystone, Kokomo, Loveland Pass, Montezuma, Mount Guyot, Mount Powell, Quandary Peak, Robinson, Saints John, Silverthorne, Tiger, Torreys Peak, Vail Pass, Wheeler

TELLER: Altman, Anaconda, Cripple Creek, Divide, Florissant, Florissant Fossil Beds National Monument, Gillett, Goldfield, Green Mountain Falls, Ute Pass, Victor, Woodland Park

WASHINGTON: Akron, Anton, Cope, Last Chance, Lindon, Otis, Woodrow

WELD: Ault, Barnesville, Big Thompson River, Briggsdale, Brighton, Broomfield, Buckingham, Cache la Poudre River, Carr, Dacono, Dearfield, Eaton, Erie, Evans, Firestone, Fort Jackson, Fort Lupton, Fort St. Vrain, Fort Vasquez, Frederick, Galeton, Garden City, Gilcrest, Gill, Greeley, Green City, Grover, Hardin, Hereford, Hudson, Ione, Johnstown, Keenesburg, Keota, Kersey, Kuner, La Salle, Latham, Lochbuie, Lucerne, Masters, Mead, Milliken, Nunn, Peckham, Pierce, Platteville, Prospect Valley, Purcell, Raymer, Rockport, Roggen, Severance, Stoneham, St. Vrain Creek, Windsor

YUMA: Abarr, Arikaree River, Beecher Island, Clarkville, Eckley, Hale, Happyville, Heartstrong, Idalia, Joes, Kirk, Laird, Vernon, Wray, Yuma